Content Matters

A DISCIPLINARY LITERACY APPROACH
TO IMPROVING STUDENT LEARNING

Stephanie M. McConachie,
Anthony R. Petrosky

Editors

Foreword by Lauren B. Resnick

JOSSEY-BASS
A Wiley Imprint
www.josseybass.com

Published by Jossey-Bass
A Wiley Imprint
989 Market Street, San Francisco, CA 94103-1741—www.josseybass.com

Readers should be aware that Internet Web sites offered as citations and/or sources for further information may have changed or disappeared between the time this was written and when it is read.

Limit of Liability/Disclaimer of Warranty: While the publisher and author have used their best efforts in preparing this book, they make no representations or warranties with respect to the accuracy or completeness of the contents of this book and specifically disclaim any implied warranties of merchantability or fitness for a particular purpose. No warranty may be created or extended by sales representatives or written sales materials. The advice and strategies contained herein may not be suitable for your situation. You should consult with a professional where appropriate. Neither the publisher nor author shall be liable for any loss of profit or any other commercial damages, including but not limited to special, incidental, consequential, or other damages.

Jossey-Bass books and products are available through most bookstores. To contact Jossey-Bass directly call our Customer Care Department within the U.S. at 800-956-7739, outside the U.S. at 317-572-3986, or fax 317-572-4002.

Jossey-Bass also publishes its books in a variety of electronic formats. Some content that appears in print may not be available in electronic books.

Library of Congress Cataloging-in-Publication Data

Content matters : a disciplinary literacy approach to improving student learning / Stephanie M. McConachie, Anthony R. Petrosky, editors ; foreword by Lauren B. Resnick.
   p. cm.—(Jossey-Bass education series)
  Includes bibliographical references and index.
   ISBN 978-0-470-43411-6 (pbk.)
1. Language arts—Correlation with content subjects. I. McConachie, Stephanie M., 1946- II. Petrosky, Tony.
LB1576.C64 2010
428.0071'2—dc22
                              2009035518

Printed in the United States of America
FIRST EDITION

PB Printing   10 9 8 7 6 5 4 3

The Jossey-Bass Education Series

To Lauren B. Resnick, founder and director of the Institute for Learning

and former director of the Learning Research

and Development Center

CONTENTS

FOREWORD

This small book may start a revolution—a revolution that ends the long and agonizing debates between "thinking skills" and "content knowledge," between "teacher expertise" and "central curriculum," between "ensuring the basics" and "reaching for the top." Arguments about these issues have been roiling the education policy world, often with little impact on the real world of teaching and teachers. Now, research has produced a new understanding of how to improve learning and build professional organizations that learn every day.

This research tells us that there is no struggle between thinking skills and content knowledge. To the contrary, we cannot effectively teach—or learn—either one without the other. Drilling on isolated bits of content knowledge, without ensuring that students use the knowledge thoughtfully, will raise test scores and keep the big, bad wolf of adequate yearly progress away from the door for another year. But the only knowledge that will stick, that will be available to build on next month or next year (or in college), is knowledge that a student has worked to understand. This is a basic principle of learning. We call it academic rigor (learning rigorous content) in the thinking curriculum (units of study in which students think and actively use knowledge on a daily basis). It's a principle you can count on.

But it is a principle that is difficult to apply alone. It calls for change in virtually every aspect of how teaching and learning occurs—from the official curriculum of a district or school, to how teachers work together to design and enact powerful teaching, to the kinds of disciplinary-specific thinking that is evidenced in well-structured student discussions. This book provides an in-depth look at a framework for making these changes. The disciplinary literacy framework, developed over eight years in collaboration with multiple, diverse urban school districts, provides the means for schools and school systems to give students at every level of entering capacity a coherent and intellectually challenging program of discipline-specific learning in the core subject matters.

The disciplinary literacy (DL) way of working is likely to be new to many working educators, although it has deep roots in the tradition of liberal education that once guided educational thinking. For this reason, the DL team has developed strategies for initiating the program that begins with professional learning opportunities—including reflection on the experience of learning new disciplinary content and collaboration in designing and implementing DL lessons. The DL framework can also be used to support district- or school-specific curriculum development efforts.

Because all DL teaching and learning proceeds from the necessary interaction between thinking skills and content knowledge, the frameworks offer promise for taming the bear of secondary school reform. The emphasis on disciplinary knowledge and habits of mind resonates with secondary teachers who value the discipline they are teaching. Students—even those with initially limited academic language capability—are given opportunities to engage in sophisticated intellectual work. As part of the curriculum and everyday teaching, teachers attend to the literacy learning needs of students within content knowledge and habits of thinking. Students experience satisfaction and motivation for further academic work when they are treated as intelligent people who come to class with knowledge and reasoning skills. Everyone benefits from this reintellectualization of school work that moves it away from the generic and remedial and brings it back to disciplines.

Content Matters presents a practical and immediately useful way to think about curriculum, teacher development, and system change. This book is for everyone who is curious about the revolution in teaching and learning, everyone who cares about the future of education—educators, college professors who teach preservice teachers and administrators, members of school boards, legislators, and parents. As you read this book, you will start to understand how and why this way of teaching and learning is so different from business as usual and why it is so important.

Lauren B. Resnick
Distinguished University Professor
University of Pittsburgh

PREFACE

Content Matters offers teachers and instructional leaders coherent, research-based, and field-tested approaches for developing literacy in disciplinary teaching. Our vision of literacy reaches beyond reading strategies into the content areas where literacy instruction more broadly conceived involves students in reading, speaking, writing, and habits of thinking as they are practiced in each of the core disciplines: English language arts, history, mathematics, and science.

This is a book, then, about teaching and learning in the disciplines. It offers cases of teachers and students in middle and high schools working together in English language arts, history, mathematics, and science in purposefully sequenced lessons designed to engage them in cognitively challenging tasks. It is a book about the ways in which the careful design and use of teaching tools and rituals and routines can promote disciplinary literacy (DL) and habits of thinking that can evolve only in classrooms where students talk with each other in rich discussions of problems using the kinds of evidence and explanations that are specific to each discipline. We make our case simply: literacy is always rooted in disciplinary content. Content matters. So do the tasks with which we engage students. And so do the ways in which students engage each other.

When the Institute for Learning at the University of Pittsburgh introduced the Disciplinary Literacy Framework in 2002, literacy instruction was almost always thought of as reading instruction. The prevailing wisdom was that students should be taught generic reading strategies to apply to any and all texts and that thinking skills could be taught separately from specific content inquiries. There was very little guidance in the field for developing lessons to engage students in the habits of reading, writing, speaking, and thinking that would help them develop content knowledge and disciplinary literacy skills. Since then, and partly through the work of the Institute for Learning in its partnerships with large urban school districts, the field has begun to shift its views about literacy development and instruction for middle and secondary school students to a disciplinary-based framework.

Content Matters presents teachers and instructional leaders with the Institute for Learning's disciplinary framework in each of the four core content areas. The chapter authors provide guidance in developing instruction and offer examples of cognitively challenging sequences of lessons grounded in the five disciplinary literacy principles:

- Knowledge and thinking—and therefore literacy development—must go hand in hand.

- Learning is apprenticeship.

- Teachers mentor students as apprentices.

- Classroom culture socializes intelligence.

- Instruction and assessment drive each other.

All of our work proceeds from these principles and the notion that disciplinary knowledge always coexists with habits of thinking—and therefore literacy skills—particular to each discipline. Teaching and learning in the disciplines, then, involves students in doing the work of the disciplines. In the mathematics chapter, for example, you will meet students in DL classrooms who are engaged in solving a cognitively challenging problem to understand the benefits of different cell phone calling plans by using mathematical habits of thinking such as drawing on prior knowledge, looking for patterns, conjecturing, and creating different representations of their solution paths—tables and equations, for instance—in purposeful ways. They propose and test ideas, tinker with calculations, try easier problems or known problems before trying the harder problem, and talk with others about their ideas, calculations, solutions, and misunderstandings. In order for this kind of disciplinary learning to occur, teachers structure and arrange students' participation through cognitively challenging tasks, carefully designed and sequenced, that reach across days and weeks of class time. Students' talk with each other to test their thinking, to share their analyses and explanations of data and sources, as well as each other's perspectives, conjectures, and interpretations, is at the heart of DL teaching and learning. Disciplinary literacy, in other words, is inquiry, and inquiry proceeds through Accountable Talk.

If, as we believe, disciplinary literacy stands as an example of an approach to teaching and learning that challenges students to participate in the intellectual work of the disciplines, and if, as we know, it invites them to engage in cognitively challenging problems through carefully designed and sequenced lessons, then in a real sense, DL asks students to apprentice to academic work and habits of thinking that they cannot yet do well. Teachers, then, have to develop the lessons and units, the tasks, and the intellectual scaffolds that provide students with the tools and the pedagogical rituals and routines that give them access to this work. Principals and other district leaders also provide teachers with the supports they need to engage students in DL. They lead by understanding the teaching and learning that is disciplinary literacy in the core disciplines. They establish communities of practice in their schools and carve time out of the days for teachers to meet, develop and redevelop lessons, observe and discuss their practice, and engage others as learners in DL lessons through networks of distributed leadership.

Content Matters, then, is also a book about instructional leadership in disciplinary literacy. It offers district leaders examples and testimonials of the ways in which our tools support administrators as instructional leaders and situates their experiences within a model of nested learning communities. Our tools offer instructional leaders methods to ensure district and school readiness for long-term engagement with all aspects of DL, including the professional learning that leads to the establishment of district and school learning communities. These communities, composed of teachers and instructional leaders, collaboratively analyze and design tasks, lessons, and units in the core disciplines. They study artifacts, professional texts, and student work samples, and they participate in observations of teaching. They design school improvement plans for DL teaching and learning, and they ensure that DL curricula and assessments align. Our book tells these leadership stories as well as those of teachers and students engaged in DL in the core subjects.

Our work in disciplinary literacy in the Institute for Learning at the Learning Research and Development Center of the University of Pittsburgh began in 2002. Since we began the DL Project, we have worked with teachers, coaches, and district leadership in over twenty-five school districts, including most recently large urban districts such as Prince George's County, Maryland; Austin, Dallas, and Fort Worth, Texas; Los Angeles Unified; New York City Region 10; Providence and a consortium of other Rhode Island districts; Bridgeport and Hartford, Connecticut; Denver, Colorado; Richland County One, South Carolina; and Saint Paul and Minneapolis, Minnesota. One of the pleasures of this book for us is that it represents our collaborative work on the DL projects and tells the stories of that work with the voices of those who conducted and participated in it.

Content Matters is divided into three sections. The first, Chapters One and Two, make the cases, respectively, for changing current practices and for the foundations of our work in DL. The second section, comprising the discipline chapters—history, mathematics, science, and English language arts—provides classroom scenarios from urban schools along with examples and explanations of DL instructional tools that teachers and students use. Finally, Chapter Seven explains how DL supports instructional leadership and provides examples of professional development models and tools. The appendixes set out the DL design principles by core academic area and the DL observation protocol and provide a summary of selected DL tools.

ACKNOWLEDGMENTS

This is a book built on the ideas, experiences, and wisdom of many people. We are grateful to the talented teachers, administrators, and students who gave us ideas and validated approaches through their disciplinary literacy (DL) work. We particularly thank the teachers and administrators of current and former partner districts who gave credence to DL practice and ideas. Following are the districts and their superintendents at the time of their Institute for Learning (IFL) work: Austin Independent School District, Pascal Forgione Jr.; Baltimore City Public Schools, Bonnie Copeland; Bridgeport Public Schools, John Ramos Jr. and Sonia Diaz Salcedo; Dallas Independent School District, Michael Hinojosa; Denver Public Schools, Jerry Wartgow; Fort Wayne School District, Thomas Fowler-Finn; Fort Worth Independent School District, Melody Johnson; Hartford Public Schools, Robert Henry; Grand Rapids Public Schools, Bernard Taylor; Kenton County School District, Kentucky, Susan Cook; Los Angeles Unified School District, Roy Romer; Minneapolis Public Schools, William Green; New York City Region 10, Gale Reeves; Pittsburgh Public Schools, Mark Roosevelt; Prince George's County Public Schools, John Deasy and William Hite; Providence Public Schools, Diana Lamm, Fran Gallo, and Melody Johnson; Richland County School District One, South Carolina, Ronald Epps; Rhode

Island Consortium, Doreen Corrente; Saint Paul Public Schools, Patricia Harvey and Meria Carstarphen; Springfield, Massachusetts Public Schools, Joseph Burke.

In addition, we are most grateful to the teachers, assistant principals, principals, and district leaders who contributed teaching, learning, and leading examples. Their contributions form the heart of this book. Here are their names along with their district superintendents at the time of their IFL work: Austin Independent School District, Pascal Forgione Jr.: Susan Barnard, Vicki Bauerle, Pascal Forgione Jr., Bobbi Gideon, Donna Houser, and Glenn Nolly; Dallas Independent School District, Michael Hinojosa: Gilda Ivonne Durant; Denver Public Schools, Jerry Wartgow: Roger Chow, Susana Cordova, and Timeri Tolnay; Grand Rapids Public Schools, Bernard Taylor: Carolyn Evans; Los Angeles Unified School District, Roy Romer: Rebecca McMurrin; Pittsburgh Public Schools, Mark Roosevelt: Elizabeth DiPietro Brovey and Jerri Lippert; Providence Public Schools, Melody Johnson: Edward Abbott, Cheryl Anderson, Becky Coustan, Deborah Petrarca, Claire Pollard, and Lillian Turnipseed; Rhode Island Consortium, Doreen Corrente: Philip Auger, Tina Brownell, and Laura Yentsch; Saint Paul Public Schools, Patricia Harvey and Meria Carstarphen: Theresa Behnke, Norita Dittberner-Jax, Micheal Thompson, and Sarah Weaver; Springfield Public Schools, Joseph Burke: Patricia Keenan.

We are also most grateful to the leading scholars and researchers who coled the original disciplinary development teams and guided the formulation of DL practice by discipline: Gaea Leinhardt, history; Margaret Smith, mathematics; Jim Minstrell, science/physics; and Anthony Petrosky, English studies.

Thanks also to leading researchers and scholars, current and former, of the Learning Research and Development Center and the School of Education at the University of Pittsburgh who shared their research findings and influenced our thinking: Mary Kay Stein, Lindsay Matsumura, Amanda Godley, Isabel Beck, Margaret McKeown, Chris Schunn, Cynthia Coburn, Jim Greeno, Sharon Nelson-LeGall, and Mariana Achugar of Carnegie-Mellon University.

We owe a enormous debt of gratitude to former IFL colleagues: Megan Hall Dooley for her contributions to the early chapters of the book; Judy Johnston, who mentored many of us on the DL team and created paths for DL practice through her leadership work in our early districts; Anita Ravi, who authored the history chapter and is dearly missed as the DL team's resident historian; Donna Micheaux, whose advocacy for equity and excellence for every student influenced DL approaches; Luise Caster, videographer extraordinaire; and Kristen Hecker, who managed everything from content development to one-hundred-person dinners. In addition, many thanks to former DL team members for their creativity and integrity as this project grew: Harold Pratt, Doug Fleming, Mary Lou Metz, Lorraine Plasse, Cheryl Parshall, John McMillan, Karen Hollweg, Dorothy Geary, Heather Nelson, and Hedi Baxter, and to Joseph Taylor and Jodi Bintz, who are also authors of the science chapter.

IFL executive director Nancy Israel provided unwavering administrative leadership for this book and for DL practice. She remained steadfast in her support when others said that DL practice was too complex and hard for students.

Special thanks to colleagues of the IFL: Kathleen McCarthy, who began the DL work and brought the DL name and foundational model to the institute; Victoria Bill, Ido Jamar, Vivian Mihalakis, and Sam Spiegel, chapter authors and DL team members, who also reviewed draft chapters of the book and made many other contributions. To all the other DL team members who contributed ideas, experiences, and are true critical friends: Nancy Owen, Annette Seitz, Clarise Brooks, Ariana Mangual, Kate Stainton, Lawrence Charap, Joan Mohr, Kenneth Shonk, Birdy Reynolds, Deborah Jordan (a chapter author), Eden Badertscher, Sandy Campo, Elizabeth Edmondson, Paul Numedahl, Rebecca Kruse, and Dave Pinkerton. To district site liaisons who make the DL content practices resonate in districts and continue to teach us about district leadership practice through their actions, conversations, writing, and reported experiences: Rosita Apodaca, also a chapter author, Beth Lief, Joanna Maccario, Patti Magruder, Fran Mossberg, Nancy Owen, and Jen Sherer. To other close colleagues whose support and work informs and improves ours: Donna Bickel, Pam Goldman, Lillie Sipp, Monica Swift, and Yitz Francus. To IFL staff who supported this project in direct and indirect ways, visible and not: IFL assistant director Colleen Briner and staff members Nancy Artz, Kate Andrew, Nancy Bee, Christopher Belasco, Heather Bell, Carol Chatman, Kathy Day, Mary Difiore, Mica Jochim, Heath Maksin, Molly Petruska, Lonny Platzer, and Missy Raterman.

Sophie Madej, IFL's knowledge manager, has made the editing and production of the book appear effortless, which we know it could not be. Many thanks to her for the intelligence and precision with which she has led the book's editing and production.

We appreciate Jimmy Nelle of Dallas, Texas, for his creative graphics in Chapter Seven.

We are grateful to Christie Hakim of Jossey-Bass Publishing for her thoughtfulness and sage advice on the book's organization and inclusion of significant topics.

Many thanks to Bruce McConachie for his comments on draft chapters, his willingness to engage with these ideas at all hours of the day and night, his good humor, and his love always; and to Ellen Bishop for her suggestions, critiques, and patience with version after version of chapters and, as always, for her love.

Stephanie M. McConachie
Anthony R. Petrosky

THE EDITORS

Stephanie M. McConachie is a Fellow at the Institute for Learning (IFL), Learning Research and Development Center, University of Pittsburgh. She currently coleads the English language arts disciplinary literacy (DL) work at IFL. As part of this project, she has designed and led professional learning and curriculum development in English studies for school and district educators in ten urban school districts and a state consortium. She has worked most intensively in the Austin Independent School District, supporting the development of teacher-led, academic-area professional learning communities to fully implement DL systemic practice. Prior to this, she coordinated IFL's development team in all four academic areas of DL. She was instrumental in developing the DL framework, design principles, and collaborative protocols. As part of IFL, she has served as a site liaison to the Springfield Public School District in Massachusetts and the Kansas City Missouri School District. In both districts, she worked with district and school leaders to improve principal instructional leadership and support the development of coherent district instructional systems and routines. Her most important work in these districts was facilitating principal-led Learning Walks. She has presented professional learning sessions at the National Staff Development Council, National Association of Teachers of English, and the Association of Supervision and Curriculum Development. She is currently coteaching the Instructional Leadership course for the University of Pittsburgh.

Before coming to IFL, McConachie led a variety of educational initiatives. She taught English and English education to students from middle school through graduate school. She has also been a middle school principal, a high school assistant principal, and an English language arts coordinator. As part of her district leadership position, she led the development of a K-12 writing curriculum. She is a past president of the Virginia Association of Teachers of English and a former codirector of a National Writing Project site. While a principal, she coached new principals as part of a National Association of School Principals' program. She holds a doctorate in educational administration and a master of arts in English education from the College of William and Mary.

Anthony R. Petrosky, associate dean of the School of Education at the University of Pittsburgh, holds a joint appointment as a professor in the School of Education and the English Department. Along with Stephanie McConachie, he codirects the English Language Arts Disciplinary Literacy Project at the Institute for Learning at the Learning Research and Development Center. He was the principal investigator and codirector of the Early Adolescence English Language Arts Assessment Development Lab for the National Board for Professional Teaching Standards, which developed the first national board certification for English teachers. He is past chair of the National Council of Teachers of English (NCTE) Committee on Research and a past elected member of the NCTE Research Foundation. His first collection of poetry, *Jurgis Petraskas,* published by Louisiana State University Press (LSU), received the Walt Whitman Award from Philip Levine for the Academy of American Poets and a Notable Book Award from the American Library Association. Petrosky's second collection of poetry, *Red and Yellow Boat,* was published by LSU in 1994, and *Crazy Love,* his third collection, was published by LSU in fall 2003. Along with David Bartholomae, Petrosky is the coauthor and coeditor of four books: *Facts, Artifacts, and Counterfacts: Theory and Method for a Reading and Writing Course; The Teaching of Writing; Ways of Reading: An Anthology for Writers;* and *History and Ethnography: Reading and Writing About Others.*

THE AUTHORS

Rosita E. Apodaca is a Fellow at the Institute for Learning (IFL), Learning Research and Development Center, University of Pittsburgh. She holds doctorate and master's degrees in educational leadership from Teachers College, Columbia University, and a master of arts in Spanish and English as a Second Language from the University of Texas. While serving as a senior cabinet-level officer in various urban districts, she led a number of significant systemic reform efforts that helped to narrow the achievement gap and increase student performance on state assessment exams. She has served in appointed and elected leadership posts at the local, state, and national levels. She has authored books for teachers on language arts in Spanish for Spanish-speaking students and has written a number of articles in journals and professional publications. During her appointment at the IFL, Apodaca has served as the liaison to the Los Angeles Unified School District, Hartford Public Schools, Austin ISD, and the El Paso ISD. Apodaca developed, with input from district teacher leaders, principals, and senior district officers, the Austin Independent School District Learning Walk classroom observation tool, to improve teacher practice while building community.

Victoria L. Bill has been a Fellow at the Institute for Learning, Learning Research and Development Center, University of Pittsburgh, since it was formed in 1995. As cochair of the disciplinary literacy mathematics team, she is responsible for guiding the development and dissemination of professional development resources and tools to large urban school districts around the country. She has worked closely with mathematics teachers, coaches, directors of mathematics, and principals to study and implement disciplinary literacy-based lessons in classrooms. She and her DL mathematics team have developed, piloted, and published a set of algebra 1 replacement tasks, lesson plans, and segments of taped lessons that illustrate the practices of disciplinary literacy mathematics. She has also published articles in *Mathematics Teacher* and *Educational Leadership* and presented at the National Council of Teachers of Mathematics and the National Council of Supervisors of Mathematics. In addition to working with the Institute for Learning, she teaches elementary math methods and an instructional leadership course for aspiring principals. She also supervises middle and high school master-level student teachers at the University of Pittsburgh.

Jody Bintz joined BSCS in 2004 and is primarily working in the Center for Professional Development. She serves as the director of the BSCS National Academy for Curriculum Leadership, a three-year professional development program designed to improve districts' capacity to design, implement, and sustain an effective high school science education program. Other areas of specialty include helping teachers improve their classroom practice, supporting districts' selection and implementation of instructional materials, and working with partner organizations to develop local school leadership in science education. Bintz has coauthored a number of articles and books in the areas of improving teaching and learning and developing leadership. Prior to joining BSCS, she served as an instructional services consultant with Loess Hills AEA 13 in southwest Iowa, where her responsibilities included school improvement and professional development planning. She served on the Iowa Support Team for Schools in Need of Improvement. Prior to her more general work with districts, she served as a science education consultant and worked with science teachers to integrate technology; align curriculum, instruction, and assessment with standards and benchmarks; create more inquiry-based classrooms; and incorporate literacy strategies.

Bintz began her career in education as a high school science teacher and coach in Treynor, Iowa. She received her bachelor of arts degree in biology and her master's degree in science education from the University of Northern Iowa, and she recently completed course work for administrative certification.

Idorenyin Jamar is a Fellow at the Institute for Learning, Learning Research and Development Center, University of Pittsburgh. As a member of the disciplinary literacy mathematics team, she has designed and facilitated professional development for teachers, coaches, and administrators in twelve urban districts around the country. Prior to working at the Institute for Learning, she was an assistant professor of mathematics education at the University of Pittsburgh and Bayero University in Kano, Nigeria. She has taught secondary mathematics in urban schools for eight years. She served on the editorial panel of *Mathematics Teaching in the Middle School* and has served on advisory boards for WestEd and the Pittsburgh Council on Public Education. She holds a Ph.D. and M.Sc. in cognitive psychology and a B.A. in applied mathematics, all from Brown University.

Deborah L. Jordan is a science educator working with BSCS in Colorado Springs, Colorado. Her work currently includes serving as a Fellow for the Institute for Learning (IFL) at the University of Pittsburgh. As a member of the IFL Disciplinary Literacy Science Team, she works primarily with Austin Independent School District and Minneapolis Public Schools. In addition, she works with the Ministry of Education in Singapore developing inquiry-based elementary science lesson packages. Her past work at BSCS has allowed her to direct the revisions to *BSCS Science TRACKS: Connecting Science and Literacy* and to provide literacy strategies for essays in *BSCS Biology: A Human Approach*.

Jordan began her career in science education as a classroom teacher. She served as a district science coordinator for six years, providing professional development and facilitating the alignment of curriculum to state standards. During her seven years as an educational consultant with Mid-Continent Research for Education and Learning, she provided professional development and technical assistance to science educators throughout the United States. In addition, she coauthored *Teaching Reading in Science,* which provides tools for science teachers to help students comprehend science text.

Nancy M. Landes is the director of the BSCS Center for Professional Development. She began her professional career as a classroom teacher and completed a master of arts in curriculum and instruction and a Ph.D. in science education at Michigan State University. She joined the BSCS staff as a curriculum developer in 1983. Since then, she has served as the project director of two major curriculum development projects—Science for Life and Living: Integrating Science, Technology and Health and BSCS Science TRACKS, both in elementary science education. In her role as the director of the Center for Professional Development, Landes oversees the professional development efforts at BSCS, which include work with the Institute for Learning of the University of Pittsburgh; the BSCS National Academy for Curriculum Leadership, a National Science Foundation–funded program in science education reform, most recently in partnership with Washington State LASER; numerous state and regional initiatives; and district-based science professional development. Landes is particularly interested in helping teachers make the connections between curriculum implementation, professional development, and student learning and in establishing the conditions that make possible the successful implementation of meaningful instructional materials and strategies in science classrooms.

Vivian Mihalakis is a Fellow at the Institute for Learning, Learning Research and Development Center, University of Pittsburgh, working with the disciplinary literacy English language arts team since 2005. She works with districts to design and present English language arts units for secondary school classrooms and develop professional development to improve the teaching and learning of English language arts classrooms. Before coming to the institute, Mihalakis worked in both public and private and urban and rural schools as an English language arts teacher. She has taught English language arts to students in grades 8 through college, and taught secondary English language arts methods courses at the University of Pittsburgh. Mihalakis earned her B.A. from Allegheny College and her M.A. in education from Lehigh University. She is a doctoral student in English education at the University of Pittsburgh and is currently working on her dissertation, "An Analysis of Conceptual Coherence and Opportunities for Interpretation in Tenth Grade Literature Textbooks."

Anita K. Ravi is the high school social studies curriculum specialist for Pittsburgh Public Schools. She was a Fellow at the Institute for Learning at the University of Pittsburgh from 2001 to 2008, where she served as the disciplinary literacy history team cochair and worked with teachers and administrators from fifteen urban school districts around the country on professional development in the teaching and learning of history as a discipline. Prior to moving to Pittsburgh, she was a high school humanities teacher at School of the Future, an alternative school in the former District 2, New York City.

She holds an Ed.M. in social studies curriculum design from Teachers College at Columbia University and an M.A. in U.S. history from New York University. Her interests include designing curriculum on comparative world history and the history of mixed-race America.

Samuel A. Spiegel is a science educator in the Professional Development Center at BSCS and the Disciplinary Literacy Science Chair at the Institute for Learning. Prior to joining BSCS, he served as director of research and development for a multimedia development company and as director of the Center for Integrating Research and Learning at the National High Magnetic Field Laboratory, Florida State University, which has been recognized as one of the leading National Science Foundation laboratories for activities to promote science and technology education. While at Florida State, Spiegel also directed the Science FEAT program, an award-winning teacher enhancement program for middle grade science teachers. His background in science education includes experiences as both a middle school and high school science teacher, conducting and supervising educational research, working with high-risk youth in alternative education and living centers, working in science museums, designing distance learning courses, and multimedia curriculum development, as well as working with the professional development of teachers. He was honored for his efforts in teacher education by the Association for the Education of Teachers of Science with the Innovation in Teaching Science Teachers award in 1997.

Joseph A. Taylor has been directing the BSCS Center for Research and Evaluation since 2007. This appointment followed a one-year tenure as assistant director of the center. He joined the BSCS staff in 2001 as a specialist in research and science teacher professional development. Taylor taught high school physics and mathematics before completing a doctoral degree in science education at Penn State University.

Engaging Content Teachers in Literacy Development

Stephanie M. McConachie
Anthony R. Petrosky

For the past twenty-five years, reading experts and educational policymakers have pressed for increased attention to adolescent literacy. There have been mandates and actions at all levels of the educational system. As an educator, you probably have taken courses or engaged in professional development on reading. Most likely you also have been part of action plans to address the reading needs of adolescent students in your community. It has also been routine for those of us in education to see whole faculties coming together to talk about reading and writing approaches in order to implement literacy strategies across the curriculum. Behind these actions has been the idea that secondary teachers can and should teach reading and writing skills as part of teaching their own subject matter. We admit that focusing every middle and high school course on literacy is appealing on a couple of fronts. For one thing, it suggests a way to extend reading and writing instruction beyond the primary grades. For another, it links literacy instruction to academic content. Both are worthy objectives.

But these general approaches to reading and advancing literacy have not worked for several reasons. One is that science and math teachers do not see themselves as reading and writing teachers. In addition, many secondary teachers quite reasonably resist the across-the-curriculum solution because they are already expected to teach more biology or American history or algebra than time permits. They do not want to add basic reading and writing skills to the list of things they need to cover (Shanahan & Shanahan, 2008; O'Brien, Stewart, & Moje, 1995; Vacca & Vacca, 1993). And they have a legitimate point: across-the-curriculum literacy instruction poses the danger of diluting disciplinary rigor if the two are set side by side in a de facto competition for time and attention.

At first, many educators and policymakers believed that improving the reading scores for younger students could be the foundation for continuing the growth in reading performance of older adolescents. However, it has not worked out that way. As Shanahan and Shanahan pointed out in their review of the 2005 National Assessment of Educational Progress (NAEP) (Grigg, Donahue, & Dion, 2007) data (2008), inoculating early in reading has not been so successful: "Apparently, strong early reading skills do not automatically develop into more complex skills that enable students to deal with the specialized and sophisticated reading of literature, science, history, and mathematics.... Most students need explicit teaching of sophisticated genres, specialized language conventions, disciplinary norms of precision and accuracy, and higher-level interpretive processes" (p. 3).

Despite these false starts, there are perspectives that hold promise for improving literacy supported by a growing body of research and an emerging classroom experience base. Taken seriously, the findings call on us to undertake challenging reforms that require major changes in school culture, curricula, and pedagogy. We will look at the findings first, then return to what we know from the classroom experience base.

APPROACHES FOR IMPROVING ADOLESCENT LITERACY

In the past three years, there has been a multitude of published reports, articles, and ongoing updates proposing multifaceted approaches for improving adolescent literacy (Moje, Overby, Tysvaer, & Morris, 2008; Slavin, Cheung, Groff, & Lake, 2008; Deshler, Palincsar, Biancarosa, & Nair, 2007; Schleppegrell, 2004; Graham & Perrin, 2007; Biancarosa & Snow, 2006). The reports have pointed out that we need to understand better what we mean by adolescent literacy in order to uncover the myths surrounding what Johnny can and cannot read (Moje et al., 2008; Deshler et al., 2007). These reports address a number of questions—for example:

- When we use the term *adolescent*, are we including students in grades 6 to 12? Or are we talking about only high school students?
- What do we know about students at those age levels in terms of what they are reading and writing in school and out of school, and what they believe about themselves in terms of their own levels of literacy?
- What does it mean in an academic setting and in society to be literate?
- What are the literacy demands of the courses adolescents are taking?
- What are students reading and writing in and out of school?

Educational and civic leaders, both traditional and nontraditional, have sought sweeping changes that could shock the secondary system into change. Their efforts have focused on creating small learning communities within high schools and middle schools. As vital as these sweeping changes can be, they cannot stop at the doors of classrooms but must continue inside to change the curriculum and instruction that students encounter. We need to understand the potential of personalization beyond appealing to the interests of students and the organizational arrangement of buildings. It is necessary also to improve each school's intellectual culture and curriculum toward using students' shared histories as a knowledge source to begin and sustain intellectual dialogues about critical ideas and topics. An expanded view of personalization would include curriculum with the potential to be responsive to shared histories and present desires, as well as to structured, instructional conversations on key ideas. These conversations require full participation and mind-engaged learners to co-construct and expand knowledge domains. And the learners need their teachers, other students, and the larger community inside and outside school to know them and believe in their abilities to participate fully in intellectual conversations. Part of thinking about issues of personalization means that we move away from binary ways of thinking that define academic literacy and out-of-school literacy as polar opposites instead of as repertoires of language to draw from and use.

Research in functional linguistics relates to this expanded view of personalization. When students learn language and grammar in these ways, their language repertoire expands. They are not replacing their informal language with more academic or formal language but gaining access to more forms of language. "In order to help students master the dialects valued in mainstream academic, civic, and economic institutions in the United States, literacy educators need to develop an approach to grammar instruction that recognizes language variation, connections between language form and meaning, and students' existing knowledge about language" (Godley, Carpenter, & Werner, 2007, p. 41).

Finally, these recent developments are helping educators to understand that content knowledge cannot be separated from learning the language used to represent it (Schleppegrell, 2004).

CLASSROOM EXPERIENCE BASE FOR DISCIPLINARY LITERACY

Disciplinary literacy (DL) has been implemented in varying degrees in fifteen school districts, most of them large and urban. Interviews, surveys, classroom observations, and anecdotal evidence provide evidence of the positive influences on teacher practice and student learning of DL systemic practice in these districts. The evidence points to improved knowledge and implementation of effective instructional practice with overall higher expectations by teachers and increased use of rigorous tasks and sets of sequenced lessons that assist students in moving from basic understanding to more complex, higher-order thinking. Teachers report higher student engagement in learning through talk, revision of work, and persistence through difficult problems and texts. In the three external evaluations of DL conducted in two large urban school districts, evaluators cite similar findings (David & Greene, 2007; Talbert & David, 2007; Talbert, David, & Lin, 2008). In several districts, achievement as evidenced on state tests has increased during the years of DL systemic implementation.

Along with these positive indicators, external evaluators have raised significant issues about sustaining progress toward implementation: "Expectations for rate of expansion and results need to be commensurate with the size of investments in building teacher, coach and administrator capacity and in providing dedicated time for focused teacher learning with coach support" (David & Greene, 2008, p. 10). As a principal in a district where teachers did not have ongoing time to learn together observed, "Teachers are afraid of the pedagogy. They might be on board using the materials, but they want to do all the talking and not let the students construct meaning. They fear that an administrator will come in to observe and not see a quiet classroom" (David & Greene, 2007, p. 17). This observation is contrasted against work in another district where administrators at the district and school levels provided time and support for teachers to inculcate DL practices in ongoing professional learning communities led by trained teacher leaders. The evaluators concluded:

> Our findings suggest that Disciplinary Literacy with Professional Learning Communities is effective in developing teacher collaboration on instruction as well as increasing the academic rigor of teaching and learning. Consistent with the literature on Professional Learning Communities (PLCs), these results derive from three related factors: (1) the DL lessons provide focus for teacher work in newly formed PLCs; (2) the task of implementing and creating DL lessons is sufficiently complex and challenging to warrant collaboration and knowledge sharing among colleagues; and, as a result, (3) teachers see benefits to their own instructional practices. Studies of PLC development document that they often fizzle because teachers perceive that required collaboration with colleagues is not worth their time. Absent joint work that is worthy of their collective effort and pays off in the classroom, teachers see time spent in PLC meetings in compliance terms and develop rituals to nominally satisfy the requirement. Serious collaboration in PLCs grows around authentic instructional challenges and tasks, and it appears that DL lessons and tools are well-designed to foster the development of teacher learning communities. [Talbert et al., 2008, p. 40]

Sustained implementation is a complicated matter that involves creating the right district conditions as well as various kinds and levels of support for teachers, administrators, and central office staff (Coburn, 2003). We return to an in-depth discussion of necessary conditions and actions in Chapter Seven.

THE LIMITS OF LITERACY INTERVENTIONS

For several years, many school districts across the country have been implementing special intensive programs of catch-up literacy for students who enter middle or high school with weak literacy skills. Typically these literacy interventions focus only on sixth- and ninth-grade students with measured reading skills several years below grade level. Such students are scheduled for literacy courses, almost always taught by English language arts teachers, in double and triple blocks—that is, more than a single period per day (Deshler et al., 2007).

Two approaches to catch-up literacy instruction in English language arts predominate. One offers students highly structured skills instruction focusing on the details of language, word and sentence structure, vocabulary, rules of composition, and the like. Special textbooks, and sometimes computer-based learning systems, support this approach. These teaching materials make it relatively easy for educators to teach the structured language curriculum adequately. However, this approach does not easily teach students habits of literacy or deep knowledge of the content of English language arts other than language itself (Graham & Perin, 2007; Langer, 2002).

An alternative to skills teaching is a workshop or studio approach to English language arts literacy development relying on rich classroom libraries to provide students with reading materials at their own level of reading achievement. This approach mixes group and individual activities with an emphasis on scaffolded written composition and book discussion. The workshop/studio approach, although often used as an intervention for weak students, could be applied to secondary English language arts students of all competency levels. However, it is very difficult for teachers to learn and is more dependent on the quality of teachers and the quality of libraries and social support systems in the schools than is the skills training approach (Biancarosa & Snow, 2006).

Whichever form of instruction is used, catch-up literacy programs reach only the neediest students and generally last for only a year or two. Furthermore, absent thoughtful restructuring of school schedules, these programs' extended time demands may drive out instruction in other subjects.

INTEGRATING CONTENT INSTRUCTION AND LITERACY DEVELOPMENT

Whether the academic area is English language arts, mathematics, science, or history, it is difficult to separate content learning from the discipline-specific ways of reading, writing, and talking needed to generate and communicate that learning. A discipline's content and habits of thinking always go hand in hand. Habits of thinking occur in disciplinary ways of reading, writing, reasoning, and talking. So the big questions for schooling have to do with the ways in which teaching in the core disciplines supports students as they work on problems situated in the content and habits of thinking of the disciplines. What, then, might English language arts departments do to better support tomorrow's learners? How can they differentiate reading and writing instruction to support varying levels of English language proficiency, including the needs of English language learners? What are ways to improve teachers' use of existing resources to empower the learning of literature and language for all students? One approach, described in detail in Chapter Six, is to integrate certain discipline-specific pedagogical scaffolding routines and patterned ways of reading, writing, and talking into sets of lessons that build sequentially (Petrosky, 2006). By finding time and expertise inside and outside the school, English language arts departments can support teachers to explore and practice this approach. Lead teachers and language arts coaches might also learn how to incorporate ideas of cultural modeling (Lee, 2001, 2008) that allow students to build from their existing knowledge of texts to use more academic ways of reading and writing. Lee's vanguard studies on the growth of intellectual reasoning among urban high school students can support the integration of cultural socialization and identity processes into middle and high school English courses.

But the high levels of literacy called for by the recent reports go beyond that associated with English language arts instruction. What are other major academic content areas doing today, and what else might they consider doing tomorrow?

In mathematics education, research done over the past decade or so has demonstrated, among other things, the importance of starting with cognitively demanding tasks, then maintaining the cognitive challenge during set-up and enactment of lessons so that students can develop deep conceptual understanding in mathematics (Stein, Smith, Henningsen, & Silver, 2000). Today, various National Science Foundation (NSF)-funded curricula that align with the National Standards for School Mathematics (2000) offer cognitively demanding tasks and lesson sequences, along with support materials that help teachers set up the tasks and assess students' work. But according to most recent Trends in International Mathematics and Science Study report (Mullis, Martin, Gonzalez, & Chrostowski, 2004), maintenance of cognitive demand during the lesson's enactment remains problematic. One of the things mathematics educators could focus on doing better tomorrow, then, is allowing students to do the intellectual work of solving challenging problems and making connections among multiple representations during lessons, with teachers providing just enough assistance and feedback for students' performance of the task without reducing the academic rigor of the experience.

In science, the National Science Education Standards (National Research Council, 1996, 2000) called for inquiry-based science instruction "combining scientific knowledge with reasoning and thinking skills" in a way that is both "hands on" and "minds on" for students. The authors were clearly hoping to reconcile a long-standing content-versus-process dichotomy in the field. But vestiges of the dichotomy persist, especially concerning the learning outcomes that a given lesson or arc of lessons can address. That is, many harbor the perception that a lesson addresses either content or process. Those who see inquiry narrowly as process do not understand how inquiry-based science can also help students understand science content. Furthermore, since many state-level, high-stakes tests emphasize low-level content outcomes that can be more efficiently taught through didactic approaches, didactics rule the day. These tests, often based on overly specific state standards, undermine the original spirit of the National Science Education Standards, which was to unburden teachers by articulating the most important big ideas and unifying themes in science and to provide flexibility in the approaches teachers could use to help students meet standards. For science teachers, tomorrow's focus might be developing students' meta-awareness of how inquiry-based perspectives and methods support their learning about science concepts and vice versa.

In most secondary schools today, support for enriching history courses and instruction has waned in the face of high-stakes tests of reading, writing, and math performance (Hess, 2008; National Center on Education and the Economy, 2007). With no national standards or assessments driving improvement efforts, history teachers have few professional learning opportunities designed to advance the teaching of history. If they are part of development sessions related to teaching and learning, it is most likely with teachers in other disciplines studying the generic reading and writing approaches and strategy instruction alluded to earlier. Consequently history instruction has not changed much from the traditional frontal model of imparting information about events and assessing students' performance on the basis of how well they are able to recall and retell what they have been told. Implicit in this model is the understanding of history as a collection of facts that one can find recorded in various textbooks and reference materials. This model obscures the reality of historical accounts as authored narratives constructed by individuals whose perspectives reflect their own situation in time and space.

What might history educators do to teach tomorrow's students how historical narratives are constructed and interpreted in addition to teaching the content of the narratives themselves? With appropriate resources and improved opportunities for history teachers to reconsider their discipline and its pedagogical content, they could mentor students to work as historians do; in other words, students would study multiple sources and perspectives to form their own understandings and explications of historical events. History has multiple meanings and definitions; for every student, learning history needs to include understanding the sources of these perspectives and articulating them. By learning to interpret and contextualize a historical document, compare it to other documents, and extrapolate ideas from these documents, students could be learning how to understand and interpret texts and how to marshal evidence to support a historical argument.

Integrating literacy and content in the core subjects is both visionary and practical. As a vision, it always involves positioning learners to solve problems by using the habits of thinking specific to the disciplines. Practically this means that teachers and students engage in discipline-specific inquiries that focus on big ideas and the reading, writing, and talking that generate and communicate their thinking. We understand few people are prepared to do this. So as both a vision and a practice, it often means moving instruction from what currently goes on to what might go on. Table 1.1 paints that movement in broad strokes.

EXPANDING THE DEFINITION OF CONTENT KNOWLEDGE

Several decades of cognitive research have expanded the definition of content knowledge to include concepts and principles, such as those arising from particular domains or subject areas, along with the skills and actions that constitute popular taxonomies. Challenging the adequacy of those taxonomies as tools for guiding students from low-level memorization to higher-order thinking, this view of learning holds that "the student's task is to connect specific knowledge with specific action" in order to develop mature, conceptual understandings (Leinhardt, 1992, p. 21).

As students advance to middle and high school, the content demands and the sources of information—whether observations of natural phenomena or significant events, solutions to mathematical problems, or reading and writing more difficult texts—become more complex. As the texts, tasks, and talk become

Table 1.1
Integrating Literacy and Content in the Classroom

Moving Instruction From:	Moving Instruction Toward:
Remedial reading classes that drill students on the subskills of reading as an end point (not purposefully linked to subject matter content), paired with basic content-area classes where students who are not performing well in reading are given less complex content and texts	Content-area classes where all students are engaged in authentic literate activity around challenging academic content, with scaffolding and content coaching provided to meet individual student needs. Differentiated support, more time, and specialized curricula address needs such as fluency and accuracy
Content-area classes where teachers "teach around" reading by lecturing or giving students worksheets and assign reading and writing only as homework—usually coupled with frustration on the part of students and teachers alike when students do not seem to read and write well	Content-area classes where teachers know how to help students develop deep understanding of a focused group of content-area concepts, teach students how to read and write to access complex disciplinary content within texts, and model in class what students are to do independently
Broad but superficial content coverage through activities that end when students demonstrate understanding and high-stakes test preparation exercises separate from curriculum	Deep understanding and generative thinking through connected inquiries that revisit key concepts from multiple perspectives, include reflection, and have been thoughtfully aligned to significant ideas, standards, and high-stakes test demands
Training students to use a few generic reading and writing strategies to learn about science, math, history, and literature	Teaching students to read, write, inquire, and reason within each discipline—as scientists, historians, mathematicians, readers, and writers

more complex, the knowledge and the ways of learning vary more across subject matters (Shanahan & Shanahan, 2008; Biancarosa & Snow, 2006; Deshler et al., 2007). "Subjects have different arrangements of facts, concepts, and constraining notational systems. A map is not a musical score, which is not like the equation for a function, which in turn differs from an evolutionary tree" (Leinhardt, 1992, p. 21). These arrangements begin with the learning demands and questions of the tasks, texts, and talk of particular disciplines or subject matter areas. They are constructed on the premise that each subject area or discipline has its own unique knowledge core, its own habits of thinking and ways of reading, writing, and thinking, and its own perspective on what constitutes literacy.

Literacy practice that takes on the challenge of preparing secondary students to achieve high levels of literacy in major academic disciplines has significantly influenced DL frameworks and tools, the systemic practice described in this book. The developers (represented among the authors of this book) coined the term *disciplinary literacy* to refer collectively to the framework and norms for literacy by discipline with the content-specific instructional materials and tools, professional development design and modules, and organizational routines needed for effective implementation of this systemic practice (McConachie, Resnick, & Hall, 2003, McConachie et al., 2006).

To make these shifts in practice so that all students in a district have sustained opportunities to learn, apply, and engage with others in content-rich learning experiences will require a new vision of instructional quality and of the necessary changes in teaching, learning, professional learning, and organizational routines (Table 1.2).

This new vision of instruction can be enacted from a number of perspectives. Teachers and principals benefit from long-term professional development, especially when it engages them in inquiries as learners in the disciplines. They benefit from studying and reflecting on their learning and the inquiry lessons in which they engaged as learners. And they benefit from studying and developing sequences of lessons as part and parcel of an inquiry curriculum because cognitively sophisticated learning more often than not reaches across arcs of lessons that can take anywhere from three or four days to weeks to unfold. The curriculum that benefits teachers and students the most as learners integrates content and instructional routines (Kauffman, Johnson, Kardos, Liu, & Peske, 2002), so that both teachers and students can use it to apprentice to a discipline's ways of thinking and working.

Table 1.2
A New Disciplinary Literacy Vision of Instructional Quality

Moving From:	Moving Toward:
Teacher as dispenser of knowledge to students	Teacher as facilitator, knowledgeable guide, codeveloper of content knowledge and habits of thinking with students
Teacher as the removed expert, only presenting and lecturing to students	Teacher as knowledgeable coach and guide assisting learners to use routines and rituals of cognitive apprenticeship (Brown, Collins, & Duguid 1989), such as opportunities to practice metacognition, engage in extended practice, receive and use intensive feedback, and revisit learning to work with students as codevelopers of content knowledge and habits of thinking
Assigning and testing many topics at a surface level	Assisting learning with frequent assessments of learning progress and needed feedback to advance and deepen understanding of core concepts
Same professional learning for all teachers on generic use of instructional strategies apart from focused study of knowledge domains	Discipline-specific professional learning of design of instruction, lessons, and units appropriate to the disciplinary problem
Teachers working alone using the textbook as the curriculum or individual lessons without modification based on student work or lesson enactment	Teacher-based learning communities meeting regularly to modify and develop lessons within units and courses based on studying lesson enactment, student work samples, and assignments
Principals as building managers who do not have time or the professional skills set to lead and develop others to lead teaching and learning in core academic areas	Principals who lead as learners and as instructional leaders of teaching and learning in core academic areas within a network of shared leadership

Curriculum, no matter how it is represented—as textbooks or sets of lesson's or units of study—apprentices teachers and students to disciplinary content and particular habits of thinking. If teachers and students work, for example, from a textbook in English language arts, then their experience of the discipline is structured by the content and teaching methods promoted by the textbooks. In the cases where there is no curriculum, teachers, especially beginning teachers, are often "overwhelmed by the responsibility and demands of designing curriculum and planning daily lessons" (Kauffman et al., 2002). In such cases where there is no specified curriculum, teachers frequently fall back on teaching what they were taught in the ways they were taught or they rely on textbooks and workbooks.

Our point is that curriculum in the disciplines is a hodgepodge. In some cases, it is a textbook. In others, it is sets of standards. In yet others, it is a district framework that tries its best to accommodate state standards and assessments, students' needs, and teachers' preferences. Our experiences in districts with DL has taught us the importance of focused, coherent curricula in the disciplines that support teachers and students with cognitively-challenging tasks organized around big ideas in the content. The use of such a curriculum, such as an NSF-designed science unit, or the development of such units, as we have seen in English language arts, requires the focused and coherent work of teachers, coaches, principals, and district-level administrators. And at least initially, professional development support for DL lesson, unit, and curriculum development is critical because it is both difficult to implement a new vision for teaching and learning and easy to "fit" such a new vision to practices that do not support it or even contradict it.

We think of this vision of teaching and learning in DL nested in learning communities throughout districts—classrooms, departments, schools, and various configurations across districts. A district's commitment to nested learning communities gives everyone in the system the support they need to study, develop, implement, and revise DL tasks, lessons, units, and curriculum.

Disciplinary Literacy

A Principle-Based Framework

Stephanie M. McConachie

In 2002, the Institute for Learning at the University of Pittsburgh's Learning Research and Development Center coined the term *disciplinary literacy* (DL) to describe the overall systemic practice it had developed and begun to pilot within a subset of its partner school districts. Disciplinary literacy was built around the belief that the definitions of literacy at the secondary level must be anchored in the specifics of individual disciplines. This was a departure from the common use of the term *literacy*—and particularly as applied in elementary education—to mean reading and writing more generally. The idea was that in middle and high school, as academic subject matter becomes more complex and differentiated by disciplines, so must the definition of literacy. Shanahan and Shanahan (2008) describe the development of literacy progression as a pyramid with the "base representing the highly generalizable basic skills that are entailed in all or most reading tasks" (p. 3). By the time students are taking high school courses, they are working to comprehend and examine texts that require increasingly sophisticated and less generalizable skills and routines:

> The constraints on the generalizability of literacy skills for more advanced readers—symbolized here by the narrowing of the pyramid—are imposed by the increasingly disciplinary and technical turn in the nature of literacy tasks. A high school student who can do a reasonably good job of reading a story in an English class might not be able to make much sense of biology or algebra books, and vice versa. Although most students manage to master basic and even intermediate literacy skills, many never gain proficiency with the more advanced skills that would enable them to read challenging texts in science, history, literature, mathematics, or technology. [quoted in Shanahan & Shanahan, 2008, p. 4]

LITERACY AND DISCIPLINARY NOTIONS

When the team of Institute for Learning Fellows, represented among the authors of this book, began working with district and teacher leaders, we used the following brief definition as the starting point from which to build understanding of DL: *Disciplinary literacy involves the use of reading, reasoning, investigating, speaking, and writing required to learn and form complex content knowledge appropriate to a particular discipline.* As adult learners quickly surmised, the definition statement that begins with common ground of process and content knowledge across academic areas finishes by stating the need for specificity by discipline.

Traditionally literacy has not included content knowledge and has been narrowly defined as the ability to read and write that involved decoding and encoding. However, today most researchers take a much broader view of literacy, suggesting that it involves mechanics such as decoding as well as higher-order thinking: conceptualizing, inferring, inventing, and testing. They argue that literacy encompasses oral communication skills, as well as reading and writing skills (Fillmore & Snow, 2000). The sociocultural perspective on literacy, which encompasses the learning and use of symbols within social systems and cultural practices, examined by Heath in the early 1980s, has recently emerged again as another significant layer of defining literacy (Banks & Members of the LIFE Diversity Consensus Panel, 2007; Goos, 2004; Nystrand, 2006; Heath, 1983). The definition of literacy we are using in this book is even broader. It advances from the established higher-order thinking and oral communication skills situated within social systems and cultural practices to acknowledge the variance of the critical thinking and language use that derives from the content problems of literacy being read, reasoned, investigated, spoken, and written about (Shanahan & Shanahan, 2008; Leinhardt & Young, 1998; Leinhardt, 1992, 1993; Resnick, 1990; Resnick & Resnick, 1989). This is an understanding of literacy and the needs of literacy instruction that takes into account that content advances through literacy understanding and that literacy advances through content understanding. The beginning definition statement remains the foundation from which to engage in disciplinary literacy by the unique requirements of scientific, historical, mathematical, and literary and grammatical inquiry.

DISCIPLINARY LITERACY LEARNING

Defining DL within instructional practice drew on accepted understandings of academic disciplines as unique knowledge communities with their own histories, epistemologies, questions, and concepts (Schwab, 1978; Grossman & Stodolsky, 1995). These knowledge communities have norms for literacy that follow from specific organizational structures, knowledge bases, and driving questions. Learners of a discipline use these norms to respond to and evaluate experiences, complex problems, the physical world, and existing text.

Disciplinary views acknowledge the value of adolescent students' learning specialized knowledge about the world: "Disciplines exist because they exert control over the social and natural world, without which social and natural phenomena remain mysterious or enigmatic, and at times unmanageable. Disciplines carve out slices of reality and explain them through rigors and standards that scholars in specialized fields determine for their community, which also become available for readership outside the discipline" (Leonardo, 2004, p. 3). Leonardo and others affirm the prevalent theory (Delpit, 1995; Scarcella, 2003) that distinct knowledge areas help adolescent students, particularly those developing academic literacy, to understand content knowledge more deeply in the selected areas they choose or are required to study.

For the vast majority of adolescents at varying points on the road to expertise in a discipline, applying domain specificity to enhance learning is an important development. Our minds work partly in terms of domain specificity; that is, we have been equipped through evolution with particular ontological categories of the world, such as "physical objects, artifacts, living kinds, and persons" (Hirschfeld & Gelman, 1994, p. 5). Working from knowledge domains assists learners to determine their ideas about the world.

Domains are built in by evolution, but they also need to be triggered by stimuli in the environment (Boyer, 1996). Dewey (1938) and Schwab (1978) both argued for the important role of disciplines in elementary and secondary education. For them, the educational status quo of static representations of knowledge and of an absence of creative knowledge-based solutions to problems needed to be changed. Once changed, disciplinary learning can lead to understandings about how disciplinary knowledge is created and verified—what Schwab called "a narrative of enquiry" rather than the old "narrative of conclusions" (1978, p. 15).

Within the study of a discipline, domain specificity and the narrative of inquiry can work together to address compelling content investigations and problems. Here, for example, Petrosky (2006) considers how to bring the teaching of literature from the past into relevance through inquiry. He situates the study of literature within "both the history of the discipline and in the kinds of intellectual work the discipline encourages and the various ways in which individuals participate in disciplinary communities when they read, study, talk and write. And although there is considerable transmission and exchange of information in discipline communities, the heart of their work resides in the problem posing and solving they invite, in the critique they encourage, and in the interpretive frameworks they establish" (Petrosky, 2006, p. 25).

For most middle and high school students, this is a very different way of learning. (Shanahan & Shanahan, 2008; Applebee, Langer, Nystrand, & Gamoran, 2003). Consequently they have little or no history of understanding how to carry on these conversations even if they do have the everyday, out-of-school language experiences that are deep and somewhat similar (Moje, Overby, Tysvaer, & Morris, 2008). Educators of middle and high school students have the challenge of engaging even students with weak academic language competence in thoughtful, cognitively demanding tasks using complex, written literary texts, historical documents, mathematics problems, and scientific treatises. Therefore, a significant initial DL practice is to engage teachers and other school and district leaders in lesson tasks from units that embody disciplinary inquiries requiring content-rich intellectual work. From their engagement, teachers reflect on their own learning in the lessons: what they did as learners and what the teacher facilitator did to support their learning. The teachers' reflections on their own learning make the subsequent discussions about what it would take for them to move from teaching by telling about what others learned to immersion in investigating, interpreting, and, as appropriate, solving situated disciplinary problems, more viable and specific. An important aspect of the discussion of "what it would take to teach this way" is about what adolescents would need instructionally and socially to learn "in these ways." What naturally follows is assisting teachers and other leaders to plan how they would go about using lessons similar to these with their own students—and then considering how they would formatively self- and peer-assess their practice in light of students' progress toward understanding core concepts as the next critical source of data in order to implement DL as systemic practice.

These lesson experiences, first for adult educators and then adapted for adolescents, have involved assisting learners to engage in representative disciplinary tasks. In history, for example, learners think as historians as they read multiple secondary accounts of an event, such as the Boston Massacre, obtaining knowledge not only of the event itself but how the event is described across these accounts by asking, "According to this author, what are the causes of the Boston Massacre?" "According to this author, what is the significance of this event in the stream of events leading up to the American Revolution?" In using the refrain, "according to this author," learners pay attention to the details included in each author's account, the discrepancies among those details, and how the differences across the accounts come to be. Finally, students construct their own account of the Boston Massacre using what they have learned from the sum of these accounts and discerning which details are most plausible in the process of constructing their own version.

The tasks and texts, as in our history example, have to be broad enough that students can draw on their home, outside-of-school cultures, along with their in-school cultures, as key social capital to draw on to expand their understanding. Students in this kind of curriculum need rich tasks, texts, and environments that permit and encourage exploratory talk and writing so that it is possible for them to use all sources of information—from both in and out of school—to bridge from what they already know, are now rethinking, or have yet to learn, to solve complex disciplinary problems. Some learners solve these problems with immersion alone; most need the guidance of explicit modeling, analysis, and practice that adheres to the norms of particular disciplines (Banks & Members of the LIFE Diversity Consensus Panel, 2007; Delpit, 1995). This kind of immersion in the real problems of a discipline is important for all adolescent learners' development as thinkers and critical consumers of knowledge. In particular, it benefits English language learners, who may be outside society's dominant culture (Banks & Members of the LIFE Diversity Consensus Panel, 2007; Short & Fitzsimmons, 2007).

School Texts Need to Be Worth Students' Time

Part of this immersion process involves "rehumanizing autonomous text" (Geisler, 1994, p. 88). This means enabling students to recast themselves as readers and thinkers who question what they are reading and find ways to extend their understanding of texts to their everyday lives. Geisler continues, "After 14 years of being taught that the text (or the teacher) has all the answers, is it any surprise that some students find it hard to understand that they must read rhetorically, that they must ask about the author's purpose and context in order to use knowledge productively? Students must actually be untaught the distrust of personal opinion and contextualized understandings that has been drummed into them through general education" (p. 58).

There are many documented instances of students seeing their assigned in-school reading as something they do not understand and have little interest in figuring out (Moje, Overby, Tysvaer, & Morris, 2008; Biancarosa & Snow, 2006). Texts, whether spoken or written, can represent the antithesis of many students' home cultures. To buy into the texts' ideas can seem a rejection of their cultures. The texts, if presented as unbridled truth, make it easier for students to stay disengaged and avoid reading altogether. If students primarily encounter content without questioning or developing interpretations, the texts they read and reproduce remain unquestioned authorities or formulaic duplications and outside the significant realm of their lives. Part of the movement toward reading rhetorically means continuing to move away from individualistic and transmission views of learning. "Because of our long history with behaviorism as the defining discourse of education, our schools have imagined disciplines principally as bodies of knowledge to transmit and learn rather than as occasions to learn and practice sophisticated kinds of thinking" (Petrosky, 2004, p. 5).

Geisler argues that students' in-school texts are stripped of the metadiscourse that would assist learners to understand them using their everyday understandings.

She reports that school textbooks are written without commentaries of differing viewpoints and without explicit attention to their construction that would make the texts explicitly authored documents that could be questioned. Given the anonymous, unquestioned, authoritative nature of school textbooks, Geisler claims that knowledge is packaged in schools "in ways that will be misunderstood or ignored by students" (1994, p. 88). When we change the texts we use to authentically authored ones with varying viewpoints and arrange instruction so students can question what they read and hear, we have the means to assist students in developing an engaging problem space of content with rhetorical process.

Habits of Thinking

Teachers must be able to teach and guide inquiry-based learning from a solid understanding of the structure and organization of knowledge within the discipline as well as its foundational facts and principles. And they need to be familiar with the means of discourse or ways of knowing and knowing how or habits of thinking within a discipline. We use the expression "habits of thinking" as an umbrella term for knowing how to work in different disciplines. The term is shorthand for the ways that members of different communities read, inquire, reason, investigate, speak, write, and co-construct their respective knowledge bases. By integrating content knowledge and habits of thinking within their disciplines, teachers can model for their students specific ways to investigate key topics. In other words, teachers must have content expertise—both the conceptual knowledge and the habits of thinking of their disciplines—plus instructional techniques and approaches or habits of practice that scaffold students' learning.

For students, disciplinary literacy involves developing expertise in the content and the rhetorical processes, genres, methods, inquiries, and strategies of a discipline (Ball, Dice, & Bartholomae, 1990; Geisler, 1994; Leinhardt, 1993, Leinhardt & Young, 1998). In ordinary language, it means learning to read, write, talk, and reason as a junior member of a particular discipline. It means understanding what counts within the discipline as a good question, evidence, problem, or solution. It means crafting arguments in the ways that members of a discipline do: for example, proofs in mathematics, document analysis in history, interpretations in literature, hypothesis testing in science. Thus, disciplinary literacy calls for mastery of both the core ideas and concepts and the habits of thinking of particular disciplines.

FOUNDATIONAL MODEL: LEARNING ON THE DIAGONAL

A foundational DL model, which borrows from Geisler's (1994) model for academic literacy, calls for teaching and learning "on the diagonal" (Figure 2.1). The idea is that developing deep conceptual knowledge in a discipline requires using the habits of thinking valued and used by that discipline. To develop strategic and powerful discipline-specific habits of thinking, one needs to be directed by one's content knowledge. So for students to develop literacy in a particular discipline, they need to grow on these two dimensions simultaneously. *Learning on the diagonal* means using content-specific habits of thinking to develop understanding of the conceptual content of each discipline.

This means that teachers must be able to teach on the diagonal. As we said earlier, teachers must have content expertise—the conceptual knowledge and the habits of thinking of their disciplines—and the pedagogical content knowledge to understand how to scaffold students' learning on the diagonal. The DL framework outlines ways teachers can support their students' development of disciplinary literacy by organizing instruction so that classrooms function as apprenticeships in a discipline. The model helps teachers understand that students need to do the

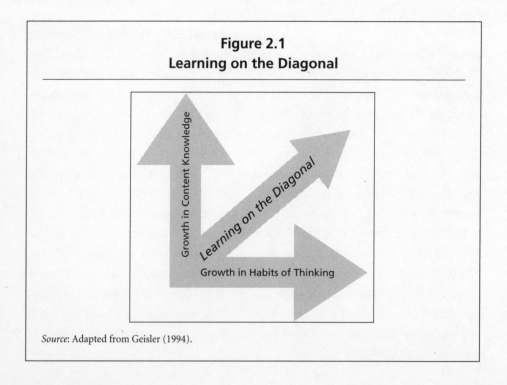

Figure 2.1
Learning on the Diagonal

Source: Adapted from Geisler (1994).

problem solving in order to develop conceptual understanding. In mathematics, the work begins with teachers analyzing features of math tasks to determine whether a task is cognitively challenging and has the potential to generate critical thinking and development of math concepts. With a challenging math task, students have the opportunity to be math problem solvers.

When learners engage in learning new mathematical ideas as they solve a cognitively challenging math task, they are working on the diagonal. To work on the model's diagonal, learners begin by joining their math content knowledge (the vertical dimension of the model) to a variety of strategies and representations to make sense of the problem (the model's horizontal dimension). In the classroom, the teacher may engineer an increase in verbal and written exchanges on the problem by organizing students into groups that the teacher can then listen to and assess how best to promote students' developing understanding with appropriate questions. The questions to the students may be related to ways of working or the habits of thinking (the horizontal dimension) or may be content questions (represented by the vertical dimension of the model). If the questions are the right ones for these learners, they will continue their learning on the trajectory to develop new mathematical conceptual understanding (represented by the diagonal). For example, the calling plans math task, examined in Chapter Four, asks learners to compare two telephone plans and determine when one becomes less expensive than the other. Students work as mathematicians, using habits of thinking represented by the horizontal dimension of the model to explore all aspects of the problem. They construct tables or graphs, or they may represent the plans algebraically. In comparing and connecting their various solution methods, they have the opportunity to consider the benefits of different approaches, joining content and habits of thinking mathematically. Like mathematicians, they look for patterns and relationships and then attempt to form generalizations. In the process, they deepen and increase their understanding of linear functions— the cornerstone of algebra 1.

FOUNDATIONAL TOOL: PRINCIPLES OF LEARNING

When teacher leaders, their principals, and other district and school leaders prepare to be part of the systemic practice of DL, they begin with the ideas and practices of the Institute for Learning's principles of learning (Resnick, Hall, & IFL Fellows, 2003). The nine principles of learning present specific ideas and a language for describing instructional environments and practices that promote rigorous teaching and learning (Exhibit 2.1). A superintendent whose district participates in DL work described their use: "We have a common language of teaching and learning. In this way, we became an effort-based, standards-based school system. We believe that effort creates ability. You become smarter by working harder in a system set up for high achievement. This is our responsibility as a public school system" (Talbert & David, 2007, pp. 2–3).

Exhibit 2.1 presents overview statements of the nine principles of learning. All nine provide teachers and instructional leaders with an image of what effective effort-based instruction looks and sounds like. The overview statements are an invitation to a deeper study of articles, videos, and student indicators of each principle. Within DL, the ideas of the principles of learning are illustrated in action through exemplar lessons and instructional video with which teachers and principals engage. The discussions about the lessons and video are specific to the four core academic areas of mathematics, science, social studies/history, and English studies. Although all nine principles interrelate in actual practice, four of them have been particularly effective in supporting learners to understand what this kind of instruction looks like for teachers and students: academic rigor in a thinking curriculum, Accountable Talk*, learning as apprenticeship, and socializing intelligence.

Academic rigor in a thinking curriculum articulates the need to combine knowledge development with attention to thinking skills and active use of knowledge at every step in the learning process. Substantial research shows that an often expressed "progressive idea"—that we can teach thinking without a solid foundation of knowledge—is misleading (Willingham, 2007; Bransford, Brown, & Cocking, 1999; Resnick et al., 2003). But so is the traditional idea that we can teach knowledge without engaging students in thinking. Students will acquire robust, lasting knowledge only if they themselves do the mental work of making sense of it. Knowledge and thinking must be joined at all stages of learning. This implies a curriculum organized around major concepts that students are expected to know deeply. Teaching must engage students in active reasoning about these concepts. In every subject, at every grade level, instruction and learning must include commitment to a knowledge core, high thinking demand, and active use of knowledge.

The principle of Accountable Talk, developed by Michaels, O'Connor, Hall, and Resnick (2002), provides tools and guidelines for building classroom talk

*Accountable Talk® is a registered service mark of the University of Pittsburgh.

Exhibit 2.1
The Principles of Learning

Organizing for effort: Everything within the school is organized to support the belief that sustained and directed effort can yield high achievement for all students. High standards are set, and all students are given as much time and expert instruction as they need to exceed or meet expectations.

Clear expectations: Clear standards of achievement and gauges of students' progress toward those standards offer real incentives for students to work hard and succeed. Descriptive criteria and models that meet the standards are displayed in the schools, and the students refer to these displays to help them analyze and discuss their work.

Fair and credible evaluations: Tests, exams, and classroom assessments must be aligned with the standards of achievement for these assessments to be fair. Furthermore, grading must be done against absolute standards rather than on a curve so that students can clearly see the results of their learning efforts.

Recognition of accomplishment: Clear recognition of authentic student accomplishments is a hallmark of an effort-based school. Progress points are articulated so that regardless of entering performance level, every student can meet the criteria for accomplishments often enough to be recognized frequently.

Academic rigor in a thinking curriculum: In every subject and at every grade level, instruction and learning must include commitment to a knowledge core, demand for high thinking, and active use of knowledge.

Accountable Talk: Accountable Talk means using evidence that is appropriate to the discipline and that follows established norms of good reasoning. Teachers should create the norms and skills of Accountable Talk in their classrooms.

Socializing intelligence: Intelligence comprises problem-solving and reasoning capabilities with habits of mind that lead one to use those capabilities regularly. Equally, it is a set of benefits about one's right and obligation to make sense of the world and one's capacity to figure things out over time. By

(continued)

Exhibit 2.1
(*continued*)

calling on students to use the skills of intelligent thinking—and by holding them responsible for doing so—educators can teach "intelligence."

Self-management of learning: Students manage their own learning by evaluating feedback they get from others, bringing their own knowledge to bear on new learning, anticipating learning difficulties and apportioning their time accordingly, and judging their progress toward a learning goal. Learning environments should be designed to model and encourage the regular use of self-management strategies.

Learning as apprenticeship: Learning environments can be organized so that complex thinking is modeled and analyzed in apprenticeship arrangements. Mentoring and coaching will enable students to undertake extended projects and develop presentations of finished work, both in and beyond the classroom.

environments that foster accurate use of knowledge, higher-order thinking about that knowledge, and learning communities so learners feel safe to take risks as thinkers and talkers in larger classroom and school intellectual and social settings. The tools of the principle of Accountable Talk are designed to help teachers turn classroom talk away from the initiate-respond-feedback (IRF) or, as it is also called, initiate-respond-evaluate (IRE) model of talk and toward genuine dialogic discussions. This model, still dominant in classroom talk, reinforces narrow views of recall of information and reproductions of existing knowledge. When students are mostly asked to respond to questions that the teacher or the texts have already answered, they have little genuine reasons for intellectual or social engagement in talk and reading to understand. They also have little reason to use what they already know from outside school to build new knowledge within school. This change from IRF/IRE to Accountable Talk is significant in the sciences and mathematics, which foster evidence-based, point-driven discussions that must begin by opportunities for students to explore and elaborate through talk as they take their first steps toward making sense of natural phenomena and mathematics tasks through public talk. In many cases, it is only after these opportunities of talking to learn that students are able to advance to the more abstract statements of math generalizations and scientific principles to reach the goals of point-driven discussions (Goos, 2004; Willingham, 2007). In the humanities areas of literature and history, talk is many times not point driven but evidence based toward support of arguments from inquiries requiring justifications of interpretations (Nystrand, 2006; Applebee et al., 2003; Wineburg, 1991). Again, as with other principles, the work begins from common ground across disciplines, but the disciplinary nature of the work changes purposes and approaches as the work advances toward higher-order learning goals.

Learning as apprenticeship draws from research on situated cognition (Resnick, Saljo, Pontecorvo, & Burge, 1997), cognitive apprenticeship (Collins, Brown, & Newman, 1989), legitimate peripheral participation (Lave & Wenger, 1991), and learning as assisted performance (Tharp & Gallimore, 1998). For many centuries, most people learned by working alongside experts who modeled skilled practice and guided novices as they created authentic products or performances for interested and critical audiences. This kind of apprenticeship allowed learners to acquire complex interdisciplinary knowledge, practical abilities, and appropriate forms of behavior. Much of the power of apprenticeship learning can be brought into schooling by organizing learning environments so that complex thinking is modeled and analyzed and by providing mentoring and coaching as students undertake to engage in academically rigorous work. Over time, through repeated classroom experiences of modeling and observation, active practice, scaffolding, coaching, and guided reflection, students become increasingly independent in carrying out academically rigorous work.

This notion of learning as apprenticeship is a powerful conceptual tool for influencing practice at the secondary level. When teachers believe that their classes should be organized in order to apprentice students to do the authentic work of their discipline, they must reconsider all classroom routines: the uses of homework, choice of materials, classroom environment, forms of discussion, who generates which questions when in the learning process, and so on. All are under inspection. Teachers must look beyond mere engagement and ask themselves to what extent a particular activity will reveal and engage students in doing the real work of history, mathematics, science, and English studies. Even those who love their disciplines must shift from performing for students to assisting the performance of students. For example, science teachers who have been arranging demonstrations of science that captivate students must now find ways to scaffold students to do their own investigations of scientific phenomena.

English teachers who have been used to presenting their own sophisticated interpretations of literary text must now find ways to model cognitive processes of "doing a reading" that make the mental work and strategies visible to students, as well as inviting and necessary. Students can no longer just memorize teachers' literary interpretations but must develop their own increasingly sophisticated interpretations of literary texts. As older, more experienced readers and writers, teachers are able to bring into the open how even accomplished readers and writers encounter routine puzzlement and necessary confusion as part of comprehending a difficult text or formulating an extended written argument. Teachers are the mentors who validate students' initial confusions about a difficult text's meaning or about how to start a writing draft as necessary and usual first steps toward understanding, interpreting, and writing text.

The DL framework has been substantially influenced by Resnick and LeGall's study (1997) of the conception of intelligence as a social practice. They drew on the work of Vygotsky and Piaget, considering both cultural and developmental theories of intelligence. In their review of intelligence, they cited the inability of learner-subjects to apply the cognitive skills they had successfully applied in defined environments to other contexts. This lack of transfer became a primary justification for the importance of developing students' habits of the intellect to promote self-realization of what to do and how to think when delving into complex problem and situations. Their work, now part of the principles of learning and the DL design principles, is based on students producing knowledge rather than on how students reproduce knowledge.

Socializing intelligence calls on students to use a full range of intellectual skills that support problem solving, even when the situation or problem is ill defined with no apparent solution paths. It is about not only having the information, represented by the vertical dimension, but also knowing how to act on it, that is, working on the horizontal dimension by rethinking the content. Moffett (1987) sees the essential purpose of an English curriculum designed to develop literate thinkers and doers as one that "teaches students to re-think or un-think." These ways of working or habits of thinking that Moffett, Resnick, Nelson-LeGall, Leinhardt, and Petrosky discuss include not only content and skills but also the discourse practices, principles, and actions socially situated within disciplines.

All four of these principles—academic rigor, Accountable Talk, learning as apprenticeship, and socializing intelligence—direct attention to the vital relationships among thinking, talking, acquisition, and application of knowledge. An extensive body of research on literacy as both a cognitive capability and a set of social practices involving reading, writing and reasoning (Goos, 2004; Geisler, 1994; Heath, 1983; Resnick, 1990; Resnick & Resnick, 1989) provides the theoretical groundwork for a broad view of disciplinary literacy that includes learning the special ways of reading, writing, and speaking that are specific to an intellectual discipline such as history, literature, mathematics, chemistry, or biology.

DISCIPLINARY LITERACY DESIGN PRINCIPLES

The principles of learning define what high-quality, effort-based instruction looks like from the individual student level. The DL design principles use the ideas of the principles of learning and then encircle them with larger instructional practices and conditions. Therefore, the DL design principles, developed to describe instructional practice by discipline, call out specific learner considerations drawn from the principles of learning.

At the overarching level, the DL design principles, relevant to all content areas, describe critical aspects of instruction, including knowledge domains, applying critical thinking to specific discipline problems, learning and teaching as apprenticeship, effort-based environments to socialize intelligence, and the integral nature of assessment to instruction.

Teachers and administrators use the DL design principles to provoke discussions about the elements of high-quality instruction, including what students need to learn and what teachers need to do to assist students to learn. They are intentionally written so that they cannot be used as a checklist for short, one-time observations in classrooms. Instead, they should be deployed (with other content-specific observation tools) to plan and observe instruction over time in order to assess structures, approaches, and patterns of ongoing, effective instruction that unfold and adjust during multiple, sequenced lessons. Initially teachers with principals and others use them, at times with accompanying video, to build awareness of DL approaches and as points of comparison between existing and desired instructional practice.

At the overarching level of the general statements, the five broad principles are separate and do not overlap in content. However, at the indicator level, the examples intentionally flow together, especially between principle 2, apprenticeship learning, and 3, teachers as mentors of apprentices. This overlap at the indicator level suggests that good instruction will often fulfill several purposes at once (see Appendix A). What follows are the DL design principles with brief explanations:

Principle 1: Knowledge and thinking must go hand in hand. Students learn core concepts and habits of thinking within each discipline as defined by standards and content requirements. All students are enabled and expected to inquire, investigate, read, write, reason, represent, and talk as mathematicians, scientists, historians, and literary thinkers about the critical questions, problems, and concepts defined by each discipline's standards and content requirements. Students experience curricula characterized by depth and consistency that are articulated across classes and grades. Students do the intellectual work involved in understanding core content and learning to identify big ideas and driving questions in a discipline.

Principle 2: Learning is apprenticeship. Learning activities, curricula, tasks, text, and talk apprentice students within the discipline. Students learn by doing the discipline—engaging in rigorous, ongoing investigation that mirrors the work of the discipline. All lessons, assignments, materials, and discussion serve as scaffolding for students' emerging mastery of discipline-specific knowledge and habits of thinking. Students can articulate how and why the activities they are engaged in will help them deepen their understanding of a disciplinary concept or in what ways they are working like members of a disciplinary community.

Principle 3: Teachers as mentors of apprentices. Teachers apprentice students by giving them opportunities to engage in rigorous disciplinary activity and providing scaffolding through inquiry, direct instruction, models, and coaching. Teachers create opportunities within and beyond the classroom that help students acquire the knowledge and habits of thinking of their discipline through active engagement in appropriate tasks. They use a variety of instructional approaches—including inquiry, direct instruction, modeling and observation, discussion, differentiated coaching, and guided reflection—to assist students' learning. They also orchestrate opportunities for students to learn from each other and from members of the discipline. Scaffolds are put in place to assist performance of tasks and are then gradually withdrawn as students become independent.

Principle 4: Classroom culture socializes intelligence. Intelligence is socialized through community, class learning culture, and instructional routines. Students are encouraged to take risks, seek and offer help when appropriate, ask questions and insist on understanding the answers, analyze and solve problems, reflect on their learning, and learn from one another. Class routines build a learning culture that invites effort by treating students as smart, capable, responsible learners. Teachers arrange environments, use tools, and establish norms and routines that communicate to all how to become smarter in their discipline.

Principle 5: Instruction and assessment drive each other. Instruction is assessment driven, and assessment is instruction driven. Teachers use multiple forms of formal and informal assessment and data to guide instruction. Throughout the year, teachers assess students' grasp of content-area concepts: their habits of inquiring, investigating, problem solving, and talking—and their learning processes and interests. Teachers use these assessments to help them tailor instructional opportunities to the needs of their learners. They also design and implement an effective classroom assessment system that begins with the end goal in mind and tracks students' progress throughout the unit and course. Students are engaged in self-assessment to develop metacognitive understanding and the ability to manage their own learning.

CONCLUSION

The DL principles send a message that teaching matters and that there is solid information from which to enact powerful pedagogy for adolescent learners. Their listing in this chapter sets the stage for the explications of each design principle in the scenarios and illustrations of teaching, learning, and tool-mediated practices in the next four chapters. The work of these content scenarios may begin from a common ground of inquiry and principles, but each quickly branches into the different representations of inquiry, reasoning, and argumentation in each slice of reality discipline.

Disciplinary Literacy in the History Classroom

Anita K. Ravi

Walk through the halls of any high school on a Friday, down the wing devoted to social studies, and you may see and hear several different scenarios. In one room, students may be "watching" a movie—shades down, heads down, teacher at his desk. The film could be a documentary, say, Ken Burns's Civil War series; or it could be a historically based fiction, say, *X* by Spike Lee, which tells the story of Malcolm X's life. Whatever the film, the students watch passively: there is no stopping to discuss at particular points, and they are not pressed to analyze what they are seeing. Although the film may be related to the content that students are studying, it is meant to fill time rather than serve as the text for instruction.

In another classroom, you may see students working silently on their end-of-week or end-of-chapter test—students focused, pencils on Scantron sheets at the ready as they try to recall the details of the chapter they are being tested on. What *were* the three main causes of the American Revolution? Will they remember that chapter next Friday? Probably not.

As you move down the silent hall, the noise of student voices begins to emerge. In this third classroom, students are seated in groups of three or four, arguing loudly with each other and pointing at the papers on their desks. They are alert and engaged. The teacher is bent down, talking with one of the groups of students, pointing to the papers on their desks, and then pointing to a series of questions written on large chart paper tacked to the wall. These students are talking about history. In fact, they are talking about the end of World War II. The papers that they point to on their desks are copies of primary source documents: letters from Manhattan Project scientists to President Truman; Truman's own correspondence with his cabinet; Truman's radio speech declaring that the bombs had been dropped; sections from a memoir of a Hiroshima survivor describing the impact of the bomb. The students are reasoning out the arguments for and against President Truman's decision to drop the atomic bombs on Hiroshima and Nagasaki in 1945. Occasionally they look to the chart paper on the wall and point to a series of questions listed up there: Why did Truman give the okay to drop the bombs, and what led up to his decision? What were some of the arguments against dropping the bomb? Was the dropping of the atomic bombs on Hiroshima and Nagasaki a necessary means toward an end to the war? In this classroom, every student is engaged in answering one or more of these questions with his or her group. The teacher moves from group to group helping students reference evidence from the texts in front of them to support their ideas, directing them toward pieces of text that might push or change their thinking. These students are engaged in historical inquiry and reasoning using standards of evidence. They are, in other words, are engaged in disciplinary literacy (DL) in history.

THINKING AS HISTORIANS

What accounts for this variance in what happens in history classrooms within schools and around the country? How might this variability relate to notions of what it means to learn history? The research on history teaching and learning reveals an identified gap between the practice of historians and the work of teachers and students in history classrooms. The work of historians resembles that described in the third classroom. Historians approach texts with certain ideas and questions in mind, setting the reason and rationale for the reading of a particular document or texts. They assemble a multitude of source information in order to test out these ideas and questions and to be true to the historical record by attending to the fragments this record leaves behind. Elements of each source then feed the production of the narrative, which is constantly checked and revised against the historian's theories about history, growing knowledge about the topic, and argumentative focus of the study at hand (Leinhardt & Young,

1996; Wineburg, 1994). Historians are also concerned with the multitude of voices, or historical actors, in any given situation.

It would not be historically sound to make an argument about Truman's decision to drop the bomb by reading only the writings and speeches of Truman. Researchers must establish the historical context in which he made that decision by questioning and consulting evidence through other voices in order to fully understand the context in which he made this decision. Historians question the authors of texts and the context in which these authors put pen to paper: What do we know about this author and the time in which she is writing? What might be influencing both her decision to write and what she is writing? Who is the intended audience for her writing, and what impact might this have on what gets written? In the research on cognition in history, this has been referred to as the *sourcing heuristic* (Wineburg, 1991; Bain, 2000). Historians do not just read and analyze the text on the page; they also read and analyze the subtext—the context in which the source was produced. The words that Truman chooses in a letter to his cabinet are inherently influenced by many mitigating factors: the Soviet race toward nuclear power, the dismal course of the war in the Pacific, pressure at home to put an end to the war, a growing consciousness in the United States and abroad of the Holocaust. All of these outside factors are brought to bear on the letter itself when Truman sits down to write it in the summer of 1945 and, again, when the historian picks it up sixty years later. This letter, a fragment of one of humanity's most momentous decisions, represents real people making hard decisions at particular moments in time.

The job of the historian is to sift through the fragments that history leaves behind to create a narrative of what happened. In creating that narrative, the historian selects and organizes the fragments—documentary evidence—to use as evidence in support of an argument. The historical narrative that results from this process is inherently argument: documentary evidence is brought to bear within the context of an argument that seeks to explain a specific historical event, movement, or phenomenon (Holt, 1990). Historical narratives (products of historians) almost always seek to tell the story of how something came to be (an event), that is, what happened, and what resulted or what was significant as a result. This chronology of events, then, is imbued with cause and effect. In the words of Tom Holt, "In history something is always developing, breaking down, emerging, transforming, growing or declining. Otherwise, it's sociology" (p. 13). Rather than a stagnant description of something that happened, the historical narrative breathes movement, growth, or decline into what it describes. There are always multiple interpretations of events and texts as constructed by historians. Not only can the story of history change with the discovery of new documentary evidence, it also changes depending on who is doing the telling.

The art of the historical craft is in how individual historians choose to bring documentary evidence to bear in their own particular argument. This process includes standards of evidence: historians are accountable to historical fact—to the words and actions of historical figures and to each other. Historians are, in fact, in constant conversation with each other and with interpretations of history over time. Within the discipline of history, not only do we seek to know history, but we also attend to the historiography of any particular subject—how historians have studied and debated a particular story over time. Just as texts are not produced in a vacuum, history itself is produced within the context of a particular time and space. Historians themselves react to the national and political climates in which they live and create their histories accordingly. Thus, we can refer to historians over time as consensus, progressive, feminist, or postmodern (Couvares, Saxton, Grob, & Billias, 2000). Patterns emerge from the perspectives that embody historical interpretations over time. And this too is part of the discipline of history.

What are the implications of the disciplinary concerns of history for students in classrooms? Most obviously, "doing" history, or practicing history, implies a movement away from rote memorization of information toward reasoned engagement with historical problems. Disciplinary literacy in history means that in the classroom, students access the tools used to understand questions such as how our national identity has been constructed and has changed over time. They work to understand, compare, contextualize, and interpret primary and secondary sources. Students extrapolate ideas from texts in the service of marshaling evidence used to support arguments about valid historical queries. The DL classroom supports them to construct their own historical narratives and enables them to make meaning about the familial, cultural, and literary history that is all around them. History, when practiced this way by students, is a process of constructing, reconstructing, and interpreting past events, ideas, and institutions from surviving or inferential evidence in order to understand and make meaningful who and what we are today. The process engages students in dialogues with voices from the past itself, recorders of the past, and interpreters today. The process also engages students in constructing coherent, powerful narratives that describe and interpret events from multiple perspectives.

Yet it is not just for the sake of doing history that such a move is so critical. Every American encounters history on a daily basis—whether we pass a historical monument on our way to work, decide to go see a historically based film at the movies on a Saturday night, or listen to a senator use lessons learned from Vietnam to make a case for an end to troop deployment in Iraq, we are, as a people, "awash in history" (Leinhardt, 2000). Disciplinary literacy in history takes as a major goal that of sending students out into the world equipped to make sense of the history they encounter every day. Yet making sense of the past in a way that is disciplinarily sound and personally relevant is not something that happens naturally (Boix-Mansilla, 2000). It is, in fact, the job of the teacher, and of the professional learning for that teacher, to create such connections in an environment that supports the learning of history in ways that remain true to how historians work. What does it mean to be an American? How has this identity changed and evolved throughout our history? How has this history been constructed and revised, and why? These are some of the central questions that drive DL in U.S. history. Because history has multiple meanings and definitions, learning history must include understanding the sources of these meanings and articulating them. By learning to interpret and contextualize a historical document, compare it to other documents, and extrapolate ideas from those documents, students learn how texts are understood and interpreted and how evidence is marshaled to support a historical argument.

In designing engaging units of study, we also take on powerful myths that culture perpetuates about history, historical figures, and learning history in school. For example, traditional classroom instruction in history/social studies often follows the stereotypical "open your books to Chapter Seven" where students read silently and answer the questions at the end of the chapter. This model perpetuates the textbook as the ultimate authority in the classroom, a belief that too many students hold as true. Our beginning work with students and with teachers seeks to explode that myth by examining four different textbook accounts of a single event in U.S. history: the Boston Massacre. Before engaging in reading any of these sources, learners are given three questions that serve as both the framework and the filter for processing what they read as they read it:

1. According to this source, what were the causes of the Boston Massacre?

2. What actually happened on that day in March 1770?

3. According to this source, what is the significance of the Boston Massacre?

Using these questions, learners read and chart what each source offers as evidence. They in fact find vast differences in the amount and type of information given and learn far more by reading multiple secondary source accounts of the same event than reading just one. The refrain, "according to this source," relocates the locus of authority in the learner (the person asking these questions) rather than in the source or the textbook. By using the questions as a tool to drive the lesson, learners are asked to take responsibility for their own learning, gather evidence, and then summarize that evidence to create their own coherent account of the Boston Massacre.

A second example of cultural myths we take on through curricular design is that of the "great individual" as the driver of historical change. Through the popularity of biography, through months meant to celebrate different groups of Americans, the great individual emerges—usually male, very seldom female—acting alone to generate watershed moments in history. These individuals are often portrayed in isolation from the societal fabric and communities that produced and supported them to become great men or women.

In a unit on the civil rights movement of the 1950s and 1960s, we seek to turn this myth on its ear by exploring the movement from the bottom up, studying how multiple groups, people, and organizations created the events we know in the traditional civil rights curriculum as the Montgomery-to-Memphis trajectory (Payne, 1998). Through a study of photographs, film, and oral history, we explore how and why different people who are usually left out of the traditional curriculum (women, children, students, workers) came together and organized for social and political change. For example, popular mythology tells us of a middle-aged woman named Rosa Parks who refused to give up her bus seat on a Thursday in December 1955 and launched a 381-day bus boycott in Montgomery, Alabama, that began that Monday. We ask learners to consider the following question: How it is that in three days—Friday to Sunday—forty thousand African Americans were organized to stay off the buses a few days later? This question leads to an examination of multiple sources, revealing that many individuals had been working for equal access to public facilities in Montgomery for decades. Popular mythology focuses on the electrifying speech delivered by the young Reverend Martin Luther King Jr. that Monday night at the Holt Street Baptist church in Montgomery. Now we ask: Who brought Dr. King to Montgomery? Who guided him, launched him as a leader of the civil rights movement, and sustained him over time? By taking on the significant moments handed to us by popular mythology, we seek to design instruction that mirrors the arguments of historian Charles Payne: that this period was about movement, not protest events, and that organizing had been a central feature of African American life and institutions since the end of the Civil War.

APPLYING DL PRINCIPLES TO THE STUDY OF HISTORY

These ideas and a curriculum for students and for professional learning emanate from DL principles applied to the study of history.

Principle 1: Knowledge and Thinking Must Go Hand in Hand

Students learn core concepts and habits of inquiring, investigating, reasoning, reading, writing, and talking within history as defined by standards:

- Students regularly engage in historical inquiry, tackling themes, concepts, and content by reading and analyzing multiple sources, both primary and secondary.
- Students learn and use skills of historical analysis, persuasion, and use of evidence in reasoning, writing, and talking about history in every unit of study.
- Historical habits of thinking are woven through each unit of study, and students are coached to use these habits with increasing complexity and ability over time.
- Students are engaged in explicating multiple historical roots of current world and local events, and conversely, they are engaged in understanding historical events, people, systems, and movements as historical phenomena situated in a specific time and place.

The ways in which students engage in this intellectual work are just as important as the work itself. If they are not apprenticed in the practice of this work, we cannot reasonably expect them to be able to produce such work on their own one day. It is the job of the teacher, the school, and the district to provide the appropriate pedagogical context for this work, which leads to the second DL principle applied to history.

Principle 2: Learning Is Apprenticeship

Learning activities, investigations, fieldwork, curricula, text, and talk apprentice students within the discipline:

- Students learn by doing history through engagement in ongoing, authentic historical inquiries.

- All materials, discussion, tasks, and homework are selected and used to support student learning of concepts, processes, and habits of thinking specified by learning standards in history and current historical scholarship.

- Students reflect on what they are doing in history and communicate their work to others. They are supported to both talk and listen: sharing their interpretations of historical documents and events, challenging those interpretations, making use of evidence, and asking questions of others to ensure their own understanding.

How are these principles put into practice in a classroom? How do teachers and school districts design a curriculum that supports rigorous historical activity in classrooms? Our example of designing DL history instruction for the classroom comes from my collaboration with a small group of middle and high school teachers in Providence, Rhode Island, during the 2005-2006 and 2006-2007 school years. After two years of attending DL institutes focused on the modules described, this core team of two high school teachers and two middle school teachers was tasked by the deputy superintendent and humanities supervisor for Providence Public Schools with designing DL units of study for grades 8 and 10, the two years in which U.S. history is taught in the district in middle and high school. To pilot the process of developing common units of study, this team decided to design one unit for each grade level, ask teachers to try it out during the second quarter of the school year, collect student work resulting from the units to analyze and calibrate across the district, then move toward designing three more units for each grade level (one to be taught during each quarter of the school year). Although the final product would not constitute the sum total of what teachers would teach in each of those courses, the four units of study in each course would be the anchor for embedding DL practices and rigor in history in all eighth- and tenth-grade classrooms, giving teachers common units of instruction to ground their practice and conversations with each other.

The first unit developed for the tenth-grade U.S. history course, which covered Reconstruction through World War II, focused on immigration to the United States in the twentieth century. Prior to designing this unit, teachers read work by scholars of immigration history and consulted their adopted standards for this topic of study: the National Center for History in the Schools, adopted by the state of Rhode Island. In consulting their standards, they realized that immigration is mentioned only once: through an examination of the large wave of immigration that began at the turn of the twentieth century and lasted through the Immigration Act of 1924. The focus in this time period was on the experiences of immigrants of Eastern European descent, the conditions in which they lived and worked (mostly in northeastern cities), and their role in political movements and the labor movement.

Within most state and national standards, immigration is flagged for study only during this period, the Progressive era. Yet in most urban classrooms, and certainly in Providence classrooms, many students are first- or second generation immigrants themselves—part of the second and third waves of immigration to the United States in the twentieth century, sparked by the immigration acts of 1965 and 1990. These students are from Latin America, the Caribbean, Mexico, East Asia, Southeast Asia, and the former Soviet Union. In a survey given to all tenth-grade U.S. history teachers in the district prior to engaging in curriculum unit design, social studies teachers were asked to rank each topic in U.S. history (identified on the survey) in order of importance: 93 percent of teachers ranked the study of immigration as "extremely important" in the teaching of U.S. history. Immigration then became the focus of development for the first pilot tenth-grade DL unit.

The first step toward designing a unit of study in DL history is to draw on recent historical scholarship for the topic at hand. The way historians have studied and characterized immigration has changed over the course of the twentieth century, just as the political climate for immigration has changed. From Oscar Handlin's theory of the "uprooted" immigrant, to John Bodnar's "transplanted," to Gary Gerstle's "coerced immigrant," each theory puts forth ideas about how and why immigrants left their homelands and came to the United States and what their experience was like once they got here (Handlin, 1973; Bodnar, 1985; Gerstle, 2001). Notions of the melting pot, which once pervaded discussions around immigration, have evolved into the "salad bowl" metaphor: immigrants are no longer forced to give up their cultural and national identities in favor of a more "American" one. Instead, they hold on to their language, traditions, ethnicity, and connection to the homeland. Of course, each theory varies for each immigrant group and for each wave of immigration. But our goal was to seek some commonalities across groups and across historical eras of immigration as well as recognize differences.

Writing in response to a backlash against multicultural studies in the mid-1990s, two prominent historians took up the case for the study of immigration through a more inclusive, ethnically diverse lens: Lawrence Levine (1996) and Ronald Takaki (1993). The United States is somewhat unique in the world when it comes to immigration in that many Americans were originally immigrants themselves (and many others came in bondage as forced migrants and slave workers). The question of what holds us together as a people is one that historians and philosophers alike have pursued over the course of our history. Levine traces this question through the writings of some prominent American and European intellectuals, from Alexis de Tocqueville to Thomas Jefferson to Frederick Jackson Turner. What emerges from his study of these writers is that each harkens back to an imagined ideal Anglo-dominated America—which never existed. The pervasiveness of such an idea then leads later to calls for immigrants to "cast off" their ethnic identity—that the failure to do so poses some threat to the imagined essence of what it means to be an American. Levine writes:

> It is currently popular to write as if those now immigrating to the United States are qualitatively different from any immigrants we have had previously and pose problems of a magnitude we have never before experienced. . . . Of course none of this is new. Every generation has produced its jeremiads about the dangers posed to the nation by the nature and actions of the current crop of immigrants, has fretted about the "barbarians" at the gates, and has predicted, in one way or another, the beginning of the end. Hyperbole and anxiety have been basic components in American discussions of immigration throughout our history. [1996, pp. 122, 124]

What is important about this argument for the teaching of immigration is the tension that has always existed between each wave of immigrants and a continually emerging notion of American identity. Because immigration and immigrants are such a vital part of who we are as a people and how we have constructed the story of American history, this tension rears its head each time debates on immigration hit the floors of Congress, which they did in every presidential administration during the twentieth century. Current debates in the Senate and in the public through the media have a long history, and arguments brought to bear in making a case for or against immigration today inherently call up this history.

The second historian we read in order to make sense of more current scholarship on immigration was Ronald Takaki (1993). Writing virtually at the same time as Levine, Takaki focused on the importance of creating a more multiethnic story of American history. In many textbooks, the contributions of nonwhite groups to U.S. history are presented as sidebars to the main text (if that), sending a message that these individuals and groups were peripheral to the history rather than central to it. But U.S. history is not a black and white story only; race, social allegiance, class, and ethnicity have been more complex than this since Jamestown. Perhaps most important, many students go through their entire history education without ever seeing themselves situated within it. When teachers and textbooks narrate a monocultural view of U.S. history, what does that say to the students who are invisible within it? Takaki calls for a "different mirror"—one that reflects the many varied histories of the students sitting in every classroom in the nation.

From our collective study of these historians, some priorities began to emerge in thinking about the construction of a unit of study on immigration for Providence Public School students. In order for students to come away with an understanding of the variety of people who have immigrated to the United States, their reasons for coming, their journeys here, we wanted to include memoirs or oral histories from these people. This would allow space for students who are immigrants themselves or are first generation to situate their own stories and the stories of their families within the narrative of American immigration. So our first priority was that students should come to understand the unique experiences of various immigrant groups across time through the voices of those immigrants. Second, we wanted students to see that debates about immigration have always been contentious and divisive—that this was not unique to 2006 (the year in which this unit was designed). Students should come to understand how debates around immigration have always been deeply linked to notions of what it means to be an American and that these debates were and always will be contentious and racially charged. Thus, we would plan for students to interact with historical debates on immigration policy emanating from Congress or the media, or both. The following inquiries emerged as the frame for our unit on twentieth-century immigration to the United States:

- What were some of the forces pushing people away from their homeland and pulling them to immigrate to the United States?

- What were some of the arguments for and against immigration in each historical period?

- What tensions did each new group encounter on arrival (economic, social, political, racial/ethnic)?

- What are the explicit connections between immigration and American politics, foreign policy, and economic interests over time?

- How has "American" identity been debated and negotiated with each new wave of immigrants? How has the notion of an Anglo-dominant American culture been contested or reaffirmed?

The team in Providence settled on the first two, arguing that for tenth grade, these questions would provide a sufficient framework for engaging in the study of immigration and understanding the nature of the debate about immigration both today and throughout our nation's history. These two inquiries would structure the entire unit of study, from the individual activities and lessons, to the sources chosen, to the design of assessments throughout. At the end of the unit, students would be able to construct an argument and support it with evidence in response to one or both of these questions. These questions were both the frame and the substance for how students would study immigration to the United States. The classroom examples that follow describe how the core content and habits of thinking are woven into instruction and result in rigorous student learning, bringing us to our third DL principle in history.

Principle 3: Teachers as Mentors of Apprentices

Instruction provides students with models, practice, and coaching in rigorous historical literacy activity.

- Teachers use various instructional approaches to teach historical concepts, processes, and habits of thinking through structured long-term inquiries, direct instruction, modeling, differentiated coaching, scaffolded activities, and independent practice by students.

- Students are engaged in multiple activities using different kinds of texts (written, visual, statistical) where they are supported to construct meaning of text, present interpretations and defend them, and engage in historical research.

- Students are supported to refine and extend their historical knowledge through revision and revisiting guiding concepts and habits of thinking.

- Students use quick writes in class or at the end of class to continually mark their learning as it evolves. They ask and answer a series of questions as they encounter primary and secondary source documents.

The Providence curriculum writing team determined that in order to reinforce habits and questions specific to the study of history, they would construct a tool that would support and reinforce specific habits of mind. This primary source analysis tool would then become the anchor for historical study throughout middle and high school (see Exhibit 3.1).

Our first case of implementation comes from Ed Abbot's tenth-grade U.S. history class at Central High School in Providence. Students in Mr. Abbott's class have been engaged in analyzing primary and secondary source documents on a regular basis. Over the course of their prior unit on the Civil War, they became skilled at using the primary source analysis tool. Abbott's colleague, Becky Coustan, was one of the authors of the immigration unit, and he has invited her to teach the first lesson of the unit in his classroom in order to see how she sets up the learning for students.

On the first day of their immigration unit of study, students are introduced to the first guiding inquiry for this unit: What were some of the factors pushing people from their homelands and pulling them toward the United States? To launch this inquiry, Ms. Coustan begins by asking students, "What are some reasons why people move to the United States?" While students are doing a quick write (in other words, using free-form writing to discover one's thinking) silently at their desks in response to this question, she writes, "Reasons people move to the United States," on the board, leaving room for lists to develop underneath. Some quick write responses from students include the following: "to have a better life and a good job," "to escape from war," and "to get a better education." Several students in the class are immigrants—from Laos, from Puerto Rico, and from the Dominican Republic. For these students, this may be the first time in American schooling that they have been given the opportunity to discuss and share their own experiences of immigration and those of their families. They work quietly and diligently, taking their task seriously.

After a few minutes, Ms. Coustan directs them to "talk to the person next to you. Share your lists." Students share what they wrote in pairs and then add new information gained from their partner to their own growing list of reasons why people move to the United States. The teacher walks around the room, prompting discussion among students to get at the core issue of why people come to the

Exhibit 3.1
Primary Source Analysis Tool
for Providence Public Schools

Name _____

Title or Name of Document _____

CONTEXTUALIZE THE SOURCE

Date of document _____   **Type of document** _____

Who created the document? _____

For whom was the document created?

_____

ACTIVATE PRIOR KNOWLEDGE

> # What do I already know about the context?

GET THE BASICS
What does the document say?

_____

_____

_____

_____

_____

_____

DIGGING DEEPER

Historians dig deep into a source by thinking and making inferences based around a set of guiding inquiries. An inference is an educated statement (or guess) based on the evidence that you have available. What can you infer from this document to bring you deeper into the guiding inquiries?

Guiding Inquiry 1	
Guiding Inquiry 2	
Guiding Inquiry 3	

What questions do you have about the document?

Question 1
Question 2
Question 3

United States. A student references Elian Gonzales, the seven-year-old Cuban refugee who, in 2000, attempted to enter the country illegally, his mother dying in transit. A custody battle between the United States and Cuba ensued, involving the Cuban American community in Miami and resurfacing the decades-old political turmoil between the United States and Cuba. Eventually Elian was returned to his father in Cuba, where he lives today. Ms. Coustan asks, "How did he get here?" Together she and the student construct the story of Elian Gonzales: that he came from Cuba on a boat, the boat sank, his mother died, and there was a fight over whether he would live in the United States or Cuba. Then she says, "So his family brought him here. So one reason people come to the United States is because their family brings them so they can have a better life." In this brief interaction, the teacher models for the student how to use some of his or her own prior knowledge to form an answer to the question. Ms. Coustan continues to circulate, prompting students to construct reasons around what they are writing: "What else? What do we have here that others might want?" Students continue to talk with each other, sharing their prior knowledge and their "educated" guesses.

After some pair sharing, Ms. Coustan brings the class together as a whole group to construct a master list for the class. She asks each pair to share one answer and directs the class to add to their notes as the list is built representing a beginning understanding of why people move to the United States:

- Education
- Job opportunities
- Benefits
- Race—"Tell us about race. How does that bring people to this country?" "So America is a more diverse country and other countries might not be."

She struggles a bit here. These are not her regular students, and she does not quite know how they will respond. When she comes to a place where a student is stuck when pressed to provide an example or "tell me about that," Ms. Coustan asks, "Can anyone add on to what she's saying?" thus prompting more students to become involved in adding to and explaining the growing list:

1. Need medical care
2. Better lives/freedom: "What do you mean by that? Can you give me an example?"

3. To escape crime

4. To get away from war

5. Poor living conditions

6. Not enough food

7. Join families

8. To marry (her own example)

After this list has been built, the teacher points to her agenda written on chart paper and tacked to the board to give students a sense of where they are headed during the course of this forty-five-minute class:

> We're starting to talk right now about reasons why people move to this country. And after we get a sense of that, we're going to look at this question, which is part of your immigration unit. We're going to look at one immigrant's story, of one person, and see what that adds to our understanding of why people move to this country. Now I understand that you guys are getting pretty good at coding—that you've been working with Mr. Krakow [Mr. Abbot's student teacher] on that. So we're going to do some coding [marking the text for a specific purpose]. We're going to do some digging deeper, seeing if that coding can take us a little deeper into understanding this question, and then we're going to share our answers out at the end of the lesson.

She then points to another piece of chart paper tacked to the board, which has the two guiding inquiries for their unit of study on immigration written on it: "Here's the question that you're going to be looking at a lot over the course of this unit. Does someone want to read it out loud?" This is the question: "What were some of the forces pushing people away from their homelands and pulling people to immigrate to the United States?"

Although the question sounds complicated, she tells students that it is really the same question that they have already answered. "What could be something that pushes someone out of their country?" she asks. Students begin to offer answers, and she then turns to the list on the board and begins labeling specific things as "pushes," such as "war" and "lack of job opportunities." She then asks the same question about "pulls" and starts to label and generate more items to add to the list based on student input, such as "educational opportunities in the United States" and "freedom of religion." As students are directing her toward which items are pushes and which are pulls, she asks them to describe an example of each. She then stops and asks students to finish labeling their lists themselves at their desks, identifying which items are pushes and which are pulls. As students finish labeling their lists, Ms. Coustan hands out the reading that makes up the core of the lesson: an oral history of an immigrant from Cuba, dated 1980, which she calls an "immigration story" (from Morrison & Zabusky, 1980). In addition, she hands out the primary source analysis tool that students will use to analyze and take notes on the document as they read and will later be used as a reference when they build interpretations across a number of sources.

Ms. Coustan first directs students to take a look at the source, what is on the page, and asks what they can learn from the title, the date, and the country of origin of the subject. The primary source analysis tool has been designed to push students to attend to specific source information, such as the date, the author, and the perceived audience. By using the tool, with the guidance of the teacher, students are being apprenticed to practice basic sourcing moves whenever they encounter a new document. She explains that the date is the date that the incident in the story happened, not the date that this story was written. They talk about the type of source: that it is an interview of an immigrant, and thus a story of an immigrant.

"Who do you think created this document?" she asks. Students answer "Augustin," the name of the immigrant telling the story. Ms. Coustan says that the author could also be the person who interviewed him, raising the issue of authorship. They do not take this topic up for further discussion in the context of this class, but it is flagged, it is on their primary source analysis worksheet, and they will return to this idea later in the unit. Her next question is, "Who was this source created for?" This one alludes to the audience and the interaction between author and potential reader. It is particularly appropriate when dealing with oral history and interviews: Why is a subject being interviewed? For whom will his or her story be relevant and why? When asked, "Where is Augustin from?" students see "Cuba" written at the top of the paper. The teacher immediately pulls down a map, asks students to identify Cuba, and then comments that it is "very close to Miami. Not quite swimmable, but close." While this portion of the class is teacher directed and driven by the tool in use, getting basic information about this source allows students to become more engaged in the content of the source on their own.

Students are then directed to read and code the source silently first; then they will share what they learned through coding with their partner. Text coding, or marking the text for specific purposes, is a literacy strategy that has been in use in the Providence Public Schools for several years to support students in actively engaging with text while reading. Ms. Coustan and her colleagues in social studies are attempting to make this strategy more specific to the practices that a historian might engage in when reading the text. When Ms. Coustan asks this class what codes they have been using, many students enthusiastically offer their list of three codes: connection, question, and comment. She then says that today, they are going to add two new codes: push and pull. She asks, "What do you think these mean?" Students respond that they are things that "pushed them out of their country" and things that "pulled them in" to the United States. In effect, they will be using codes derived from the guiding inquiry for this unit to interact with this first text, an immigrant's account of his experience coming to the United States from Cuba.

Ms. Coustan reads through the first few sentences of the document, then stops, and models her thinking and her coding. She thinks aloud about what her comment would be and what she would write in the margins. A student offers a "connection" she would make: that her uncle took a boat from Puerto Rico to the United States just as Augustin took a boat from Cuba to the United States. In fact, Augustin was one of the participants in the Mariel boat lift of 1980, when Premier Fidel Castro agreed to allow boats to carry those who wanted to leave Cuba and go to the United States. Although there is debate around whether this was an attempt to rid Cuba of criminals or of dissenters, the boat lift represented a significant moment in the immigration history of Cuba and a significant moment in relations between Cuba and the United States. Those who came had political, social, and economic reasons for leaving their homeland. They were all anti-Castro. Thus the stories they tell, the oral histories they provide of their experience, carry these perspective or biases.

After working silently with the text for about ten minutes, Ms. Coustan asks students to turn to their partner and share the passages they coded as push or pull and explain their reasoning. There is a space for them to write about pushes and pulls on their primary source analysis tool. On a piece of chart paper at the front of the room, Ms. Coustan has made a chart with two columns: one for push and one for pull. As students talk to their partners, she again circulates around the room, pushing students to explain why certain passages are labeled push or pull, marking for students how they would capture their reasoning in writing on their graphic organizers: "So that's another point you may want to put down here. Exactly what you said. If the country was open-minded about him speaking out against the government with his group, then he wouldn't have to leave, right? He's saying that he is not free to criticize the government of Cuba." After a few minutes of partner talk, Ms. Coustan asks each group to write one push and one pull on the chart paper at the front of the room, along with evidence within the document to support that push or pull. As students stand at the chart, discussing what they will write, they refer back to the text and make sure they write evidence in support of their point. Students who are not up at the board continue to work through the text at their desks, recording their ideas.

In the remaining five minutes of class, Ms. Coustan pulls the class together and asks students to share what they wrote and the reasoning behind it. When a student offers as a push "government was too controlling," Ms. Coustan asks, "Does anyone have an example of the government being controlling?" She reads from the chart: "'They're not allowed to express their feelings; you work and stay quiet.' What do you mean by that?" The student who wrote the comment responds, "He said that his father had, like, told him to work hard." The student quotes from the text: 'Life would be different now, very hard. Just learn to work and be quiet.'" Another student explains his comment: "They made a lot of money, but they have no place to spend their money, so they start speaking out against Castro." Both students have offered documentary evidence for pushes they identified while reading. By the end of the forty-five-minute period, students have explored the first guiding inquiry of the unit: by accessing their own knowledge (and experience) of why people leave their homelands and come to the United States. Then they added to their understanding of this inquiry through reading, coding, analyzing, and talking about one immigrant's story. They have begun to explore features of the source itself, including its structure, purpose, and relationship between author and purpose. They have also learned to ask questions of the text that help them begin developing an understanding of immigration and the immigrant experience.

The carefully crafted inquiry for this unit, derived from historical research on immigration, invites students into the historical process of making sense of a variety of immigrants' experiences. They are being apprenticed to make arguments and defend those arguments by using evidence from the text. And the students in this classroom who are immigrants themselves have begun to see how their own experience, and that of their family, fits into U.S. history; they see themselves in the curriculum, perhaps for the first time in their lives. The groundwork has been laid for them to develop their own historical narrative of immigration throughout the rest of this unit of study.

As the classroom example demonstrates, not only are students engaged in the core content and habits needed to engage in historical practice, they are being guided and apprenticed by the teacher and the instructional design of her lesson to do so. They are treated as smart, capable learners. The teacher operates under the assumption that all students will be able to read, comprehend, analyze, write and speak about this text regardless of their classification (as an English language learner or a special education student, for example). This is at the heart of DL principle 4.

Principle 4: Classroom Culture Socializes Intelligence

Intelligence is socialized through community, class learning culture, and instructional routines:

- The teacher creates a community within the classroom where students are active participants in explaining, debating, discussing, and analyzing historical problems and issues.
- Students understand and value learning from one another and from the teacher.
- All students are treated as smart, capable readers and writers of history.
- Students regularly reflect on their learning and their methods of learning in class.

Within a single class period, students are supported to build from prior knowledge and experience and use a model for how to work with a guiding inquiry and a primary source. Each teacher-guided whole group session is meant to model a way of working and thinking (and the teacher talks for no more than two to three minutes at a time). Students have multiple opportunities to work with a partner or two, try out ideas, and add to others' understanding. By the end of class, they are expected to use evidence from the text they read to support a reason that the author left his homeland. Each pair or threesome contributes one reason to a class list that builds to eight or ten examples. Within a single class period, they have moved from individual prior knowledge to a collectively developed interpretation of a primary source document in response to one of the guiding inquiries for the unit.

As students progress through this unit on immigration over the course of four or five weeks, they read and analyze several first-person accounts of immigration. Using the strategies of text coding and structured note taking on the primary source analysis tool, students learn to pull information from these interviews and oral histories in order to build their own account of each immigrant's experience. Examining the work that students do tells us how they are processing and learning from each activity within the unit, leading us to the final DL principle.

Principle 5: Instruction and Assessment Drive Each Other

Instruction is assessment driven and assessment is instruction driven:

- Teachers research and assess student understanding of historical content, concepts, and interpretations by analyzing students' use of inquiry strategies, reading, writing, and reasoning strategies.

- Teachers use multiple forms of formal, informal, and formative assessment data to guide instruction.

- Students receive formative feedback from the teacher on their progress and process of creating historical interpretations.

- Students regularly reflect on what they have learned (content) and how they have learned (habits of thinking) and how their thinking on both has changed.

Ms. Coustan used multiple means of assessing student understanding during the lesson. First, she used student responses to the initial quick write (reasons that people move to the United States) to assess student thinking about the guiding inquiry for the unit before engaging them in the actual content of immigration. After modeling how to label which factors on the list were pushes and which were pulls, she asked students to label the factors on their own lists, walking around to check if they understood these concepts as they applied them to their own lists. Each time students are asked to work with a partner, the teacher is afforded the opportunity to walk around and listen for understanding, stopping to question and probe students who need additional guidance and support. As students work through the oral history of Augustin, the immigrant from Cuba, Ms. Coustan does this: listening to determine if students can identify the reasons that Augustin wants to leave Cuba and come to the United States. Finally, as each group writes one push and one pull on the board at the front of the room, along with evidence from the text for each, the teacher can assess how well they have applied these concepts and their close reading of the text in order to understand the text itself. Each of these informal and semistructured activities and tasks in the classroom—student writing, student talk—is an opportunity for the teacher to assess student understanding as the lesson unfolds.

As students progress through a unit of study in history, more formal assessments are designed to ascertain the depth and level of student understanding over time of the guiding inquiry (or inquiries) for the unit. The following examples of written assessments and student work in history are from Deborah Petrarca's tenth-grade classroom at Hope High School in Providence. It is spring 2007, and the immigration unit is now officially part of the Providence tenth-grade curriculum after being piloted in the previous year. Ms. Coustan is now the instructional coach at Hope High School. She has been supporting Ms. Petrarca's teaching of the immigration unit. After describing how Ms. Petrarca has amplified the unit, a close analysis of the resulting student work will be provided.

Ms. Petrarca began the unit by modeling the historical reading and analysis of the oral history of Augustin from Cuba. Students have read eight other oral histories of immigrants, ranging across time and geography. From Germany in 1925, to Nigeria in 1969, to Vietnam in 1975, students have delved deeply into the experiences of these immigrants to learn about their reasons for leaving, their journeys to the United States, and their experiences on arrival and settlement. Ms. Petrarca has added to the primary source analysis tool the following categories for which students are to gather evidence from each source:

- Immigrant nationality and date of immigration
- Situation in this immigrant's homeland
- Why this immigrant traveled to the United States
- Who traveled with the immigrant and who did not (family members? friends?), and why
- A description of the immigrant's journey to the United States
- The immigrant's first impressions or first experiences in the United States
- The hardships the immigrant suffered
- Highlights from the story

Students have taken notes on each of these on their primary source analysis tools as they read and discussed each source in small groups. Engaging in this minihistorical study across multiple sources, students begin to see similarities and differences emerge across documents, ethnic groups, geographical regions, and time. Those fleeing war and persecution tend to immigrate with their families. Their reception in the United States depends very much on American attitudes toward that war or that region of the world. In his notes on a Cambodian immigrant's first experiences on arrival in the United States in 1975, a student writes, "It wasn't very good because refugees were often robbed and beaten." In his notes on a Cuban immigrant's experiences, the same student writes, "Found a job doing what he knows how to do plumbing. This made him happy."

Toward the end of this unit, students are asked to write a response to the first guiding inquiry for the unit: "What were some of the forces pushing people away from their homelands and pulling people to immigrate to the United States?" They are directed to write an introduction, a thesis, and a conclusion that discusses the patterns they noticed across their documents and provide three examples from three different immigrant stories within the body of the paper to support their thesis. This same student begins his response in the following way:

> People always try to find better ways of life. Many people escape the hardships and struggles and turn to face a bright new future. When immigrants come to America they are searching for a life that does [not] consist of what they already endure in their homelands. Some of the forces that push people away from there homelands are fleeing from wars, escaping from hunger and starvation and seeking a higher education.

The student then goes on to give an example of each of these three reasons using evidence from the documents he read and analyzed. For his first example, the student cites an oral history from an El Salvadoran refugee who came to the United States in 1981:

> The forces that pushed her and her family away from El Salvador were the problems with making money, getting a good job or a higher education. They also had a danger of a war that was raging and the soldiers were killing people at random.

For his second example, this student summarizes the experiences of a German immigrant, suffering from starvation, who came to the United States in 1925 to escape the Russian invasion. And for his third example, the student describes a Cambodian refugee who came to the United States in 1976 to escape the Khmer Rouge:

> Over 2 million people were killed during this time. She and her husband who was a soldier were forced to leave. Losing family on the way made it even harder to survive. They came to America in an airplane. The church that had sponsored them had helped them get a job and a house. She had never cooked with electricity and never had a refrigerator before.

The student concludes by restating the reasons that people leave their homelands that constituted his thesis statement. In summing up what is common across these documents, and some truths well beyond these documents, he states:

> These are only some of the immigrants who have made it to the U.S. There are plenty who have made an attempt to come to this country, but never reach their destination. America is the answer for these immigrants. Life has been so hard for the people who have suffered so many horrible things in their homelands. . . .

Because of the way the guiding inquiries, the instruction, and the final unit assessment were structured, the student is able to provide specific examples about different experiences of immigration that can also highlight patterns and trends across immigrant experiences in the United States. In the final assessment, students were also given choice as to what kind of evidence to use and how to go about constructing their argument. So while this student read and analyzed seven immigrant stories, he chose the three highlighted in his essay because they spoke to the argument he sought to advance.

This type of reasoning, inquiry, and analysis is at the heart of historical practice. The notion that immigration as a phenomenon crosses time and space, yet has specific features that are unlike other types of historical phenomena, is embedded in instruction and evident in the resulting student work. In examining this student's work, we learn that the student is also aware of the distinct differences among these immigrants' experiences and how the circumstances of leaving the homeland are connected to that immigrant's experience on his or her journey and the reception he or she receives in the United States on arrival.

The second guiding inquiry for this unit pushes students to consider the context in which each group of immigrants arrived and to explore the nature of debates around immigration during specific periods in our nation's history: "What were some of the arguments for and against immigration in each historical period?"

In a related assignment within the same unit, students engage in an in-depth study of the period surrounding the Chinese Exclusion Act of 1882 with the goal of answering this guiding inquiry through a case study of a single period in immigration history. Students interact and code a set of documents from the period containing two political cartoons, an oral history of a Chinese immigrant, and a portion of the debates on the Senate floor around Chinese immigration. On the first cartoon, entitled "The Great Fear of the Period," dated 1860s, a student writes the following comments in the margins: "Why did the artist draw the foreigners with big humongous heads?" "I think this man is Irish—they make them look like monkeys." At the bottom of the page, the student writes, "This cartoon shows that the fear in that the Chinese are taking over the market for all labor." The cartoon depicts an Irishman and a Chinese man eating Uncle Sam, then the Chinese man eating the Irishman, all the while taking on certain features of the men being eaten. It is a striking symbol of exactly what the title depicts.

On the second document, an autobiographical sketch of a Chinese immigrant published in 1903, the student makes as many as ten comments, questions, and connections on each of the three pages. These comments range from informational questions—"I wonder where Mott Street was located"—to personal connections—"I didn't know English either when I came"—to summative comments about the person's experiences—"This is interesting because he had to learn something [the laundry business] in order to survive in USA." Each comment demonstrates that the student is actively engaged in reading, processing, and interpreting the text, incorporating what he is reading into what he already knows and stretching to figure out the things he does not yet know.

As a way of assessing how students can reason across several documents, Ms. Petrarca developed an informed reaction piece writing assignment in which students were asked to make connections across all three documents on the Chinese Exclusion Act using evidence from the documents themselves. The same student described above provides a detailed analysis of each document in the set, as well as explanations of how they are all related. A second cartoon is described, and the student's writing reflects his own progression in understanding what life may have been like for Chinese immigrants in the latter half of the nineteenth century. He states: "According to Lee Chow in 1903 the Chinese were hard workers and that's why other laborers did not like them.... They were discriminated against because they could not bring their wives to the U.S. and they couldn't marry out of their race. They were also accused of not being good citizens when they were truly not allowed to be good citizens at all." In this short piece, the student shows an understanding of the chronology of discrimination against the Chinese, as well as the specific reasoning used to make a case for Chinese exclusion on the part of native whites. By delving into a single period and examining three seminal types of documents in the study of immigration history, the student has gained the ability to see how immigration has always been central to the debate around what it means to be an American. In looking to the words of immigrants themselves, to public opinion as expressed in political cartoons, and to debates among those who make immigration policy, the students in this class have been apprenticed in how to go about understanding any key period in U.S. immigration history.

Taken together, these two writing assignments—the response to the first guiding inquiry for the unit using evidence from multiple immigrant experiences and the informed reaction piece—give the teacher a window into how students are able to construct historical arguments and marshal evidence to support them in writing. The supporting classwork and homework—the primary source analysis tool, quick writes, small group work, whole-class sharing—help teachers see how these abilities are developing before students are ever asked to write formally. By studying student work together, teachers can also gain insight into their own teaching practice, the design of writing assignments, and how they might standardize expectations across all classrooms. This, in fact, is how Ms. Petrarca's student work was used at Hope High School: as a means toward developing common and high expectations for all students and then conveying those expectations to students in a rubric specific to these assignments in their immigration unit of study.

CONCLUSION

Disciplinary literacy in history as a framework for curricular design and classroom instruction gives teachers and students the tools, habits, and routines they need to make sense of events, trends, and people in history with an eye toward their own place in the construction of that history. It asks teachers and students to take an active role in their learning, struggle with difficult ideas and content, and develop a set of discipline-specific habits of working and thinking. In the process of taking an active role in the learning of history, teachers and students become empowered to interact with the historical record—expecting and seeking out multiple interpretations—while having a viewpoint and a stake in how history is constructed, how the story is told, and who is included.

The case study from Providence shows not only the potential of such an undertaking, but the need for it for the sake of our students. First, by engaging with recent historical scholarship on immigration, teachers of history take into account the practices and arguments of those who form the discipline they teach. By questioning these historians, teachers themselves engaged in a sort of conversation with these historians, with their ideas. The translation of these big ideas into inquiries for students then sets the stage for students to engage with the big ideas that emanate from the discipline as well. Yet the translation and the creation of guiding inquiries must take into account the students themselves: their experiences, their own histories, who they are as Americans, and what may be missing from their understanding of U.S. history. In the example in this chapter, Ms. Coustan began with the prior knowledge students bring to the question of why people leave their homelands and come to the United States. She then built individual prior knowledge into a class-generated list. It is only after students have considered what push and pull might mean in this context in reference to their list that they turn to a historical source: an oral history of an immigrant. This becomes the example and model for how they will use the guiding inquiry to make sense of the experiences of multiple immigrants across time and space. In effect, students are supported to act as historians do by using a set of criteria (in the form of inquiry) to interrogate and make sense of documentary evidence.

At the end of the unit, students are called on to organize what they have learned about immigration to the United States into an argument as supported by examples, or evidence from the historical record. Again mimicking the practice of historians, they engaged in constructing their argument, picking examples, and creating a coherent historical narrative. In the process of reading and analyzing sources to get ready for this final task, the primary source analysis tool supports their ability to question and interact with a set of oral histories. Through carefully constructed inquiries, the modeling of how to analyze primary sources, and a tool that supports independent analysis of sources, students are enabled to think, talk, and write like historians. In doing so, they are empowered to interact with and create a historical record of their own. In the case of the immigration unit, they take a part in that history, seeing their own experiences and those of their families in the historical record that is produced.

The case described in this chapter serves as an exemplar of how one school district and one set of teachers can together take an active role in producing the environment and opportunity for rigorous disciplinary study in history.

Disciplinary Literacy in the Mathematics Classroom

Victoria L. Bill
Idorenyin Jamar

Most of us have vivid memories of our high school mathematics classes. The routine was fairly predictable.

Students entered the class and took out their homework. The teacher walked up and down the rows with his grade book in hand. He glanced at students' work and inserted marks in his grade book. He wrote answers on the board for those problems that most students missed, perhaps explaining the correct procedure, and then moved on to the day's lesson.

The teacher worked two example problems on the board, describing the procedure for each step. Following the description, he asked if everyone understood, and students nodded their heads, even if they were confused. There was an unspoken agreement among classmates that they would not ask questions because that meant that another example would be worked and they would not be able to get to their homework before the bell rang. Students were then given several problems to solve individually, and the teacher, or a few students, worked the problems on the board. Everyone was expected to check his or her own work; however, many simply copied the solutions from the board so they could study them later or have an older brother or sister, or their parents, explain the work. Before the bell rang, the homework for the next day was assigned—something like, "Do all of the odd-numbered problems on page 376." Some started the homework in class, while others pretended to be working (they were planning to copy a friend's paper prior to tomorrow's class). Bringing in a completed homework paper on time counted for 25 percent of the course grade.

Unfortunately, this is not just a page out of the past. Episodes such as these were still found to be more the norm than the exception in U.S. classrooms, according to data from the Third International Study of Mathematics and Science (National Center for Education Statistics, 1999): students often are expected only to master fixed and prescribed skills, processes, and structures (Stigler & Hiebert, 1999; van Oers, 2001) and learn to use them in predictable ways.

Years later, we ask ourselves what we actually learned as students in math classes. How much of what we "learned" did we truly understand? What did we come to think about what mathematics is or what it means to engage in mathematics? How did we come to view our own ability to "do mathematics"? Unfortunately, for many of us, mathematics was an endless stream of procedures and facts to be memorized, and, we hoped, recalled and applied correctly when needed. But it remained a mystery.

The way in which most of us learned mathematics is an issue not only for us as individual learners, but also for United States as a nation. The requirements of an ever-changing workplace dictate that basic skills and routine expertise will not be sufficient for today's students as they become tomorrow's workforce. Instead they will need "the levels of knowledge and understanding that can support transfer to new problems, creativity and innovation, something that we now recognize as 'adaptive expertise'" (Pellegrino, 2006, pp. 1–2). Students will need to know both specific content knowledge of mathematics—for example, facts, concepts, skills, procedures, and notations—as well as strategic action knowledge—and how to use that content knowledge in a generative way to construct new understanding and solve novel problems (Leinhardt, 1992, p. 21). Students will also need to acquire a willingness and ability to work with numbers and quantitative and spatial relationships according to accepted values in the mathematics community, and "above all they will need to be willing to pursue the quest for certainty, to apply the norms of non-contradiction, systematicity, generalization, modeling, and so on. In short, they will need to demonstrate the mathematical attitude" (van Oers, 2001, p. 78).

For students to develop these capabilities, they must have an opportunity to engage in true mathematical activity in the classroom. But what is mathematical activity? "Mathematics," according to the American Association for the Advancement of Science, "can be characterized as a cycle of investigation that is intended to lead to the development of valid mathematical ideas" (1993). This involves investigating patterns, experimenting, forming and testing conjectures, and developing and debating convincing arguments that both prove and explain (Silver, Kilpatrick, & Schlesinger, 2005; Stylianides & Silver, 2004). For students in classrooms such as that profiled at the start of the chapter, their experiences do not provide opportunities for them to engage in these ways of working as a means of developing their mathematical understanding.

In a disciplinary literacy (DL) classroom, mathematical activity involves the processes of mathematical inquiry—for example, pattern finding, conjecture, generalization, proof, and refutation—by enacting learning practices such as discussion and collaboration, proposing and defending mathematical ideas and conjectures, responding thoughtfully to the mathematical arguments of peers, and pointing out and correcting their own and others' errors (Goos, 2004). In short, the classroom becomes a community of inquiry where thinking, reasoning, sense making, and problem solving are socially constructed activities.

In order for students to engage in inquiry around important mathematics content, they have to develop a mathematical attitude and mathematical habits of thinking. These habits of thinking must be ones that are valued within the discipline of mathematics: individual reflection and self-monitoring, working backward from the end point (Goos, 2004), looking for patterns, visualizing, trying to understand how and why something works, tinkering (guessing and checking) (Cuoco, Goldenberg, & Mark 1996), reasoning from and between representations (Boaler & Humphreys, 2005), persevering through difficulties, and drawing on prior knowledge. These practices make it possible for learners to figure out solutions to problems and make sense of mathematical ideas.

Processes of thinking cannot be learned in isolation. In a recent analysis of the difficulty in teaching critical thinking, Willingham (2007) notes that "people who have sought to teach critical thinking have assumed that it is a skill, like riding a bicycle, and that, like other skills, once you learn it you can simply apply it in any situation. Research from cognitive science shows that thinking is not that sort of skill. The processes of thinking are intertwined with the content of thought" (p. 8). In addition, teaching habits of thinking in isolation from the content does not work because students do not come to understand when, and how, to apply them.

Directly teaching content alone is not the answer: "Clearly, teaching the underlying principles alone does not improve performance, but equally clearly, performance proficiency does not produce conceptual understanding. One suggestion is to consistently teach these different kinds of knowledge together in action, explicitly acknowledging how the different forms of knowledge work together" or are intertwined—students learning about linear functions, for instance, by examining a visual pattern to determine what makes the pattern linear. "The pieces of needed knowledge are seen as working together when the acts of problem posing, solution, and learning are public and shared [Leinhardt, 1992, p. 21]."

We refer to the learning of content through habits of thinking as *working on the diagonal* (Geisler, 1994)—that is, the merging of content and habits of thinking. The two—disciplinary content and habits of thinking that are valued within the discipline—go hand in hand. One cannot be learned without the other. We will illustrate what it means to work on the diagonal in a mathematics classroom as we examine students' engagement in Ms. Scott's algebra 1 class in an urban school.

However, it is first important to consider the types of tasks that students engage in if they are to have an opportunity to work on the diagonal.

The Task Matters

One goal of disciplinary literacy is for students to develop habits of thinking that they will call on when addressing a range of mathematical situations both in and out of the classroom. For this to occur, it is important that we provide opportunities for them to solve mathematical tasks in school that require the use of mathematical habits of thinking. Not all tasks require this kind of thinking. The Trends in Third International Mathematics and Science Study video data (National Center for Education Statistics, 1999) found that "in the United States, content is not totally absent, ... but the level is less advanced and requires much less mathematical reasoning than in the other two countries" (Stigler & Hiebert, 1999, p. 27). In contrast, there are tasks that provide opportunities for students to construct deep connections among knowledge of actions, skills, concepts, and principles as they engage in figuring out a solution and determining if their solution is reasonable. Such tasks provide the opportunity for students to explain the reasoning behind their solutions and compare their methods and thinking with their peers'. We refer to such tasks as *high-level tasks* (Stein, Smith, Henningsen, & Silver, 2000). Many high-level tasks can be approached and solved in multiple ways, and as a result, students need to recall prior learning, tinker, sometimes guess and check, try one representation—a graph, a table, an equation—then another, and persevere in the face of difficulty. Thus, providing opportunities for students to engage in high-level tasks is critical if students are to learn habits of thinking as they learn mathematical content. The National Council of Teachers of Mathematics' *Illuminations* Web pages (2008) are one source of such tasks (see http://illuminations.nctm.org/ActivitySearch.aspx).

A DISCIPLINARY LITERACY CLASSROOM: WORKING ON THE DIAGONAL

The remainder of this chapter examines vignettes from an urban eighth-grade algebra 1 class as a means of illustrating what it means for students to work on the diagonal, that is, to use mathematical habits of thinking to understand mathematical content. Student engagement in the calling plans task, parts I and II, provides examples of how self-monitoring, looking for patterns, visualizing, and other habits of thinking facilitate students' understanding of properties of linear functions and linear systems, for example, such as constant rate of change (slope), y-intercept, and point of intersection. A particular method for solving the task was not given to students; instead they were to figure out their own solution methods and explain them to others.

These are the tasks presented to students:

> *Calling Plans Part I:* Long-distance Company A charges a base rate of $5 per month, plus 4 cents per minute that you are on the phone. Long-distance Company B charges a base rate of only $2 per month, but charges 10 cents per minute used.
>
> How much time per month would you have to talk on the phone before subscribing to Company A would save you money?

> *Calling Plans Part II:* Create a phone plan for Company C that costs the same as those of companies A and B at 50 minutes but has a lower monthly fee than either of the other plans.

Students exhibited a variety of habits of thinking and inquiry practices as they worked to understand the relationship between the two phone plans while they worked individually, in their small groups, and during the whole-class discussion. We will focus on a discussion of the mathematical habits of thinking that these students used when working in small groups and then discuss methods of apprenticing students so that they learn to acquire the habits of thinking. The value of allowing students to work in multiple configurations (individually, in small groups, and as a whole group) will be addressed in our discussion of the phases of a lesson later in the chapter.

In this example from the lesson, students work in groups of four to attempt to figure out how many minutes they would have to talk before plan A became cheaper than plan B. The students in this group began by creating a table that includes the cost of both plans for a small number of minutes, beginning at one minute and increasing by one-minute increments up to ten minutes (Table 4.1). The table then helps one student to see how the cost increases but also suggests to other students that they will need to find another approach, in this case using an equation, since extending the table will clearly take "a long time" to find out when plan A becomes the cheaper plan.

Jamal: I get it now, because the 2, 'cause so a minute is 2 and 10 cents and then you wrote 20 and then 30, 40, 50, 60, 70, 80, 90, but that's gonna take a long time, I know, but like . . .

Sonja: Let's see what happens at 100 minutes.

Keisha: That's gonna take a long time.

Sonja: If we do like, like, keep on adding and adding.

Keisha: That's why we need to do an equation for it.

Jamal: What?

Keisha: An equation.

Sonja: An equation for it. Otherwise you'll just keep on adding and adding. . . .

Keisha: So it keeps going up by 10 cents.

Jamal: How do you know that?

Keisha: Look in the table: 10, 20, 30, 40.

Fred: But it says $2.10, $2.20, $2.30.

Keisha: The two is where it starts at. Every one starts at two.

Fred: It changes by ten cents each minute.

Sonja: So it is $2.00 + .10m$. Try it for 5 minutes and 10 minutes first to make sure it works. Then we can do 100 minutes.

Keisha: Then we'll have to do it for plan B too and see.

Table 4.1
Calling Plans Part I

Minutes	Company A	Company B
1	$5.04	$2.10
2	5.08	2.20
3	5.12	2.20
4	5.16	2.30
5		2.40
6		2.50
7		2.60
8		2.80

In this segment of their discussion, students used the following mathematical habits of thinking:

- Tinkering
- Using representations in purposeful ways
- Understanding how and why something works
- Proposing and testing ideas
- Trying easier problems or known problems before trying harder problems
- Drawing on prior knowledge
- Talking with others

Students in this group call on many habits of thinking as they work together to construct a solution to the problem. The use of multiple representations, a table and an equation, serves many of the same purposes for these students that they serve for mathematicians: the opportunity to stabilize ideas; the opportunity to edit, refine, and produce clarity and elegance; the opportunity to communicate with others; and the opportunity to discover (Eisner, 1998, cited in Boaler & Humphreys, 2005). Students tinkered, trying different numbers of minutes to see how it changed the outcome—"Let's see what happens at 100 minutes" and "We'll have to do it for plan B too and see." This tinkering and trying led them to recognize that they needed to find another approach because they figured out that their approach was "gonna take a long time."

These students used representations in purposeful ways. The students knew to make a systematic table, one that was organized in a logical incremental sequence, as a way to organize data so that patterns are evident. While some of the students used the increments of 10 cents to create the table, once the table was constructed, the visible pattern helped Jamal understand what was occurring in the context: the relationship between the "$2 and 10 cents."

The table was a good starting point, but it was not long before Keisha realized that it was going to "take a long time" to find the point at which plan A becomes a better deal because the plans grew by increments of $.10 and by $.04. If they continued to extend the table, which goes by increments of one minute, it would take a long time to "see what happens at 100 minutes." As a result, she proposed that they create an equation. Keisha shows her habit of thinking: to know that she can change her approach to the problem and use an alternative representation—the equation. She knows that the equation is a generalization of the pattern and can be used to calculate the cost of any number of minutes directly. Sonja created an equation, "so it is $2.00 + .10m$," and she proposed that they test the equation by trying a known case (the cost of 5 or 10 minutes). Sonja proposed that they test their equation by trying "it for 5 minutes and 10 minutes first to make sure it works." "Then," she said, "we can do 100 minutes." Once she validated the correctness of the equation by checking the results with those at her table, she felt confident that she could use the equation to solve for the cost of 100 minutes. Sonja has the habit of thinking to know to try easier problems before solving for larger amounts. The equations are a way to formalize the functional relationships—the relationship between the number of minutes and the cost for each plan; otherwise the students would have to rely on the recursive relationship of adding 10 cents for each minute, "adding and adding." Sonja drew on prior knowledge of multiplication when she realized that for every minute talked, 10 cents was charged, thus the cost of m minutes would be $10m$, plus the base fee, $2.00.

Not all students in the group understood how Keisha and Sonja arrived at the equation that they would use to solve for the cost of 100 minutes. Jamal and Fred knew they had the right and responsibility to understand how and why ideas worked. Jamal asked, for example, "How do you know that [it keeps going up by 10]?" Keisha points to the increments in the table—"10, 20, 30, 40"—but Fred again challenges her when he states, "but it says $2.00, $2.20, $2.30." He knows he has the right to hold Keisha accountable to the data, and she clarifies her thinking that "the two is where we start." In this exchange, we see students valuing engagement in problem solving while co-constructing and discussing solution paths with their peers. Explicating one's reasoning like this in words or in writing makes it public and available for others (or oneself) to assess, critique, question, or challenge (Michaels, O'Connor, Hall, & Resnick, 2002).

These students were not explicitly "taught" particular mathematics concepts. Instead, they came to grapple with several mathematical ideas as they worked together to solve this task (and several others solved previously). As they analyzed the situation and formed the equation, students asked themselves what remains constant and what is changing. As they did this, they grappled with the ideas of constant (y-intercept) and rate of change (slope, the cost per minute) of the linear functions. Although the teacher had not yet explicitly mentioned these terms, the nature of the task and students' mathematical habits of thinking made it possible for a foundation to be laid for them to understand the terms through their use of the mathematical actions that they represent.

LEARNING AS APPRENTICESHIP

Students in Ms. Scott's class were in the process of acquiring both the mathematical habits of thinking and the content knowledge necessary to solve high-level tasks. These do not develop unaided. Habits of thinking are the ways of working in a discipline, so the best way to learn these skills is by working alongside someone who is proficient in using them to accomplish his or her work. Some may argue that the relationship that needs to exist for such learning to occur resembles that of an apprentice and master. To be apprenticed implies that cognitive and metacognitive processes are acquired through assisted engagement with a sensitive and knowledgeable adult (Brown, Collins, & Duguid, 1989).

In the classroom, these practices must be modeled and nurtured by the teacher or a more skilled peer. The teacher carefully observes the knowledge and skills of each student to determine the student's zone of proximal development (ZPD)—the "distance between a child's problem-solving capability when working alone and with the assistance of a more advanced partner" (Goos, 2004, p. 262). This interaction between the adult and child within the child's ZPD that enables novices to solve problems beyond their unassisted efforts is called *scaffolding* (Goos, 2004). Once the teacher determines what students know and can do individually without assistance, as opposed to what they can accomplish with the assistance of a more knowledgeable other, the teacher focuses on arranging and structuring children's participation in activities, so that children's responsibilities shift from joint problem solving to independent problem solving (Rogoff, 1990). Such interactions also provide opportunities for formative assessment, which "refers to frequent, interactive assessments of student progress and understanding to identify learning needs and adjust teaching appropriately" (Shepard, 2008, p. 281). Thus, formative assessment can be viewed as assessment for learning rather than assessment of learning (Leahy, Lyon, Thompson, & Wiliam, 2005). We will highlight some instances of formative assessment as we elaborate the notion of apprenticeship.

Although there are many ways of structuring learners' participation in learning, we have selected for discussion just three of the ways that Ms. Scott apprentices students into the practices used by mathematicians:

1. Cognitive prompts
2. The phases of a lesson
3. The sequencing of lessons in a unit

Cognitive Prompts

The ultimate goal of teaching is to develop a self-regulated learner who exhibits the potential to use her or his knowledge for a variety of purposes in different situations (Zimmerman & Schunk, 2001). Question prompts, when used routinely and internalized by students, can guide students' attention to specific aspects of their learning process (Rosenshine, Meister, & Chapman, 1996), thereby helping them to monitor and evaluate problem-solving processes (Ge & Land, 2004). Metacognitive prompts, delivered in various ways, can also encourage students to reflect on their problem-solving processes, inquiry methods, and explanations (Collins, Brown, & Holum, 1991; White & Frederiksen, 1998). Such prompts have an indirect impact on student learning. For example, in White and Frederiksen's work, students who routinely answered reflective assessment prompts developed greater understanding of both the subject matter and the inquiry process. We refer to these as *cognitive prompts,* because if students internalize them, they can help focus students' thinking and attention on critical aspects of problem solving and content. Over time these prompts may become habits of thinking for students.

Ms. Scott consistently used cognitive prompts such as the ones that follow to support students as they engaged in problem solving:

- What is this problem about, and what are you trying to find out?
- How might you go about solving this problem?
- How is this problem similar to or different from others that we have solved?
- What patterns or relationships exist in the problem?
- How might you represent the situation using a visual model, verbal description, a graph or table, or an equation? What might this representation allow you to see that the other ones do not?
- Can you write an equation that you can use to represent the problem's context? This might help you think about the problem.
- Can you make a conjecture? What is your conjecture based on? How can you determine whether your conjecture is valid?
- Is the solution to the problem reasonable? Does it make sense? How do you know?

In a small group discussion, we can see that students have internalized one of the teacher's cognitive prompts: "How is this problem similar to or different from others that we have solved?" The students relate the mathematical ideas within the calling plans task to two visual pattern tasks that they solved earlier in the month: the hexagon and counting cubes tasks.

Marcus: It's like the other problem; it's like the hexagon train. It has a constant too.

Janetta: Five dollars is the base fee.

Marcus: Two was the constant in the hexagon problem. Remember the ends: there were two of them. Five dollars is the constant in this problem; it is a one-time fee.

Samuel: In the cubes problem, there was always one cube in the middle. It was constant too.

Marcus and Samuel have clearly asked themselves, "How is this task similar to other tasks that we have solved?" in an attempt to work more intentionally when solving the task. Students who purposefully and systematically approach their work and consider ways in which their ideas are or are not well understood are likely to be more successful at knowledge integration than students who merely forge full-speed ahead without engaging in these metacognitive activities (Davis, 2003). Ms. Scott knows that Marcus and Samuel have internalized at least one of the cognitive prompts because they used the prompt to guide them when problem solving. She also knows that they have acquired the habit of thinking to question and reflect on their learning.

When a cognitive prompt is used while students are solving tasks, it will carry with it the context in which it was used. Thus, cognitive prompts take on deeper meanings for students as they are used, and students begin to appropriate them when solving similar tasks. An example from Ms. Scott's lesson helps illustrate how cognitive prompts might gain deeper relevance to students. In this example, Ms. Scott prompts a small group of students to make a sketch of a graph of a function. Then the sketch is shared with the rest of the class, and the students work to name aspects of the graph and make connections between their method and the sketch. Finally, Ms. Scott has students reflect on the potential benefits of the habit of thinking: sketching the graph to visualize the pattern.

The following example helps illustrate how students may learn to appreciate a problem-solving strategy and a habit of thinking. In this segment of the lesson, Ms. Scott decided to encourage a small group of students to sketch a graph because at one point in the problem-solving process, she saw that they had become mired in the details of the problem, spending most of their time figuring out the cost for various numbers of minutes and creating tables and not progressing to a point where they could compare the two plans. When she heard the group mention "the line," she saw this as an opportunity to prompt them to think about the power of representing the problem situation a different way: as a graph instead of as a table. By prompting them to create a different representation of the two plans, she hoped that students would consider the base fees and the per-minute charge of each plan as they made the graph. She posed a cognitive prompt: "Is there a different representation that might help you to think about the problem in a different way? I heard you mention line. What else do you think you could do instead of making a table?" After some deliberation, they created a sketch of the graph of the two phone plans (Figure 4.1)

The scenario also illustrates the power of formative assessment to adjust teaching in response to student needs. By asking the group to share their thinking, Ms. Scott was able to understand what they were grappling with (focusing on the individual costs in the table) and then to introduce an idea that helped them move

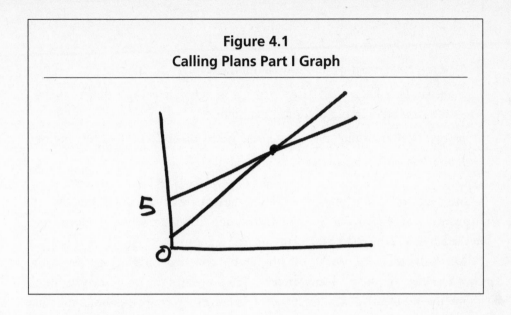

Figure 4.1
Calling Plans Part I Graph

5

forward: "So, what I'm hearing is maybe you wanna start by doing a graph?" It is also important to note that in this case "teaching" is truly "scaffolding" (Rogoff, 1990). The teacher arranged and structured the children's participation in the specific activity at that point in time and in response to their current needs in a way that allowed their thinking to move toward the mathematical goals of the lesson.

Later, in the whole-class discussion, the small group's solution path provided an opportunity for Ms. Scott to ask the class to consider how their graph represented the calling plans context:

Teacher: (to the class) How did this group know what the graph of the data would look like?

Sandra: I'm thinking if you look at the table, and it's going by the same number, it must be a linear line—it must—so they must have made it like that and since it had an intersection point they made it cross.

Teacher: The intersection point, okay. Could someone else add on to what she said? What else helped them make this graph?

Roberto: What helped her like get Company A and B they started out with that 5 and 2. It says so in the table.

Teacher: Okay. So you know from the table that Company A and B start off at 5 and 2 at zero minutes, and how did she show that on the graph?

Sandra: 'Cause where it said "0," they just moved up like two spaces up a little bit, and they wrote 5 where the other started.

Teacher: What else did they know about the plans?

Tameika: They knew to make each plan a straight line because they go up by the same amount of money for each minute.

Joshua: They knew that one was steeper, 'cause it is ten cents for every minute.

Keith: One was four cents, so it goes up a little bit.

Students explain the intersection point, the base fee of each graph, and the rate of growth of each plan. One student makes connections between the information in the tables and the cost of the plans and the graphs.

Ms. Scott took the work with the graph one step further. She asked the class to reflect on the problem strategy: "So how does the graph help us think about the problem in a different way? What can you see in the graph that you couldn't see as easily in the table?" Working with graphs is relatively new to the students. Therefore, spending time comparing and making connections between prior knowledge, the construction of a table, and the construction of a graph may help more students see that graphs are important tools for analyzing and describing the behavior of functions. In this transcript, students reflect on the benefits:

Teacher: So how does the graph help us think about the problem in a different way? What can you see in the graph that you couldn't see as easily in the table?

Feonna: You can see how it goes up.

Mia: Yeah, you can see one is more slanted.

Teacher: One is steeper than the other. One has a greater rate of change. Say more about this.

William: One is ten cents for every minute, and one is four cents for every minute.

Teacher: Do you agree? Show us. (Student points to the graph of plan A and plan B.)

Kimberly: I know this one is ten cents per minute because it is more slanted. This one is four cents per minute, and it does not go up as fast.

Teacher: Okay, what else was helpful about making a graph? How did making a sketch of the graph help you visualize the plans?

Jeanne: You can see when the plans are the same cost 'cause they intersect.

Teacher: Can you see that in the table?

Joshua: Not as easy 'cause you may never get there.

Timmy: You can see how it goes up, but in tables, you have to know that the numbers go up.

Teacher: So when solving other problems, you might try visualizing the relationship, or you might make a sketch of the relationship.

In this example, we see how Ms. Scott engages students in comparing the insights that they gained from the graphical and the tabular representations of the phone plans. Based on their comments, the students seem to have made connections between the different rates of growth of the two phone plans and the slant of the two lines. They also seem to recognize the different base fees and the y-intercepts of the two graphs as well the point of intersection representing the time when the two plans have the same cost. Ms. Scott emphasizes that a sketch might have helped them visualize the plans. She hopes that students will recall this information as a cognitive prompt when they solve other problems.

Ms. Scott will know if the scaffolding that she has provided to the small group and in the whole class discussion is enough to help students use the habit of thinking "visualize the pattern by making a graph" only if they transfer and use the knowledge independently when she observes them in solving problems in small groups or individually, as we observed when students recalled their discussion of the problem that they solved previously.

The examples clearly illustrate the central role of formative assessment in Ms. Scott's classroom. The use of questioning allows her to gauge her class's understanding as instruction unfolds. She thus is able to continually modify the direction of the whole-class discussion in response to student understanding. The lesson is continually formed, and reformed, but always with the goal of the lesson in mind. She has a clear understanding of the central mathematical understandings that she is aiming for—a deeper understanding of slope, y-intercept, and point of intersection.

Cognitive prompts, as these examples illustrate, cannot stand alone. A list of prompts posted in the classroom, for example, is not sufficient for student learning. Instead, students must build meaning as they actively engage in problem solving over time with the help of cognitive prompts.

Phases of a Lesson

In addition to the routine use of cognitive prompts, students in Ms. Scott's classroom know that they will engage in solving problems daily in predictable ways. The daily flow of activity that supports mathematical investigation and problem solving in Ms. Scott's classroom has a setup phase, an explore phase, and a share-and-discuss phase. Each phase has explicit expectations associated with it. Students know the ways in which they will engage in the problem-solving process with one another, and the teacher as well, as the rationale for working in these ways. Formative assessment also plays a key role in each of these phases.

In the setup phase, the teacher makes sure that students understand the expectations of the task by not only clearly explaining them—either orally or in writing—but also by assessing students' understanding of the instructions by having them restate the expectations in their own words. It is important to stimulate students' curiosity and motivate their active participation. In this phase of the lesson, students in Ms. Scott's class know that she will not suggest an explicit pathway for solving the task. Students tolerate the ambiguity that often exists because they know that they will have time to work with peers to figure out a way to solve the task.

During the explore phase of the lesson, students work first individually and then with their peers to solve the task. During the explore phase, Ms. Scott listens and makes note of students' use of and understanding of strategies, habits of thinking, and content as she circulates asking questions that allow her to assess what students know. Once Ms. Scott assesses student understanding, she uses the cognitive prompts to challenge and press students to share their reasoning, make connections to previous learning, apply new problem-solving strategies, or use their habits of thinking as they explore new concepts. This use of questions to both assess and advance student understanding (Smith, Bill, & Hughes, 2008) is another example of the central role of formative assessment.

During the explore phase, the teacher ensures that students adhere to the norms of participation so that each one will be responsible for his or her own learning and for the learning of his or her teammates. As a result, students serve as coaches for one another in preparation for the point when the teacher will ask a question of the group. The success of individuals in the group is viewed as the success of the whole group. Students coach each other in small groups because they know that anyone in the group may be called on to give an explanation of the group's solution path.

Following the explore phase of the lesson, the teacher engages students in sharing and discussing various solution paths. During this share-and-discuss phase of the lesson, Ms. Scott selects a focus for the discussion based on her mathematical goals for the lesson. She selects and sequences students' solutions so that she can orchestrate a discussion that progresses in a coherent and planned way. When selecting the solution paths, she is mindful of the learners' current state of knowledge and carefully selects solution paths that allow many learners early entry into the discussion of the mathematical concepts within the task (Smith, Hughes, Engle, & Stein, 2009). In orchestrating this discussion, Ms. Scott uses questioning as a way to assess the class's understanding of the emerging mathematical ideas. Within the same classroom, she is able to determine which students do and which do not understand the mathematical concepts, and she and the others in the class engage in a discussion of the concepts until many students' understanding evolves. As more students are able to talk about the mathematical ideas within the first solution path, Ms. Scott selects yet another of the students' solution paths for discussion—one chosen with the goal of deepening students' understanding of mathematical ideas. She continues the process of assessing students' understanding and works to engage all students in making sense of the solution path and mathematical ideas within the task. She consistently makes on-the-spot decisions to reshape the discussion if necessary, based on her assessment of the class's needs (Smith et al., 2009). Thus, formative assessment is another important feature of this phase of the lesson.

The discussion of the graph in Figure 4.1 is an example of a portion of a share-and-discuss phase of a lesson. When solution paths are shared, students are invited to ask questions, repeat others' ideas, or put the ideas into their own words and add on to the ideas or clarify others' thinking. The discourse differs from the typical talk patterns in classrooms, which often involve the teacher's initiating a question, getting a response, and then evaluating it and initiating another question (Mehan, 1979). The discourse patterns that we refer to as Accountable Talk (Michaels et al., 2002) involve students in investigating the underlying meaning of concepts as a community of learners. The classroom talk mirrors more closely a group discussion. Students know that the teacher and their peers will press for accuracy and the underlying meaning of concepts. They also know that they in turn are expected to demonstrate their understanding of the concepts and skills in the share-and-discuss phase as well as in future lessons. This consistent way of working, which includes a consistent culture of questioning, justifying, investigating, and reworking, socializes students to work individually in ways similar to those in their small groups. Learning is an interactive and interpretative process whose development is determined by the social and cultural context (Bruner, 1986; Vygotsky, 1978). Students are socialized by the norms and routines in the classrooms to work in these ways. The students in this classroom construe themselves as intelligent. They believe they have the right (and the obligation) to understand things and to make things work (Resnick & Nelson-LeGall, 1997).

Sequencing Lessons in a Unit

It would be naive to think that phases of a lesson or cognitive prompts alone set the expectations and make it possible for students to be apprenticed into the habits of thinking that mathematicians use. In an apprenticeship relationship, a master structures the content and habits of thinking to be learned in order to ensure that the apprentice's learning builds in incremental ways on prior learning. In the same way, a very skilled teacher arranges learning opportunities within a unit of study so that they build toward important mathematical goals.

Consider the instance above when the student referred back to the hexagon task and the counting cubes task—the visual pattern tasks that the students had solved as they began to explore linear functions. The teacher chose to have students solve these tasks early in their study of functions because, according to English and Warren (1999), visual pattern tasks help students move from a recursive description of a pattern (that is, to add four each time) to a functional description (that is, to find the perimeter of a hexagon train you multiply the train number by 4 and add 2). Next Ms. Scott moved to the use of a real-world context, because students had a basic understanding of patterns developed from the visual pattern tasks; she wanted them to then connect to a familiar context of cell phone plans. In addition, this task allowed them to build on their emerging understandings to focus more explicitly on slope (rate of change), y-intercept (base fee), and point of intersection (the number of minutes when the two plans would have the same cost). Building a table, a graph, and an equation, and making connections among these representations, as well as the context, helps to deepen these ideas. By thinking back over the set of tasks, students referred to the hexagon task: "It's like the other problem; it's like the hexagon train. It has a constant too."

Students noticed they all had something that remained constant in the pattern as well as a constant rate of growth. They would begin to see how these related to the constant and the coefficient in the algebraic representation. When students make these types of connections among lessons, they are beginning to see their learning as a set of connected ideas, not merely isolated bits of information. Through this set of related tasks, students' understanding of features of linear functions—the primary focus of the algebra 1 curriculum—begins to develop.

Organizing a curriculum around arcs of related high-level tasks is not a simple task. It is important first to identify the big ideas of the subject and the intended mathematical understandings for a lesson or arc of lessons (Charles, 2005) and to think of the teaching, and learning, building over time toward these ideas and understandings. For instance, the calling plans task helps build students' understanding of the big idea of relations and functions:

- Mathematical rules (relations) can be used to assign members of one set to members of another set.
- A special rule (function) assigns each member of one set to a unique member of the other set.

The calling plan task provides an opportunity for students to develop some of the specific mathematical understandings related to this big idea (Charles, 2005). While teachers could work individually or in groups to identify the big ideas and mathematical understandings central to their course and the lessons, many districts are now providing curriculum guides that identify these big ideas. Teachers can then work together to find, or develop, tasks that build toward these ideas. Keeping a public charting of these big ideas in the classroom as they emerge, and frequently referring back to them, are ways to sustain thought over time and keep the key ideas alive in the minds of students (Henningsen, 2000).

PRINCIPALS' SUPPORT FOR TEACHING AND LEARNING DL MATHEMATICS

We now turn to a discussion of how principals can support teachers and students who are working to develop a culture of DL in their mathematics classrooms. Their ability to provide this support will depend on their vision of DL mathematics teaching and learning and what they understand about how DL classrooms should look and sound.

We hope that this chapter has provided a clear vision of DL mathematics for principals. Mathematics is no longer merely a set of rules and procedures to be practiced and mastered. Rules and procedures are still important, of course, but now students are given the opportunity to construct them, building on their prior knowledge whenever possible. A school subject that once asked students to focus only on the learning of facts and formulas now includes curricula and instruction that ask students to recognize the importance of finding patterns, discuss relationships, make sense of mathematical ideas, and see the connections among those ideas. The aim is for students to develop ownership of the knowledge and thus be able to use it in a wide range of situations in school and in their out-of-school life. This is not the way that most adults learned mathematics. Therefore, for practicing teachers to embrace these new practices and learn to facilitate such learning requires that they be provided both time and opportunity. The principal, as the instructional leader of the school, is critical in this process. With this vision in mind, he or she will need to:

- Guide the selection of resources
- Arrange learning opportunities for teachers that extend and build on district-wide professional development opportunities
- Maintain the focus and coherence on teaching and learning
- Serve as a critical link between lessons learned in professional development and those applied in the classroom

Resources vary from district to district. Some districts have identified for students a healthy diet of high-level tasks, such as those described earlier in this chapter. However, if the adopted curriculum is not constructed around high-level tasks, the principal can provide the opportunity for teachers to work together to select or create high-level tasks that supplement and amplify the district's curriculum. A mathematics team that agrees to give students opportunities to engage in solving such tasks ensures that students will have the opportunity to regularly engage in thinking, reasoning, sense making, and connection making in their mathematics classrooms.

Merely providing access to high-level tasks is not enough, however. It has been found that when teachers try to implement high-level tasks, students have the opportunity to engage in the intended high-level thinking only 37 percent of the time. The other 63 percent of the time, the intended high-level thinking and reasoning is not achieved due to several classroom-based factors (Stein et al., 2000). Thorough lesson planning is one way that teachers can be better prepared to engage students in high-level thinking and reasoning, thus actualizing the lesson's potential. Principals can be instrumental in arranging time for teachers to meet regularly with colleagues to plan, observe, and reflect on how they will or did teach the lesson and what they heard from students that let them know that students engaged in and understood the key mathematical ideas. The principal can also be instrumental in maintaining the focus and coherence of teachers' planning meetings and ensuring that other district and administrative demands do not impinge on this crucial work.

Teachers' lesson planning builds on central office professional development that teachers have attended throughout the year. These development opportunities that develop over time and focus on the elements of lesson design are what teachers then strive to carry through in the lesson planning sessions at the school level. A principal can and should serve as a critical link between the lessons that teachers learn in districtwide professional development and the ideas they take from these sessions and apply in the classroom. Often teachers are exposed to new pedagogical practices in professional development, but these practices do not become a regular part of teachers' practice. The opportunity for focused and ongoing planning and reflection by teachers is just one possible means of increasing the likelihood that teachers will apply new practices in their day-to-day work. In addition, the principal can provide opportunities for teachers to visit each other's classrooms, providing another pair of eyes and ears, as teachers try the new practices and give each other feedback. Artifacts from the classroom could be shared and reflected on by teachers. For instance, a visiting teacher could take evidence-based notes that focus on the pedagogical practices that the teacher is trying out; if a teacher is trying to improve his or her monitoring of small group work, the visiting teacher may note the assessing and advancing questions that the teacher used and what the students did and said after the teacher left their group. The principal might also observe classrooms with the understanding that the feedback and follow-up debriefing will be limited to the practices learned during professional development. While teachers might initially view this as a form of evaluation, by tightly linking these observations and conversations to the professional development opportunities, the principal will help the teacher to apply and reflect on lessons learned from professional development and to set, accomplish, and celebrate their professional development goals.

Through these processes, both teacher and principal benefit. The principal has an opportunity to learn about mathematics teaching and learning and to gain insights into mathematics instruction across the set of mathematics classrooms, with the goal of achieving instructional coherence within the building. The teachers benefit from the feedback they receive from others and learn the benefit of being a reflective practitioner.

CONCLUSION

In this chapter we have explored the kind of learning that disciplinary literacy focuses on: the learning of content through habits of thinking—both discipline specific and general. By combining both dimensions in pedagogical practice—and instruction organized to support student learning on the diagonal—students learn content by working like mathematicians. It is our hope that all students will be able to engage in these ways in their mathematics' classrooms. We leave you with the following image of what it means to be apprenticed to work like mathematicians.

The teacher is leading the class in a comparison of different plans that will all cost the same amount ($7) as plans A and B at 50 minutes. The students have listed several plans, and the teacher is pressing them to examine the patterns that have emerged:

Teacher: How will I know this [the plan with no "head start"] is going to be steeper just by looking at the equation? Yes, Stephanie?

Stephanie: Since they all have to reach $7 at 50, since there's no head start at monthly fee they have to always, there has to be more to, for the, per minute so it's going to go up faster. It's going to be a higher slope.

Teacher: Did you hear what she said? Can you say that one more time?

Stephanie: Since there's no head start or monthly fee, you have to pay more for the amount per minute, and so the slope or the line will go up faster 'cause they all have to reach $7 when 50 minutes. Do you see that?

Teacher: All plan C's have to go through here, so if I'm going to lower this monthly fee, what has to happen to go through here?

Jerome: The amount per minute has to go higher.

Teacher: Good. Jake, you had an interesting theory about that very thing. Can you share it?

Jake: I came up with the theory that each time you take 50 cents from the monthly fee, you have to add 1 cent to the, um, to the, um, the yeah, the rate.

Teacher: Can you explain, 'cause I'm writing it here? Let me stop you there because I'm going to write the equations up here. Someone have another one here?

Marie: $Y = .13x + .50$.

John: It's going down. (Multiple students talk at once.)

Teacher: Where? What else do you see? What patterns do you see?

Jamilah: Like 11, 12, 13, 14.

Teacher: So .11, .12, .13, .14—put that into words. What's happening to the rate when you do that?

Jamilah: By 11 cents, by 12, by 13—

Teacher: Okay, now I want you to look at what Jake said. You add 1 cent per minute.

Camilla: Subtract 50 cents from the monthly fee.

Teacher: Subtract 50 cents from the monthly fee. Look up there. What's happening there at the graph or the table?

Corey: It decreased by 50 cents.

Teacher: It's decreasing by 50 cents. Let's see if we can figure out why this is happening. Talk to your neighbor.

Multiple students talk quietly at once.

Disciplinary Literacy in the Science Classroom

Samuel A. Spiegel
Jody Bintz
Joseph A. Taylor
Nancy M. Landes
Deborah L. Jordan

Although knowledge of science is identified as essential to the success of our nation's economy and future workforce (Committee on Science, Engineering, and Public Policy, 2007; BSCS, 2007), a majority of Americans still report their high school science experience as alienating and lacking—having spent much of their time listening to lectures or reading chapters in a textbook, answering multiple-choice questions at the end of those chapters, participating in a few disconnected laboratory experiences, taking tests that focused on memory of science facts, and heaving a sigh of relief when it was all over. Because instruction does not support students in connecting important science concepts and the nature of science to their own lives, many students leave their high school science courses with the sense that science is too hard to understand, that it is important and interesting to only a few of the brightest students, and that it has no connection to their own daily lives (Rhoton & Shane, 2006). In fact, in a recent survey of 1,304 adults, only 26 percent believe they have a good understanding of science, and 70 percent do not believe the United States is the world leader in science advancement (Chicago Museum of Science and Industry, 2008).

Those of us involved in science education know that the perception of science as difficult, unimportant, or irrelevant can change when students become involved in classroom science experiences that value them as learners and embody the principles of disciplinary literacy (DL). Even twenty-five years after the release of *A Nation at Risk: An Imperative for Educational Reform* (National Commission on Excellence in Education, 1983), the challenge for students to become scientifically literate is still an unattained national goal; nevertheless, it can be achieved (National Research Council, 2006). Research shows that science classrooms, such as those that embody DL science principles and promote rigorous learning for all students, show significant gains in achievement and help to close the achievement gap (Coburn & Russell, 2008; Banilower, Cohen, Pasley, & Weiss, 2008). Before we consider specific practices that lead to science achievement, we look inside a DL classroom and consider the research on learning to provide a lens for reflecting on DL science.

DEVELOPING A VISION OF DL SCIENCE: SNAPSHOT OF A PHYSICS CLASSROOM

Picture a group of high school physics students seated in clusters of three or four discussing the results of an investigation they just conducted on the relationships among force, mass, and acceleration. Through this and subsequent lessons, students are gradually building an understanding of the physics concept that change in the velocity of an object is proportional to the applied force and inversely proportional to the mass. Specifically, the students conducted a series of experiments using rolling carts in which they could change the mass and force applied. They analyzed the motion of the carts using motion sensors and considered changes in velocity (acceleration) with variations in the mass and applied force. They point to a graph they generated and debate what the data mean. All students are focused on their results and making sense of their data. The teacher moves from group to group, sometimes listening closely to students' ideas and other times asking questions that probe or help them clarify their thinking.

Next, the teacher draws everyone together and focuses the students' attention on the wall-mounted chart papers that display each group's results. The task for students is to compare their group's data with the data of the other groups. The teacher helps the class look for patterns in the data, specifically addressing the question, "What is the relationship between the mass of the object, the force applied, and the acceleration?" After a brief whole-class discussion, the teacher prompts students to turn to a partner and talk about possible explanations for the patterns in the data.

After they have some time to talk with a partner, the teacher instructs each group to write an explanation of the relationship among mass, applied force, and acceleration, citing the evidence that supports their assertions about the relationships. In addition, he asks them to describe the scientific reasoning they use to connect the data to their assertion or claim. Occasionally they look to the large sheet of paper on the wall that has the following prompts:

1. What do you already know about the relationships among force, mass, and acceleration? Why do you think this?

2. What did you learn about the relationships among force, mass, and acceleration from your group's investigations?

3. What did you learn about the relationships among force, mass, and acceleration from examining the class aggregate data?

4. How does your current explanation connect to other ideas you learned in this unit?

5. How does your group's explanation compare to those of the other groups?

6. Did you revise your explanation at any point? If so, why?

7. Why is your explanation about the relationships among force, mass, and acceleration important to the study of mechanics?

8. What do you understand now that you didn't understand in question 1?

9. What experiences did you have in these lessons that helped you increase your understanding of mass, force, and acceleration?

REFLECTING ON THE LESSON: WHAT THE RESEARCH TELLS US

In reflecting on the experiences of these physics students, it may help to look more closely at research on how students learn science. The following notable findings from *How People Learn: Brain, Mind, Experience and School* (National Research Council, 1999) and *How Students Learn: Science in the Classroom* (National

Research Council, 2005) provide some guidance and are consistent with the research and theoretical underpinnings of DL science.

- *Students come to the classroom with preconceptions about how the world works.* In question 1 from the class list, the teacher explicitly asks students to think about what they know (or think they know) about mass, force, and acceleration and the relationship among them. The research about learning science is very clear that students (as well as many adults) have conceptions that are scientifically limited or incorrect when compared to what scientists understand about phenomena (Schneps & Sadler, 2003; Driver, Squires, Rushworth, & Wood-Robinson, 2006). In this situation, a common preconception is that force is a property of an object (the object possesses "force") rather than an interaction between two objects. When students share their initial ideas in a respectful environment, the teacher and students can identify their thinking related to the understanding of the science concepts to be developed in the unit. Later in this chapter, we examine how DL practices and routines, such as Accountable Talk (Michaels, O'Connor, Hall, & Resnick, 2002), can elicit student conceptions and advance their understandings to be more consistent with current scientific understanding.

- *With respect to science, everyday experiences often reinforce the very conceptions of phenomena that scientists have shown to be limited or false, and everyday modes of reasoning are often contrary to scientific reasoning.* Students have daily experiences with forces and changes in motion, but they often associate those experiences with lay meanings of the terms, such as force being associated with resistance or coercion (Driver et al., 2006). The students consequently think that if a force exists, there is always resistance or that forces may somehow have a negative consequence. This is complicated when students consider force along with motion. Their everyday experiences lead to common but incorrect beliefs that if there is no motion, there is no force acting on the object, that a moving object stops when its force is used up, and that a constant speed requires a constant force. These ideas are not consistent with the scientific understandings articulated in national standards and benchmarks related to Newton's laws of motion (see National Research Council, 1996; American Association for the Advancement of Science, 1993). Inquiry science lessons need to provide new experiences that allow students to make sense of these ideas that run counter to their beliefs and how these ideas fit with their existing understandings and everyday experiences (Bybee, 2002). Questions 3, 4, and 8 help students compare their prior thinking to new ideas.

• *Students should build a deep foundation of usable knowledge and understand facts in the context of a conceptual framework*. In this example, the teacher did not ask students to define the terms *force, mass,* and *acceleration* outside of actual experience. Rather, the teacher asked students to investigate the relationships among those concepts and then develop explanations from classroom data. Such knowledge is more likely to become usable because students put their ideas together by investigating, speaking, writing, and reasoning. Question 7 in the list supports students' development of a conceptual framework. It also provides opportunity for students to talk about their emerging understanding of relationships among force, mass, and acceleration in the larger context of mechanics.

• *Students should have opportunities to learn science as a process of inquiry*. This involves observation, imagination, and reasoning about the phenomena under study. It includes the use of tools and procedures in the context of authentic science inquiries. These tools and procedures become devices that allow students to extend their everyday experiences of the world and help them organize data in ways that provide new insights into phenomena. In this physics classroom snapshot, students conducted scientific inquiry with their classmates by focusing on a scientific question; conducting investigations; gathering and analyzing evidence as a group and as a class; developing explanations based on that evidence; and communicating their understanding through sharing their explanations. The teacher helped students understand the importance of these practices by asking them to reflect on questions 2 through 6 on the classroom chart.

• *Students should be taught explicitly to monitor and take control of their own learning—often referred to as* metacognition. Questions 7 through 9 on the classroom chart clearly exemplify metacognitive processes. Those questions ask students to connect their current understanding to what they knew at the beginning of the unit, how they came to their current understanding, and what these ideas have to do with the larger ideas in the study of mechanics. These types of questions help students recognize that they can learn important ideas in science, how they learn, and that they are responsible for that learning.

- *Students should understand the tendency of us all to attempt to confirm rather than rigorously test (and possibly refute) our current assumptions.* Creating a learning environment that promotes genuine testing of assumptions is one example of a metacognitive approach to science instruction. The approach is deepened when students learn why and how to create models of phenomena that can be put to an empirical test. In a classroom that honors students' ideas and encourages them to test, compare, and communicate those ideas, students have numerous opportunities to rigorously test their assumptions about scientific phenomena and possibly change their ideas based on evidence and reasoning from their own experiences and the reasoning of others.

These findings reinforce the interplay between reasoning and developing content knowledge as described in Chapter One. The research findings shift responsibility for learning to the learner, recognize the importance of students' prior conceptions and experiences, and consider how to build on those prior understandings as students develop their content knowledge as well as their understandings of science as an enterprise.

DL SCIENCE AND THE NATURE OF SCIENCE

The vision of a DL science classroom is distinctive from what we might see in many of today's science classrooms. A DL science classroom envisions different roles and levels of learning for the students than has been the norm. The students do the cognitive work rather than relying on the teacher to tell them. In a DL science classroom, all students develop deeper, conceptually grounded understandings of science content (subject matter), apply scientific reasoning, and engage in the practices of science—all elements essential to success in the modern workforce (Committee on Science, Engineering, and Public Policy, 2007). DL science is grounded in the principles of learning (POLs) (Resnick, Hall, & IFL Fellows, 2003). As such, it:

- Acknowledges the importance of activating and assessing prior knowledge (the POLs are academic rigor in a thinking curriculum and active use of knowledge).

- Clearly defines rigorous academic goals for students (the POLs are clear expectations, academic rigor in a thinking curriculum, and commitment to a knowledge core).

- Requires that learners become engaged in rich and rigorous learning experiences that allow and encourage students to cognitively wrestle with foundational concepts and processes (the POL is socializing intelligence).

- Provides opportunities for students to demonstrate their competency through authentic science products and performances (the POL is learning as apprenticeship).

- Affords students the opportunity to reflect on their own learning (the POL is self-management of learning).

For this vision to come alive in science classrooms, a teacher must be grounded in the nature of science as well as in the DL principles of learning and have a strong understanding of the content. Inquiry is at the heart of science and scientific ways of knowing. What are the distinguishing characteristics of science as inquiry that set it apart from other disciplines and lay the foundation for learning science in classrooms? First, scientists believe that the world is understandable: "Science presumes that the things and events in the universe occur in consistent patterns that are comprehensible through careful, systematic study" (American Association for the Advancement of Science, 1989, p. 25). Science is not the search for the truth, but the search for more and more precise ways to explain and predict how the world works. The practice of science employs logical reasoning to connect evidence with conclusions. Science is all about sense making—using logical reasoning to connect observations and data with accepted scientific principles. Furthermore, scientists make sense of the world by engaging in scientific inquiry. According to *Science for All Americans* (American Association for the Advancement of Science, 1989):

> Scientific inquiry is not easily described apart from the context of particular investigations. There simply is no fixed set of steps that scientists always follow, no one path that leads them unerringly to scientific knowledge. There are, however, certain features of science that give it a distinctive character as a mode of inquiry. Although those features are especially characteristic of the work of professional

scientists, everyone can exercise them in thinking scientifically about many matters of interest in everyday life [p. 26].

Science has these features:

- Science demands evidence.
- Science is a blend of logical reasoning and imagination.
- Science explains and predicts.
- Scientists try to identify and avoid bias.
- Scientific ideas are subject to change.
- Scientific knowledge is durable.
- Science cannot provide complete answers to all questions.

National Standards in Science

Fortunately for those of us in science education, we have clear and well articulated national standards that help us translate the nature of science into the practice of science in classrooms. The *National Science Education Standards* (NSES) (National Research Council, 1996) and *Benchmarks for Science Literacy* (American Association for the Advancement of Science, 1993), which serve as frameworks for most state-level science standards: and provide guidance in understanding what is important to know (the science content) and do (the practice of science) in a science classroom. Scientific inquiry is at the heart of developing scientific literacy in students and, in conjunction with the POLs and DL principles, it is the keystone of DL science. Inquiry has specific meaning within science and is a part of both the content that a student should learn in science class and the pedagogy that teachers employ in teaching science. This means that science literacy for students includes both "doing science," that is, engaging in the inquiry practices of science, and understanding the nature of scientific inquiry as part of the content of science, along with understanding core science concepts (subject matter).

Five Essential Features of Classroom Inquiry in Science

To further define and support students and teachers in the practice of scientific inquiry, the National Research Council (NRC) published *Inquiry and the National Science Education Standards* (2000) as an addendum to the NSES. In this document, the authors propose a working definition of inquiry "that distinguishes inquiry-based teaching and learning from inquiry in a general sense and from inquiry as practiced by scientists" (p. 24). This definition incorporates five essential features of inquiry that apply across all grade levels and in all disciplines of science:

- *Essential Feature 1:* Learners are engaged by scientifically oriented questions.

- *Essential Feature 2:* Learners give priority to evidence, which allows them to develop and evaluate explanations that address scientifically oriented questions.

- *Essential Feature 3:* Learners formulate explanations from evidence to address scientifically oriented questions.

- *Essential Feature 4:* Learners evaluate their explanations in light of alternative explanations, particularly those reflecting scientific understanding.

- Essential Feature 5: Learners communicate and justify their proposed explanations. [p. 25]

These five essential features of classroom inquiry (5EFs) provide a framework to integrate scientific inquiry into the classroom while advancing student learning of subject matter and scientific inquiry. A key aspect of the 5EFs is that all five are essential to fully experience scientific inquiry. Often in science classrooms, we do engage learners in questions and allow them to gather and explore some data. Where we traditionally fall short, however, is in not allowing students to first articulate and struggle with their own understandings (prior conceptions) of the phenomenon before inviting them to consider alternative explanations that may better explain how the world actually works (a more scientific explanation). These alternative explanations emerge when students apply logical reasoning to the results of their investigations—their evidence—and develop their own explanations for what they have observed. Students then refine and justify their explanations based on more evidence from others' investigations, their interactions with their classmates, and information provided by teacher, such as currently accepted ideas within the scientific community.

A DEEPER LOOK INTO SCIENTIFIC INQUIRY AND DL SCIENCE

In a DL science classroom, learning activities, assignments, and assessments work together to engage students in a science apprenticeship while deepening their content knowledge. However, students are not scientists, and science education has different goals from those of science. Science education for K–12 students is primarily about helping them to understand both the content (core subject matter) of the disciplines of science and the nature of science. Frameworks such as the five essential features of classroom inquiry provide opportunities for students to learn the content of science through the eyes of a scientist. Students ask and answer core questions in a discipline rather than completing arbitrary worksheets or chapter tests. Daily, the subject matter tasks, texts, and talk that engage students involve them more deeply in the nature of science as they think and as scientists do. The content is coherent across an arc of lessons that builds conceptual understanding while keeping the learning on the diagonal. (See Chapter Two for a description of learning on the diagonal.) The term *arc of lessons* is used to represent a conceptually cohesive sequence of learning activities. These may be encompassed in a chapter, unit, module, or other organizing scheme depending on the instructional materials. Within the arc of lessons, students may spend time engaged in a variety of practices: reading, writing, discussing, and experimenting, for example. The quintessential aspect of the arc of lessons is around the learning. Are the students using the practices (reading, writing, speaking, investigating) to learn and form conceptual understandings of the content and practices of science? Is the learning cohesive and rigorous?

BUILDING THE VISION OF DL SCIENCE IN A SEVENTH-GRADE LIFE SCIENCE CLASSROOM

To develop a richer vision of DL science in practice, we will examine a seventh-grade science classroom whose students have been investigating interactions between living (biotic) and nonliving (abiotic) things in ecosystems. In this midyear unit on the behavior of organisms in changing environments, students build toward an understanding of a core science concept: that heredity and experience limit the behavioral responses an organism can make to changes in its environment. The teacher, Ms. Thompson, has begun to implement DL practices and routines in her classroom and is concentrating specifically on using Accountable Talk moves. (See Table 5.1.)

In the following section, we highlight specific Accountable Talk moves within the classroom dialogue. In general, Ms. Thompson emphasizes the first two sections of Accountable Talk: (1) to ensure purposeful, coherent, and productive group discussion and (2) to support accountability to the learning community. As

Table 5.1
Accountable Talk Moves and Functions

Teacher Move	Function	Example
To ensure purposeful, coherent, and productive group discussion		
1. Marking	Direct attention to the value and importance of a student's contribution.	"That's an important point."
2. Challenging students	Redirect a question back to the students or use students' contributions as a source for a further challenge or inquiry.	"What do *you* think?"
3. Modeling	Make one's thinking public, and demonstrate expert forms or reasoning through talk.	"Here's what good readers do . . ."
4. Recapping	Make public in a concise, coherent form the group's achievement at creating a shared understanding of the phenomenon under discussion.	"What have we discovered?"
To support accountability to the learning community		
5. Keeping the channels open	Ensure that students can hear each other, and remind them that they must hear what others have said.	"Did everyone hear that?"
6. Keeping everyone together	Ensure that everyone not only heard but also understood what a speaker said.	"Who can repeat . . .?"
7. Linking contributions	Make explicit the relationship between a new contribution and what has gone before.	"Who wants to add on . . .?"
8. Verifying and clarifying	Revoice a student's contribution, thereby helping both speakers and listeners to engage more profitably in the conversation.	"So are you saying . . .?"
To support accountability to accurate knowledge		
9. Pressing for accuracy	Hold students accountable for the accuracy, credibility, and clarity of their contributions.	"Where can we find that . . .?"
10. Building on prior knowledge	Tie a current contribution back to knowledge accumulated by the class at a previous time.	"How does this connect. . .?"
To support accountability to rigorous thinking		
11. Pressing for reasoning	Elicit evidence and establish what contribution a student's utterance is intended to make within the group's larger enterprise.	"Why do you think that . . .?"
12. Expanding reasoning	Open up extra time and space in the conversation for student reasoning.	"Take your time . . . say more."

© 2009 University of Pittsburgh. (Michaels et al., 2002).

she practices, Ms. Thompson will incorporate all of the Accountable Talk moves over time and help her students gradually employ them as well.

In this lesson, which takes three class periods, Ms. Thompson builds on a common task that is consistent with her course goals and sequencing (Educational Services Incorporated, 1966). She uses mealworms to provide students with a concrete experience that reflects the learning goals and the core concept of the unit. The specific learning goals of this lesson relate to (1) the concept that organisms react in predictable patterns to changes in their environment (growth in content knowledge) and (2) to students' abilities to generate scientifically oriented, testable questions and corresponding experimental procedures (growth in habits of thinking in science).

Session 1: Developing a Scientifically Oriented Question

As we enter, groups of students are huddled around several tables, apparently curious about the mealworms Ms. Thompson has just displayed.

"Before we get started," Ms. Thompson begins, "who can remind us of the big question we've been investigating?" A chart is posted on the wall with the following overarching questions for the unit:

• How do changes in the environment affect the behaviors of organisms living in it?

• How do changes in an organism's behaviors affect its ability to obtain and use resources, grow, reproduce, and maintain stable internal conditions?

A chorus of students sings out responses. To be clear, however, Ms. Thompson asks again: "Who can remind us of the big question we've been investigating? One at a time, please" (Accountable Talk move 6, keeping everyone together).

Juan raises his hand and responds upon a nod from Ms. Thompson: "We want to know how organisms might behave if their environment changes."

Ms. Thompson points to the first question on the class chart and says, "Okay, that's what we want to know. Thank you, Juan, for the helpful paraphrase of our first big question. So how do you think we're going to be working with these mealworms over the next few days?"

"Checking out their properties," Marsha volunteers.

"And why would we do that?" Ms. Thompson encourages (move 2, challenging students)

"'Cause that's how ecologists find out what things are," Marsha continues.

"And we're doing ecology," adds Dante, his gaze fixed on the mealworms.

Like the rest of his classmates, Dante appears eager to get to work.

"Okay. What I want you to do, then," Ms. Thompson begins, "is to observe the behavior of your mealworms and come up with some questions about them. You remember last week we talked about criteria for a good experiment question, right?" The students turn to a second chart. This one reads:

Good Questions to Guide Our Experiments
1. Start with "what" or "how."

2. Include something to compare.

3. Include something to measure.

Ms. Thompson knows how important it is for students to craft relevant questions to guide their experiments. Providing students with opportunities to ask and investigate their own questions is motivating. Because she has English-language learners in her classroom, Ms. Thompson uses "experiment" questions rather than scientifically oriented questions to limit the language challenge. The concept is the same.

In groups of two or three, the students observe the movements of the mealworms. Ms. Thompson circulates from group to group, encouraging them to write a list of their questions, listening to their ideas, and occasionally asking a question or elaborating on a comment to make sure language issues are not interfering with any student's ability to fully engage in the task.

"That's kinda the same as this question," she hears at one table. "Let's make them one."

"That's a helpful suggestion, Julie," Ms. Thompson responds (move 1, marking).

"Whoa, that's a good one!" comes a cry from another group. "Let's do that."

Ms. Thompson notices that the class is more engaged than usual. She suspects they like having a sense of control over what they are learning. One of the challenges Ms. Thompson faces is that students have viewed her—the teacher—as the answer giver. And indeed, with so much material to be covered, giving answers is a temptation. But Ms. Thompson knows that is not how students learn, so she has been working to shift how they view her role and help them assume more responsibility for their own learning. "I'm not going to do the thinking for you," she has told them. "You have to stew.... You have to talk to one another.... You have to work for the answers" (move 3, modeling). She has also gradually been introducing them to Accountable Talk strategies to help them learn how to push each other's and their own thinking through productive discourse. As she works on her Accountable Talk skills, she sees how they help to keep the discussions focused, rigorous, and flowing.

Soon all of the groups have posted two or three of their favorite questions. Ms. Thompson calls them back together to consider which questions are testable and link back to the overarching questions. Following some spirited discussion about how to distinguish what is testable from what is most interesting, the class reaches consensus on a question they really want to investigate: How fast do mealworms move if you put them on something warm?

"All right," she says. "If this is the question you want to pursue, you'll have to revise it to meet the criteria we identified. I'll help you think about how to do that, but I'm not going to revise the question for you. What tools do you have to work with?" (move 2, challenging students).

"What makes a question an experiment question?" Jaime suggests, pointing to the chart of criteria for experiment questions.

"It should help us learn about the overarching questions," adds Georgia, pointing to the question sheet.

"We could look up some of our old questions," suggests Christina, leafing back through the pages of her notebook. "Make them the same."

"That's an important point, Christina," remarks Ms. Thompson (move 1, marking). "Connecting to what you've done before is a mark of a good scientist" (move 3, modeling).

"What did you come up with?" asks Ms. Thompson.

Juan reads his group's agreed-on question: "What effect does changing the temperature of the surface the mealworm is on have on mealworm speed?"

Ms. Thompson asks, "Did everyone hear that?" (move 6, keeping the channels open). Students all look up as Ms. Thompson asks the question.

"Who can restate what Juan just said?" Ms. Thompson challenges (move 6, keeping everyone together).

Georgia responds, "I think the question asks if mealworms will change how fast they move."

Julie raises her hand and adds, "I think the question is about two things: first, the temperature of the surface—how warm or cold the surface is—and second, how fast the mealworms move on warm or cold surfaces."

After ascertaining that students understand the intent of the question, Ms. Thompson writes a refined question on the board so all can see it: What effect does the temperature of the mealworm's surface have on a mealworm's speed? Before proceeding, she asks for confirmation from Juan's group that she has not changed their intent. She is satisfied that the question can support a well-designed experiment to test how surface temperature affects a mealworm's speed as it moves across the surface.

Session 2: Designing a Scientific Investigation

Before proceeding, Ms. Thompson asks students to predict how mealworm speed will be affected by changing the temperature and to write their predictions in their science notebooks. She also asks them to record why they made the prediction. What do they know that makes them think that will be the result (move 10, building on prior knowledge)?

Next, she asks the students to write a plan for conducting their investigation. The students know they need warm and cool surfaces on which the mealworms can crawl, and after some brainstorming, they identify a safe way to conduct the investigation using moist paper towels: (1) from a freezer, (2) from the microwave (set at low power and monitored by Ms. Thompson), and (3) at room temperature. Ms. Thompson challenges the students to develop a more precise plan by giving a measurable definition for "warm" and "cool" based on the temperatures of the paper towels from the three sources (move 2, challenging students). She also asks them to create and describe a precise method for measuring mealworm speed.

Creating Data Tables   Ms. Thompson asks the students to think about how they will display their data so they can compare data across all groups. Although the students are eager to begin their investigations with the mealworms, they know that the preparation will make their classroom discussion much easier the next day.

"What do you need to think about in creating a data table that will help you organize your data for this investigation?" Ms. Thompson asks as she points to the question they have agreed to investigate.

"We need to think about the variables," offers Dante.

" . . . how hot or cold the paper towels are," Tan Ying continues.

" . . . and how fast the mealworms move," Juan adds.

"Excellent!" Ms. Thompson responds. I am glad to hear you name the specific variables" (move 1, marking). Ms. Thompson then asks students how they might design an appropriate data table for this investigation. Some students page through their science notebooks looking for examples of data tables they completed for other investigations.

Matthew suggests, "I think we can use a data table like the one we made when we looked at how far a marble rolled down an incline." He reads the date from the top of his notebook page. "We had three inclines—almost flat, medium incline, and steep. That's like having the three temperatures—cold, room temperature, and warm."

"Are you saying that we need three rows in our data table?" Ms. Thompson clarifies (move 8, verifying and clarifying). "What do the rest of you think about Matthew's idea?"

After a number of students concur, she asks for volunteers to come to the board to draw possible data tables for this investigation. After some comparison and discussion, the class agrees on the table shown in Table 5.2.

After all students have copied the data table in their science notebooks, Ms. Thompson interjects, "I have one more question before you begin your investigation. Is one data table going to be enough for this investigation?"

"This data table is good only for one mealworm's results," Julie responds. "We need to test more than one worm, don't we?"

A chorus of students answers Julie's question. They agree that they need to test at least three mealworms. They all want to test as many as possible in the time allotted and are chomping at the bit to get going. Ms. Thompson smiles because she realizes that students understand something critical to the nature of science: scientists perform multiple trials in any investigation. She knows she is making progress.

Table 5.2
Student Data Chart Template

Temperature	Mealworm Speed		
	Distance	Time	Speed
Cold (about 10°C)			
Room temperature (about 26°C)			
Warm (about 40°C)			

Collecting and Recording Data   On completing their investigations, laboratory groups transfer their data tables onto large sheets of paper and post them at the front of the room. Students examine others' data, noting similarities and differences. Table 5.3 is a sample of one lab group's data tables.

Session 3: Analyzing Data

Ms. Thompson guides a class discussion about why the results might not all be the same. Students have had these discussions before and recognize that there is variation in the organisms, the temperature of the paper towels, and their own

Table 5.3
Student Mealworm Data

Mealworm 1

Temperature	Mealworm Speed		
	Distance	Time	Speed
Cold (10°C)	75 cm	2 minutes	0.63 cm/sec
Room temperature (26°C)	168.5 cm	2 minutes	1.4 cm/sec
Warm (40°C)	120 cm	2 minutes	1.0 cm/sec

Mealworm 2

Temperature	Mealworm Speed		
	Distance	Time	Speed
Cold (12°C)	100 cm	2 minutes	0.83 cm/sec
Room temperature (28°C)	150 cm	2 minutes	1.25 cm/sec
Warm (37°C)	115 cm	2 minutes	0.96 cm/sec

Mealworm 3

Temperature	Mealworm Speed		
	Distance	Time	Speed
Cold (8°C)	65 cm	2 minutes	0.5 cm/sec
Room temperature (25°C)	175 cm	2 minutes	1.5 cm/sec
Warm (42°C)	130 cm	2 minutes	1.1 cm/sec

abilities to collect data accurately. The mealworms, for instance, do not move in a straight line. Ms. Thompson ends with the reminder that each laboratory group must use its own data to write an answer to their original question: What effect does the temperature of the mealworm's surface have on a mealworm's speed? She also reminds them to look at the predictions they wrote at the beginning of the lesson. How do their actual results compare with their predicted results?

Later, after all lab groups have formed an answer to the class question about mealworm behavior and posted their ideas on chart paper, Ms. Thompson conducts another class discussion, helping students clarify their thinking and reach consensus about scientific ideas from evidence they collected during the investigation.

Students have begun to share with one another their ideas about mealworms' responses to temperature change. One student spoke on behalf of her group: "The mealworms moved faster when the paper towels were at room temperature and slowed down a little when they got too warm and a lot more when they got too cool." Another student asked the question that Ms. Thompson has modeled time and again: "How do you know?" (move 11, pressing for reasoning). The response was just as she hoped: "It's what we saw in our data." "See," a student says while pointing to the data chart posted on the wall, "when the temperature went up or down, the mealworm speed slowed down." Another student chimes in. "It's what we saw too." With gentle prodding from Ms. Thompson, the student follows by giving specific examples from the team's data and calculations. After discussions of their data, students generate additional questions about factors that affected the behavior, including an organism's need for food and water. Students write about their learning so far and then read more about other factors that bear on mealworm behavior, growth, and reproduction.

One of Ms. Thompson's fundamental beliefs about teaching and learning is that for real learning to occur, "students have to own it, possess it, and use it several times."

Reflecting on the Lesson and Student Learning

This lesson provides a concrete example of how a change in the environment has an impact on the behavior of an organism and helps students respond to the overarching question of the unit. Based on evidence they collected themselves, students learn that a change in an environmental condition (temperature) affects the behavior of mealworms (the speed of their movements). Later lessons in the series (arc of lessons) will ask students to consider how this particular behavioral response affects the mealworm's ability to use environmental resources, grow, and reproduce, connecting this experience to the second overarching question of the unit.

This one lesson serves as a small bridge between students' prior knowledge about how living and nonliving things interact in the environment and the concepts related to behavioral responses and evolution implied in the overarching questions described previously. The students also furthered their understandings of scientifically oriented, testable questions and how to design a scientific investigation. This lesson will help them communicate as scientists do by developing and defending explanations that address the overarching questions posed at the beginning of the unit. Accountable Talk strategies help keep the discourse productive and focused.

Ms. Thompson commented during a discussion after the lesson, "In past years I would spend too much time on behavior management. They would get tired of hearing me talk or just not be engaged in learning. With this approach [DL science], students stay more focused so it gives me more time, all of us more time, to learn science."

INSTRUCTION AND ASSESSMENT DRIVE EACH OTHER

Learning activities, assignments, and assessments that engage learners in scientific habits of thinking (for example, developing scientifically oriented, testable questions) while learning about natural phenomena (for example, how organisms respond to environmental conditions) help students become apprentices in science. Accountable Talk can help keep the discourse productive toward the learning goals.

In DL science, assessment is an integral part of the learning process. DL science infuses both informal assessment strategies, such as listening to student discussions and reading responses to quick write prompts, and formal assessments, such as written explanations and unit summation tests. These formative strategies enable teachers to assess and monitor student learning so they can adjust instructional practices or sequences if necessary; these strategies also provide an opportunity for students to assess, monitor, and adjust their own learning. Students are guided to assess their own learning and the learning of their peers to plan and engage in the next steps of their learning.

Ongoing informal assessment during instruction gives students time to do important tasks and teachers time to observe, review, and assess what the students learn from those tasks. For example, Ms. Thompson assessed the quality of the student-generated questions and, based on her assessment, knew that she must help students revise their questions so that the questions embodied the features of scientifically oriented questions. Because the students talked to one another about their ideas, Ms. Thompson had many opportunities to learn what and how students were thinking about both the content and scientific inquiry.

The next section examines a classroom that is investigating somewhat similar content but at a much more sophisticated level. Ms. Thompson's lesson focused on the first two of the 5EFs. The next lesson emphasizes the development of scientific explanations and provides a fuller picture of inquiry and DL science. Consider how this process provides rich assessment opportunities for both the students and the teacher.

THE ROLE OF SCIENTIFIC EXPLANATIONS

In reviewing the 5EFs, you may have noticed that explanations are a key feature of inquiry and are explicitly mentioned in four of the five features. Explanations within science have a specific meaning that students might confuse with general definitions they may use in other content areas such as mathematics, English language arts, or history. Within science, one develops an explanation to make sense of the data, following either experimentation or an analysis of data gathered from someone else's experiment or observations. Scientific explanations are always evidence based; that is, they are based on the data gathered and interpreted to answer a question. The explanation is the answer to the scientifically oriented question being addressed. At a minimum, the explanation should include the claim one makes about the question under investigation, the empirical evidence used to support the claim, and the scientific reasoning used to justify logical connections between the evidence and the claim (Kuhn & Reiser, 2005; McNeil & Krajick, 2006).

Recently a number of science educators have published significant research related to the nature of scientific explanations and how to scaffold student learning in developing, communicating, and justifying their explanations. In a study of the research related to scaffolding scientific explanations conducted by

McNeill, Lizotte, Krajcik, and Marx (2006), the authors synthesized the following findings:

- Explanations are rarely a part of classroom practice (Kuhn, 1993; Newton, Driver, & Osborne, 1999).

- Students have difficulty using appropriate evidence (Sandoval & Reiser, 2004) and including the backing for why they chose the evidence (Bell & Linn, 2000) in their written explanations.

- Students typically discount data if the data contradict their current theory (Chinn & Brewer, 2001).

- During classroom discourse, discussions tend to be dominated by claims with little backing to support them (Jiménez-Aleixandre, Rodríguez, & Duschl, 2000).

- Understanding of scientific principles is linked to the ability to develop explanations.

The last finding is worth highlighting. Students' understandings of science principles are directly linked to their abilities to develop and articulate explanations. As Kuhn and Reiser (2005) note, "Explanations are both the goal of the activity and the means to get there" (p. 1). Students' construction of scientific explanations is integral to their understanding of scientific principles. Sense-making activities and social interaction are keys to the development of explanations. Consequently socializing intelligence and engaging in Accountable Talk practices enhance students' development, communication, and justification of explanations. Students make sense of content knowledge in science as they develop explanations. Sense making and the articulation of explanations are part of the same process in science and should be viewed not as sequential but rather as an iterative process (Kuhn & Reiser, 2005).

A DEEPER LOOK AT DL SCIENCE IN A HIGH SCHOOL BIOLOGY CLASS

Consider a classroom at the local high school in the same district. Like other teachers in the district, Ms. Barton is working to more fully integrate DL science practices and routines into her classroom to promote more rigorous learning for all of her students. She has made considerable progress in integrating Accountable Talk into her practice and has noticed that her students are engaging in it as well. She is now focusing on the use of scientific explanations in her inquiry-based teaching.

Ms. Barton, who teaches both biology and chemistry at this urban high school, agreed to an observation of one of her biology lessons. The focus of the observation was the development of explanations and the role of DL in furthering student understandings. The lesson is one that builds on students' previous experiences from middle grades around ecosystems and how organisms interact with their environment, similar to what we saw in Ms. Thompson's classroom. This will afford an opportunity to look at a lesson in greater depth and consider conceptual cohesiveness within the unit of study, as well as consider how concepts are developed across grade bands.

The lesson is part of the final unit of the biology program in the district. One of the aspects that differentiates DL science from DL history/social studies or English language arts is that for DL science, there are several choices of well-developed, commercially available instructional materials. So rather than focus on the development of instructional materials or arcs of lessons, we focus on more effective implementation of those programs (analysis, selection, adaptation, pacing, and chunking).

The overall goal of this unit is to more deeply understand the concept that living systems interact with their environment and are interdependent with other systems. Students have completed the first chapter of the unit, building on their prior understandings of the carbon cycle, food webs, and matter and energy as they examined an island system, a simulated pasture, and their own local environment. In each instance, they considered how human activity within the ecosystem had an impact on the entire system, including humans.

Ms. Barton has been using the instructional materials with reasonable fidelity—that is, in ways that are generally consistent with the overall design of the program. At this stage of the program design, lessons are intended to help students begin to make sense of scientific principles by constructing explanations. In this case, students construct an explanation based on a scenario titled "Tri-Lakes" (BSCS, 2006).

In the arc of lessons in which the Tri-Lakes scenario resides, students investigate the role that science plays in the complex decisions that humans make as part of the ecosystems. They consider systems analysis approaches as they explore the direct and indirect impacts of various factors within a system. Ms. Barton's specific learning goals for the lesson are:

- Students will recognize that systems are complex and dynamic but can be studied through a systems analysis approach called *factor analysis.*
- Students will recognize that decisions they make can have consequences on ecosystems. Students learn how to be good environmental citizens.
- Students will develop stronger evidence-based explanations.

During the lesson, students consider the Tri-Lakes ecosystem and factors that might have an impact on the bass population within the lake. They are presented with a scenario that begins with a letter from the Tri-Lakes Bass Association (Exhibit 5.1).

Planning and Reflecting on the Lesson to Advance Student Thinking

In preparation for this lesson, Ms. Barton and her DL science coach worked together to more clearly define the factors that might have an impact on the bass population in the lake. The focus of the conversation was on Ms. Barton's thinking about the lesson, with the coach shifting the discussion from content to pedagogy to the learners as they consider the lesson. This cyclic pattern—content to pedagogy to learner—is referred to as the *coach discussion cycle* and is one of the DL routines and tools used in moving the work into the classroom.

The coach and Ms. Barton considered what would constitute "stronger" (Ms. Barton's emphasis) explanations from the students at this juncture. With some probing and joint effort, they drafted three focus questions to help orient the students' analyses of the data and focus their explanations:

1. What can we determine about the ecosystem and changes that have occurred over the past ten years?
2. How are the organisms within the lake responding to changes within the ecosystem?
3. What has caused the changes in bass catch rates within the lake?

In scientific inquiry, the question both engages the learners and drives where the learning will go through the inquiry.

Exhibit 5.1
Tri-Lakes Letter

The Problem at Tri-Lakes
TRI-LAKES ASSOCIATION

Dear Biology Students at Tri-Lakes High School:

The members of the Tri-Lakes Association are very concerned about a confusing problem we have in the Tri-Lakes region. In general, the fishing is good, especially for bass. But people are not catching as many bass as they did years ago. As a result, our reputation as the bass-fishing capital of the world is suffering. Reservations at local resorts are down by 25 percent. This has had disturbing financial consequences for our area.

I know that, under the leadership of your very dedicated teacher, the biology classes at Tri-Lakes High have kept records on the water quality of the lakes for many years. The members of the association have noticed something about the change in the number of bass fish being caught. This change seems to have happened along with, or as a result of, a number of other changes around the area. We hope that your data about the lake and your scientific abilities will help us determine what is happening, or at least give us a sense of what questions we need to study.

The members of the association, some of whom are scientists, have made the following observations. We hope this information helps:

► Small invertebrate animals such as *Daphnia magna* and *Gammarus* are less common in the lake than they used to be.
► The lake is greener for more of the year than it used to be.
► Like the bass, perch in the lake seem smaller, and they are less colorful than in previous years.

In addition to those observations, I am sending data packets with information gathered from local papers and lake study records. These packets contain information that the association members pulled together in an attempt to understand what might be happening to our region. Some of the data may look familiar. We pulled some information from your annual report to the association. We hope that this combination of local, national, and historical data will provide enough clues for you to identify our problems so that we can begin working on solutions.

Our next association meeting is in two weeks. We look forward to hearing from you at that time. Because many of you and your families are involved in the fishing and resort industries, I am sure you understand the seriousness of this situation. I eagerly await your response.

Sincerely,

Chris Tackle

Chris Tackle
President, Tri-Lakes Association

Source: BSCS (2006, p. 1).

Teaching from the Planning

After reading the letter and considering possible factors that might have an impact on the scenario (for example, pollution, too much fishing, introduction of an exotic species that is outcompeting the bass), the students reviewed the data that are available about the lake system. The data are organized into a complex sixteen-page data packet (Exhibit 5.2) that requires the students to analyze and

---

Exhibit 5.2
Organization of Data Sheets

NEED TO KNOW

Information Sheets

Study the information sheets that you decide are likely to help solve the mystery at Tri-Lakes. You also can use other available resources.

1. Tri-Lakes Advertisement
2. *Tri-Lakes Tribune* Article, January 29, 1996
3. *Tri-Lakes Tribune* Article, June 17, 2000
4. Location of Tri-Lakes Resorts
5. Zone Map of the Average Temperature
6. Largemouth Bass
7. Yellow Perch
8. Total Number of Fish Caught Annually, 1982–2002
9. Number of Largemouth Bass and Yellow Perch Caught Annually, 1982–2002
10. Average Length of Fish Caught Compared with Legal Limit
11. Table of Dissolved Oxygen and pH for Tri-Lakes, 1982–2002
12. Algae and Cyanobacteria
13. *Daphnia*
14. *Gammarus*
15. Pesticides
16. Acid Precipitation

You do not have to read everything in the data packet. Compare the titles of the information sheets with the questions you raised. Which information sheets are likely to be helpful for answering your question? Sort through the large quantities of information critically to find the important pieces. This is a valuable scientific skill.

Source: BSCS (2006, p. 639).

interpret the data, evaluate data sources, and reorganize and make sense of the data they decide are relevant to the question they are answering. The class also conducted experiments on *Daphnia* (water fleas), a primary food source for fish such as young bass.

With the data packets in hand and the data generated from the experiments with *Daphnia,* the students, working in triads, have begun to develop written explanations around one of the focus questions. Ms. Barton is moving among the groups, monitoring their conversations and periodically stepping into a conversation with a group. Occasionally a group calls Ms. Barton to join their discussion or ask a clarifying question.

Cognitively Wrestling to Advance Understanding

As the groups move into their discussions around the data, they need to cognitively wrestle with the data and the science concepts behind them. The struggle is important to help the students build onto their existing constructs and expand their understandings. They are working with a multifaceted problem, one that does not have an easy or clear answer. It requires the students to consider complex interactions between biotic and abiotic factors within an ecosystem. As they personally engage in the cognitive wrestling, they also engage at a group level. The group discussion pushes them to become clear about their understandings in ways they can articulate to others, as well as to make sense of what others are saying. Ms. Barton includes time for the discussion based on her experiences in teaching and in her work with DL science, noting the importance of socializing intelligence and effort-based learning as articulated in the POLs (Resnick et al., 2003). Let's listen in on one group's discussion around some of the data to experience this sense making through cognitive wrestling and discourse:

> *Vincent:* When concentration is increased due to pollution, some bacteria and algae may have a population explosion. So like, then it says, as the populations increase, many of the algae and higher bacteria die off. Oxygen-using decomposer bacteria increase the numbers, which drops the level of oxygen levels in the lake. Okay, look at the chart.
>
> *Tomeka:* Is that this page?
>
> *Vincent:* Look at the chart, and it says the oxygen levels were decreasing and pH was increasing.

Tomeka: pH is decreasing.

Vincent: Increasing.

Tomeka: No, the pH is decreasing. It's becoming more acidic. But if it was the power plant making the pH decrease, it wouldn't just be by 0.5; it would be really, really low.

Ryan: But it says, umm, here on page 4–125, it says nitrates and phosphates support nutrients that are normally present in low concentration.

Tomeka: Wait, when they [nitrates and phosphates] increase, algae has population explosions, which means the algae count goes up, which means there will be more oxygen in the water. So it can't be due to nitrate pollution, because oxygen levels are going down.

Ryan: Yeah, but keep reading. Then it says, "Oxygen-using decomposer bacteria then increase in numbers, which drops the oxygen levels in the lake."

Tomeka: It's not the power plant.

Ms. Barton: It's not the power plant, okay, so what can you agree on? Is there any evidence that you can say, "Okay at this point . . ."?

Ryan: Something to do with the nitrates and phosphates.

Ms. Barton: So what is it about the nitrates that make you think that the change has something to do with that?

Ryan: First, it says the normally formed lakes have low concentration of nitrates and phosphates, and then when they increase, because of the pollution, cyanobacteria and algae may have population explosions. Explosions of these organisms give the water a green color, which it said over in the beginning data sheets—look how green the lake is. Don't the bass eat algae for food?

Tomeka: I understand what you're saying that the nitrate does have something to do with it, the nitrates and phosphates, because it does say if the nitrates and phosphates go up, then the algae will die, and then there's no more oxygen, and the fish will die off. Right? But I still think that if the nitrates and phosphates were being produced by the power plant, there would be more of an effect on the pH.

Ms. Barton: And so what is the pH trend that you're seeing? What's your evidence on the pH trend?

Tomeka: It's becoming more acidic, and it's only gone down 0.5. I think if it had something to do with the . . . you're not saying the paper mill, you're saying the power plant, right?

Vincent: Yes. See, on page 4–117.

Tomeka: But they didn't even tell us when the power plant was there. They only told us that the mill was built in '97. We don't know how long the power plant's been there. So if it's been doing this all the time, then this trend should have been lower by now.

What role might the focus question have played in directing the discussion? How did the students' use of Accountable Talk further the discussion? What understandings were represented in the discussion? These are the kinds of questions that would focus a reflective discussion throughout the class. The students used a variety of Accountable Talk moves alongside the teacher. Note the sophisticated moves and variance from teacher moves to student moves as the students work to understand each other and make sense of the science to formulate their explanations. Accountable Talk helped move them beyond the concern raised in the McNeill et al. study (2006) that classroom discourse tends to be dominated by claims with little backing of evidence or reasoning.

The students also used a variety of habits of thinking. For example, they used evidence to support their assertions, determining which data (that is, the observations, measurements, and recordings that are captured about a natural phenomenon that is being studied) were relevant and sufficient to support their claim, engaging in understanding natural phenomena through a scientifically oriented question, and formulating and articulating their reasoning along with their evidence to develop a scientific explanation. There was evidence (the data that the student researcher uses to support his or her claim) in their discussion that they have moved beyond a mechanical discussion of protocol or procedures and are cognitively wrestling with the science. The students were not outlining what they did or how data were collected. Rather, they were working to make sense of the data and synthesizing this material to further understand the problem within the lake. In addition, they were struggling to make their understandings explicit so their classmates could grasp their perspective.

Building Knowledge and Thinking Through Explanations

In the remainder of this section, the focus is on students' thinking as they formulate, revise, communicate, and justify their explanations (essential features 3 to 5). Working in groups of three, students generated and recorded draft explanations on chart paper. To provide an opportunity for students to make their thinking public, all groups posted their explanations around the room in preparation for a gallery walk, when students review each other's work and provide constructive feedback. In this way, students communicate their explanations and consider alternative explanations posed by other groups in the class. Students engage in peer assessment as they provide feedback on explanations posed by others. Through this process, they critically reflect on their own representations and understandings in comparison to those of others and then use the feedback to revise their own explanations.

Two samples of draft explanations developed by the students are presented in Exhibit 5.3. As the students reviewed the drafts, they began to recognize that there were not enough data presented in their own explanations to support the claims they made. For example, one student noted, "We put all the discussion about nitrates and phosphates in our reasoning, and they put the data about that stuff in their evidence section. I wonder where it should go. I don't think we made it clear why we were talking about them [nitrates and phosphates] in our paper."

Similar to this student, others noted that their reasoning was not sufficient to help readers understand how they came to their claims based on the evidence they presented. This is consistent with the research findings outlined earlier in this chapter around explanations: that students have difficulty justifying their rationale for choosing evidence. By comparing their ideas with those of others, students began to work out how they could make their thinking clearer, and in the process, they further develop or refine their own thinking. In addition, students were able to monitor their own thinking (self-assessment) and build metacognitive skills. The experience provided rich opportunities for the teacher to assess student understandings and reflect later on her instruction.

Consistent with the use of formative assessment strategies, Ms. Barton provided feedback for each of the explanations, marking segments she wanted to reinforce and posting wonderings or questions to push student thinking where it was not consistent or sufficient. She noted on group B's explanation in Exhibit 5.3 that the students emphasized acid rain as a primary factor and was concerned about

Exhibit 5.3
Student Draft Explanations

Group A

Question: How are the organisms within the lake responding to changes within the ecosystem?

Claim: Nitrate and phosphate levels in Tri-Lakes have been rising. The rises in nitrate and phosphate levels are resulting in the death of fish and other organisms.

Evidence: Drainage from industrial and residential areas that deposit high concentrations of nitrates and phosphates in the water. Reduced catch rate of bass in the lakes.

Reasoning: Nitrates and phosphate levels are rising. Oxygen levels are declining. Fish and other animals are dying.

Group B

Question: How are the organisms within the lake responding to changes within the ecosystem?

Claim

- Temperature changes and acid rain are causing low population.

Evidence

- Low temp does not affect the organisms.
- High temp. affects the organisms.
- "Acid" pollution affects a lot.
- "Pesticides."
- *Daphnia* = sensitive to changes in their environment.

Reasoning

- The organisms are responding to the change by dying, due to acid rain causing water to turn green. There is a change in the water which causes the food chain to die off

For example: *Daphnia* feeds off of smaller organisms. *Daphnia* is food for fresh water fish. The pollution is killing what each organism is taking in which is cutting out on their food supply. Causing them to die.

their understanding or confusion about the source of the acid rain and its effect on the system. So she pushed their thinking to press them for their reasoning: "I wonder how the acid rain causes the water to turn green." She also asks the group, "Why would green water cause the food chain to die? Be sure to state your reasons in your explanation so we know what you are thinking about the effect." Ms. Barton noticed that group A had focused its explanation around the nitrates and phosphates. She wanted them to expand their data and reasoning so they did not lose the intended understanding about the complexity of the system. She asked the group if any other factors might be contributing to the effects they were attributing to the nitrates and phosphates and also wondered what factors might be leading to the shifts in the nitrates and phosphates in the lake. To address this question, students returned to the data packets and discussed various biotic and abiotic factors and how they interact within the system.

The students then had an opportunity to make initial revisions to their explanations. In the next lesson, they gained greater insight around the core concepts of the unit as they examined another aquatic system. The class then made final revisions to their explanations as part of the last lesson of the unit. These revisions included an emphasis on the connections made to scientific principles. As part of this lesson, students conducted a poster session where they presented and justified their explanations around the Tri-Lakes scenario. All groups were asked to address the focus question: "How are the bass and other organisms in Tri-Lakes responding to changes within the ecosystem that have occurred over the past ten years?"

The two explanations in Exhibit 5.3 changed through this spiraling process of considering alternative explanations, revisions, feedback, discussion, readings, refining the question, and reflection. The samples in Exhibit 5.4 show only the claim and reasoning to emphasize the students' thinking. Unlike the earlier example from Ms. Thompson's classroom, Ms. Barton's students were provided the focus question, since the emphasis of this lesson was on the reasoning and development of the written explanation, not on developing scientifically oriented questions.

The groups provided reasonable and sufficient evidence by including charts and graphs from the data packets, data tables from their experiments, and citations from reliable science sources such as the U.S. Geological Survey. For example, group B included the charts shown in Exhibit 5.5. These charts were extrapolated by the students from the Tri-Lakes data packets. They used mathematical

Exhibit 5.4
Student Final Explanations for Claim and Reasoning

Group A

Claim

The changes in pH, temperature, and pollutants in the lake have lead to a decrease in *Daphnia* which may be causing the lower bass catch rates in the lake.

Reasoning

We think that the *Daphnia* behavior (heart rate, swimming pattern, movement rate) changes when the pH of their H_2O changes. As our pH shifted from 6.0 down to below 4.5, our *Daphnia*'s heart rate became very rapid, and they swam more slowly through a smaller volume of H_2O. Below 4.5, they die. The pH of the Tri-Lake has dropped from 6.0 to 5.5 since 1982 (pH data from H.S.[high school]). Lower pH is known to affect *Daphnia*'s ability to feed (*Daphnia* info sheet) because *Daphnia* feed by moving their legs. Our experiment verified that in a low pH environment the *Daphnia* moved very little. The letter to the H.S. said that *Daphnia* populations are decreased on the lake. According to the Bass info sheet young Bass eat *Daphnia*; less *Daphnia* means less food for Bass, so fewer bass are coming to maturity. Low pH can contribute to this problem.

Also, the data reported by the Tri-Lakes association shows the temperature in many of the more shallow areas of the pond where the bass live is 22°C, resulting in a possible change in *Daphnia* behavior, maybe even death of the *Daphnia*. Direct observation showed that the change in temperature changes the behavior of the *Daphnia* (see data table 1), evidence (p. 126) shows that temperature above 20°C are fatal to *Daphnia*, the average temperature in many of the shallow areas of the Tri-Lakes area are 22°C (p. 116) and bass prefer to live in shallow areas (p. 119). The temperature of the bass habitat could be too warm for the *Daphnia* population to survive.

From our evidence we can conclude that the numbers of *Daphnia* are decreasing due to low pH levels of the water and the raised water temperatures. This will reduce the bass food source, causing the bass population to be less. There is also evidence that the drainage from the industrial and residential areas of the lake are contributing to the pH and temperature shifts. Pollutants from the factories may also be increasing nitrate and phosphate levels (p. 128). The increase in nitrate levels will lead to reduced dissolved oxygen levels in the lake. The dissolved oxygen levels in the lake were 10.2 mg/L in 1982 and have been steadily reducing to a level of 8.8 mg/L in 2002 (p. 124).

We think additional research is warranted in the lake. Areas of further study should include doing collecting additional temperature data across the lake, tracing the pollution sources, monitoring nitrate and phosphate levels, and recording weather and industrial activity in the area.

Group B

Claim

The *Daphnia* and bass are dying (population is reducing) in Tri-Lakes due to the changes that have been happening in the lake system over the past ten years.

Reasoning

Daphnia are affected by temperature and pH changes (data sheet 3). Our experiment showed that *Daphnia* began to have a change in heart rate at pH of 5.5 and when temperature reached 23°C. The *Daphnia* data sheet also reported that they do best in water with temperatures of 20°C. *Daphnia* movement is important to its survival because they are nourished by leg motion to produce currents around themselves. Our experiment found that *Daphnia* movement was less at temperatures above and below 20°C.

The temperatures in the lake have been getting warmer (temperature change chart and table) and are above safe limits for *Daphnia* in shallow areas. The pH of the lake has been going down as shown in Table 2. The reduced pH will also affect the *Daphnia,* based on our experimental results.

Bass feed on *Daphnia.* If the *Daphnia* are dying the bass will die because they have less to eat. We saw this in the "Gulf of Maine" activity where the fish lost their food source and started to die. The bass are connected to the *Daphnia* and they both need clean water at right temperatures to survive.

(continued)

The lake is being affected by a lot of activities and changes around the lake. There are factories (paper mill and prosthesis plant) that have been built at the lake and more boaters that are leading to more pollution in the lake. The lake was reported as being very green (4–116). This may be due to a population explosion of cyanobacteria and algae from the pollution increase (4–125).

We think additional research is warranted in the lake. Areas of further study should include:

• Trying to find the reason for the temperature and pH changes

• Checking pollution levels to see if these might be directly affecting the bass

• Looking for data to see what other organisms are being affected by changes in the lake

representations and graphs to make sense of the data and communicate the evidence as consistent with their findings, thus supporting their claim.

Group A was able to articulate a richer understanding of some of the factors that may be affecting the bass in the Tri-Lakes ecosystem. They appropriately focused on patterns in the data that revealed a correlation between an environmental factor (for example, pH) and changes in organisms (for example, *Daphnia* behavior). Their reasoning logically linked the evidence to their claim and scientific principles, thus demonstrating a reasonable understanding that multiple factors are likely affecting the bass and the lake. The conclusion within their explanation began with text modeled by the teacher ("We think additional research is warranted. Areas of further study should include . . ."), as did most of the other groups. This is part of the scaffolding process. In subsequent years, when Ms. Barton introduces explanations earlier in the school year and as students work with explanations across grade levels, their ability to generate language for strong explanations will become more sophisticated. For now, using these templates for scaffolds helps focus student learning and manage time and resources in the

Exhibit 5.5
Daphnia movements as water temperature changes

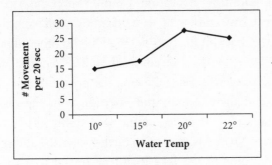

Water Temp	# Movements per 20 sec
10°	14
15°	18
20°	28
22°	24

pH shifts in Tri-Lakes 1982-2000

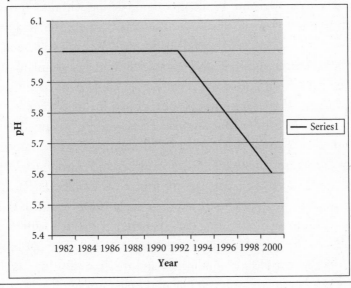

lesson. The scaffolds should eventually be faded away so the students can stand on their own (McNeill et al., 2006).

Compare the depth and connections that group A makes to the group B examples (see Exhibit 5.4). Group A incorporates more sources and patterns of data and makes interpretations consistent with scientific understandings as they link factors to potential impact on the bass population and other organisms in Tri-Lakes. For example, they make the connection between the nitrates and phosphates to dissolved oxygen levels (following the press for accuracy by Ms. Barton noted earlier) and then support the assertion with the dissolved oxygen data in the third paragraph of their reasoning (see Exhibit 5.4).

Group B addresses the query from Ms. Barton to further describe and support how the cause of the green color of the lake might be linked to changes in populations of organisms within the lake. They also drop the language about acid rain in their final version. While they could define acid rain, the group had trouble articulating clear and direct connections between the acid rain, other abiotic factors in Tri-Lakes, and organisms within Tri-Lakes. In a good scientific explanation, the claim is built around the assertions one is willing to defend and support. The claim is supported with evidence and linked to scientific principles through reasoning. If a clear connection cannot be made in the reasoning, it is not a strong one. Assertions that are less certain can be identified as areas for additional study. So group B is correct in eliminating the acid rain discussion from their explanation. They have enough evidence and reasoning to support the claim they assert, which is appropriate for this arc of lessons. The acid rain was a distracter to them that did not add to their explanation. Some of this group's struggles may be due to discounting data that are inconsistent with their beliefs, a trend noted in the research (McNeil & Krajcik, 2006). Ms. Barton does not choose to address their ideas around acid rain further at this time, as she knows the students will explore this topic in one of the chemistry units next year.

Although group B did not write as sophisticated an explanation as group A, group B's thinking nevertheless significantly advanced from the draft to the final version. In addition, both groups show evidence of mastering the learning goals. They demonstrate their recognition that systems are complex but understand that they can study systems through scientific approaches.

The written explanations are just one form of assessment. From the student explanations, their discussions, and other student-generated responses (laboratory notebook, essay, quizzes), we can say that all students demonstrated an adequate understanding of the learning goal: many decisions they and others make have consequences within ecosystems.

ON THE PATH TO DL SCIENCE

Think about the classroom scenarios described in this chapter and consider the classroom culture. Is there evidence that the learning environment in those rooms might help students learn? In what kinds of talk were students and teachers engaged? How was the discourse connected to the texts and tasks with which they were working? Might the students learn by thinking of themselves as apprentices, using the same conceptual tools scientists use to solve problems or to investigate phenomena? What norms and routines appear to be established, and how might those routines invite student engagement and effort?

Two key questions drive the work in disciplinary literacy in science:

1. How do we provide learning experiences that support all students in rigorous content learning where they are simultaneously learning core content knowledge and scientists' habits of thinking?

2. How do we support teachers in providing these kinds of learning experiences in their classrooms?

What does the path to rich DL science classrooms look like? Glimpses into a DL science classroom can reveal a wide variety of activity. Small groups of students are actively engaged in collaboratively solving a question through an investigation, individual students may be quietly reflecting on how a reading connects with their current understandings of a concept, or perhaps the whole class is engaged in a spirited discussion around explanations of scientific phenomena. Although there is not one specific type of activity that denotes a DL science classroom, the combination of activities should result in all students working together to make sense of science content. They should have opportunities to understand the nature of science by working like scientists. This type of classroom inquiry can be described in part by the five essential features of classroom inquiry (National Research Council, 2000) and involves focusing study through a scientifically oriented question; analyzing data to develop, communicate, and justify an explanation; and connecting the explanation to current understandings in science.

In DL science, teachers plan and implement arcs of lessons (units of instruction) using well-developed instructional materials built around important science concepts, such as those described in the *National Science Education Standards* (National Research Council, 1996) and the *Benchmarks for Science Literacy* (American Association for the Advancement of Science, 1993). These materials are also guided by research, such as the findings from *How People Learn* (National Research Council, 1999). Instructional practices are grounded in the principles of learning and the DL principles in science.

Administrators Supporting DL Science

DL science is enacted in collaborative learning communities. Such communities are best established at the classroom and school levels, where students and faculty see and know that the primary function of the school is learning for all. Administrators play a key role in establishing and maintaining this environment. (Chapter Seven elaborates on the general aspects of advancing and supporting DL.)

This chapter illustrates several examples of DL science classrooms. The featured teachers all needed time and support to learn about DL science. They also needed encouragement and accountability to enact the practices in their classrooms. This does not happen without the support of an informed administrator who is an instructional leader—someone who leads by example as an active learner and provides guidance and focus.

As part of DL, administrators have opportunities to develop an understanding of the foundational theory and practices of DL (for example, POLs and Accountable Talk). This is typically the focus of their initial study in DL. In addition, they have opportunities to experience aspects of DL science in an effort to help them understand and support its enactment in their schools. Through administrators' active participation in professional development specific to DL science, they experience DL science as learners, which helps them understand firsthand how students learn science concepts and how teachers design successful learning experiences. Then they can effectively reflect on the instruction they should see in classrooms and how they can support teachers and students in moving toward a full enactment of DL science.

The paths an administrator might take to learn DL science vary from district to district, but the key is to actively engage administrators in the learning and leading of science. The paths to DL science vary because of the adaptive assistance model that DL uses to address the unique needs and structures of each district. Some of the experiences include participating in DL science leadership sessions, DL science institutes, and in-district DL science sessions.

Another route along the pathway to effective DL science is for administrators to engage, alongside their teachers, in school or district study groups, that is, professional learning communities or communities of practice. Study sessions may focus on science teaching and learning through collaborative practices, such as studying current science educational research, participating in science Learning Walks, engaging in studying student work, and participating in classroom observations. Topics of study include practices and tools specific to science—for example, scientific inquiry and the nature of science, studying student work in science, and science classroom observations. The goal is to form sustained, intensive, cohesive, and collaborative professional learning communities across the district and within the schools to advance student learning. The more often that administrators are immersed in DL science, the greater the opportunity is for them to understand the tools and protocols. When administrators have a greater understanding of DL science, the deeper the work penetrates into the system and the more likely DL teaching and learning will be sustained throughout the school and district.

Ms. Barton's principal attended all of the general DL and DL science professional development sessions. In addition, he participated in several DL science sessions alongside the teachers, and he periodically walked into Ms. Barton's classroom or chatted with her in the hall. These brief conversations allowed the principal to assess Ms. Barton's progress in incorporating DL into her classroom and let her know that DL science was important to him. His experiences with DL science prompted him to ask questions such as these:

- What concepts are your students working toward understanding? How does the instructional sequence support students in building new understandings and provide common experiences to delve into the science?

- How have you assessed their current understandings? How are you changing or altering instruction to support the students who are not getting it?

- What are you doing to ensure that your students are doing the mental work—the work that helps them make sense of and explain the science?

- When will the students have an opportunity to analyze evidence to build a scientific explanation and make deeper sense of the concept?

These kinds of questions help to push thinking around teaching and learning. The principal developed these questions through his understanding of DL,

DL science, and use of the protocols and tools. He understands that to effectively lead an initiative such as DL science, he must be a vital part of the process by modeling active learning, showing that the work is important, being involved enough to know the work and what to expect from the initiative (realistic outcomes and how to monitor progress), and leading the teachers in the effort.

In addition to professional development and learning support, administrators play a role in ensuring that teachers have access to strong instructional materials and appropriate equipment that will support students in rigorous learning. There are well-developed instructional materials that support DL science learning and teaching, often referred to as reform-based programs. These programs use research-based instructional designs (for example, learning cycle, the BSCS 5EF instructional model) and inquiry-based sequences (arcs of lessons) that are conceptually cohesive and provide engaging opportunities for students to develop deep understandings of the science standards. These resources support teachers and students in their learning. Equipment and consumables are essential to the science classroom and are required each year. There need to be an established budget and clear procedures for ordering, receiving, storing, and handling equipment and consumables. Often this issue of management is overlooked and leads to diminished experiences for the students and frustration for teachers. Administrators are made aware of these issues and consider strategies and approaches to address them through the DL science professional development.

Achieving DL Science

In a DL science class an administrator should expect to see and hear:

- Students having time and structure (prompting questions, engaging experiences linked to concepts) to think about the concepts and focus questions and to express and reflect (orally and written) on their current understandings

- Teachers listening to students and, when probed, articulating what they are listening for (specific common misconceptions, what the concept is, what accurate representations of the concepts are) and how they will guide the students to build on the students' current understandings

- Students engaged in lessons that provide new experiences to explore science concepts, make sense of their own understandings in light of scientific principles, and clarify their thinking

In short, the entire class is engaged in inquiry-based science learning, using Accountable Talk and other DL strategies and routines to advance their own learning with guidance and support from the teacher.

CONCLUSION

DL science is complex and dynamic. It requires a focus on content, habits of thinking, and the learners; this cannot be done in an isolated or linear fashion. DL science is an iterative, intertwined, and spiraling process. The path to DL science in a school or district requires commitments from teachers, building administrators, central office staff, and district administrators. It requires teamwork from all of these participants, but especially from teachers, who take the responsibility to study their practices as they implement science inquiries in their classes. And, of course, it requires time—time for teachers to study collaboratively, time for administrators to observe teachers teaching science inquiries, and time to support students with the tools and routines that can enable them to become scientifically literate in the modern world.

Disciplinary Literacy in the English Language Arts Classroom

Anthony R. Petrosky
Stephanie M. McConachie
Vivian Mihalakis

W̲e begin this chapter with a group of teachers and administrators who are discussing a selection from Gloria Anzaldúa's book *Borderlands/La frontera: The New Mestiza* (1987), a rich and complex text that invites inquiry and engagement. Their conversation is excerpted from a professional development session on teaching difficult texts where the teachers engaged as learners in an inquiry on voice in the Anzaldúa selection and its relationship to writing and the writer. They are responding to the question, "What is voice, and what does it have to do with writing or the writer?"

Anzaldúa, a Chicana writing to understand her selves and her heritage, says, "I will no longer be made to feel ashamed of existing. I will have my voice: Indian, Spanish, white. I will have my serpent's tongue—my woman's voice, my sexual voice, my poet's voice" (p. 81). We pick up their conversation about midway. Prior to engaging in this discussion, each participant composed a quick write in response to the inquiry question, citing references in the text to support claims. Then participants shared their responses with two or three colleagues at their tables. As you read, notice the ways they grappled with the text, their various interpretations, and their interactions with each other. They are engaged in exactly the kind of inquiry work that can engage students. Their talk and habits of thinking mirror the talk and habits of thinking of students in inquiry learning:

Facilitator: Have we answered the question about what is voice and what does it have to do with writing or the writer?

Ben: She feels the need to legitimize her voice in writing. That the legitimacy of having the multitudes of different voices, that it's not standard English, it's not standard Spanish. Because what she says is, "Until I am free to write bilingually and switch codes without having always to translate when I still have to speak English or Spanish, when I would rather speak Spanglish and as long as I have to accommodate the English speaker rather than having them accommodate me, my tongue will be illegitimate."

Gabriela: I had a real hard time with this exercise because I really could not tell where one voice ended and the next began. I can certainly see your point where she makes those distinctions, but I would add a few other things. She's being very analytical here. She's doing a social commentary here. She came across to me as very academic in some ways.

Facilitator: Where did you see the academic voice for instance?

Gabriela: Well, just in the way she is very clear about the distinctions in different linguistic patterns.

Sarah: As Gabriela says, it's a multidimensional persona, and through that persona, each persona has its own voice through the writing process. So at one time she's the poet writing through that persona. The next time she's the woman. The other time she's the Spanish person. Each of those personas gets their chance to speak through the writing process.

Facilitator: From our experience teaching writing, voice is a very difficult thing to talk about, and it gets really difficult in the stage where you have to say what it is and where you see it in a piece of writing. So if I could ask you to try your hand at that.

Chris: That's what I was going to comment on. Basically when he was reading, I guess it was Ben who commented when she was going into that whole section on language. I saw that as partly her white voice, the white academic voice coming through. It seemed out of place in a way, yet it seemed purposeful, like she had to address this academic portion. There were a couple other passages that caught my attention. On page 36, just above overcoming the tradition of silence in italics. That whole Spanish sentence: *"El Anglo con cara de inocente nos arrancó la lengua."* In Spanish, I saw that as her Spanish voice. Translated it's, "The white with innocent faces rips out our tongues." I saw that as her Spanish voice coming through loud and clear and angry.

Facilitator: That's the first time we've heard the emotion actually named, but there seems to me to be an angry voice here. I guess also, as I read it, a voice of desperation, of someone who's holding all these threads together in the fear that any one of them will spring out from her grasp because she wants them all.

Mary Louise: I don't think we can have an intelligent conversation about voice if we don't have a common definition. If I define *voice* as identity, then we're all a multiplicity of voices, and what we're hearing is a voice which has different identities embedded in it. I don't find it useful to tease those out because I think we are all complex beings, and as complex beings, we're all a multiplicity of voices, and we choose when to adopt one voice or another depending on the context that we're in.

Facilitator: So what does writing have to do with it then?

Andrew: What Mary Louise said is real interesting 'cause I think the form here allows those voices to come out and to be seen. If you write—and maybe I'm completely crazy here—but if I was going to write a novel, I don't see a multiplicity of voices, except explicitly created within a novel, the way I see in these essayistic pieces. I think this expository form provides a means for the writer to see those things come up. Just an idea about the form. Maybe there's a connection with the writing there. The form you choose allows you in different ways to explore different parts of your identity, voice, or however you want to define it.

Facilitator: That's interesting because in a way, it's a kind of a collage, and it begins with this dentist's voice.

Jackie: And in that sense it's not very smooth in a traditional sense. It's abrupt, and it uses different forms. You don't have the transitional devices. It's a very complex piece, I think, in its texture.

Before going on to discuss the place of such interpretive discussions in English language arts (ELA) disciplinary literacy (DL), we draw attention to both the content and progression of this excerpt. A facilitator participant begins by asking whether the question has been addressed. From there, the discussion touches on Anzaldúa's need to legitimize her voice; a participant's thoughts on why it was difficult to see where voices end and begin; a mention of Anzaldúa's angry, social, and academic voices, the multiple dimensions of her personality speaking; her Spanish voice; the relationship of voice to the form of writing—in this case, a multigenre essay without transitions. These turns of talk pivot on the participants' responses to each other. They listen, in other words, to each other's comments; then they respond to them, build from them, and revisit them. Finally, at the end, a couple of the participants draw conclusions about voice and the form of writing. In DL, the nature of their talk and the kinds of thinking it generates are as important as the content of what they say.

All three aspects of their talk—its interpretive nature, the thinking it generates, and its content—work together in a dialogic knowledge construction. Inquiry in this sense is more about "making" than "learning" (Wells, 1999). When learners are engaged in genuine inquiry, as our participants were, "learning is an outcome that occurs because making requires the student to extend his or her understanding in action—whether the artifact constructed is a material object, an explanatory demonstration, or a theoretical formulation" (p. 65). This "understanding in action" can also be thought of as another way of describing cognitive apprenticeship where learners apprentice to the making of knowledge that occurs in such interactions as our professional development discussion.

Disciplinary literacy means learning to read, write, talk, and reason as a junior member of a discipline's community. It means understanding what counts within the discipline as a good question, evidence, problem, or solution. It means crafting arguments in the ways that members of the discipline do: for example, articulating understandings and documenting analyses of texts, writing as an investigative reporter does, forming and warranting interpretations within and across texts, and interpreting texts from different perspectives. The participants in the discussion express interpretations and arguments in a social situation where they act as members of an ELA community working together to understand Anzaldúa's selection through the question posed and through each other's various perspectives.

We refer to this type of intellectual work as *inquiry learning:* teachers and students inquire into the content knowledge and habits of reading, writing, and speaking. To do this, they work in nested layers of courses, units, and lessons that have been built around overarching inquiries, or big ideas, and purposely sequenced texts that make it possible to "do" the work of reading, writing, talking, and reasoning in streams of activities that require increasingly sophisticated levels of intellectual and social engagement.

This engagement extends John Dewey's (1938) idea of the importance of doing authentic work by asking teachers and students to also understand and inquire into the concepts and insights that supported the processes they used to metacognitively understand how they did the work. Teachers and students work together, as the adult learners did in the example, on challenging texts and ideas as part of tasks that give them the authority to form their own interpretations and understandings. They also have multiple opportunities to inquire into their learning, revisit their ideas and concepts through different lenses, and study the roles played by the teacher and the students at key points in their studies.

Following is an excerpt from the same discussion where the participants step back to reflect on what and how they learned. Notice their comments on the questions, the facilitator's and participants' roles, and the habits of reading, writing, and talking they used: taking marginal notes, rereading, listening, responding to big questions, individual writing, group sharing, and the assumptions about the participants:

Ralph: So as I read, I took margin notes about the big ideas and what I was thinking as I came along. It kind of—when I looked at the six or seven bulleted items, it kind of really puts it all in perspective as to what we were talking about. What I bulleted was the following: code switching, identity, what is literacy, multiple literacies, conformity, and judgment with regard to language. I didn't realize that until I just went back and looked at it, but right from the start, it captured it all.

Gabriela: I think it's really up to me as the facilitator, because often when we ask our students to reread a passage, they find it very frustrating, but the clear purpose, the clear defined purpose, is really helping me to facilitate the work that I will do back in my district in working with the students because I'm an impatient person. But having to read it for a second time with a clear purpose really made a difference.

Sarah: It's not just rereading. This was three readings, and many students don't even realize that it's okay and that you can glean more from what you've read by rereading and that it's okay. You might not have understood something, and you'll understand more the more you read it.

Chris: He [a facilitator/participant] also didn't summarize or paraphrase some of our questions or responses. I think a lot of times facilitators do that. They feel the need to validate what the participants are saying. But I think not doing that makes it feel like our learning community, and he's just kind of the guy on the side.

Mary Louise: I also think that the questions that were chosen helped to focus our reading skills. I think it really points to the importance of choosing and creating the proper questions when you're creating an assignment for a student.

Andrew: He was bringing us back by saying, for example, "So what does writing have to do with it?"

Mary Louise: You do get instances of that. . . .

Jackie: It's very important to go for the big question right away that a more traditional mode of teaching might be asking a lot of particular comprehension kinds of questions that most people find kind of boring to answer, but instead going right for the glory right away. He compared that to playing basketball. That one approach is to work on dribbling over and over and over again to get that right, but if you don't shoot the ball every once in a while, it doesn't become very exciting. And what you want to do is get out there and play and experience the whole thing.

What I found here was there aren't too many questions, but they're big questions, and the two or three ways to look at the work all are very big kinds of questions, but they all sparked a different point of view, at least for me; I found that I looked at it a little bit differently each time.

Sarah: What I find interesting and wonderful about the questions is that they assume that the audience has a level of intelligence and expertise to be able to participate in the process, as opposed to being talked to in the process. These questions, "What do you mean? Help me understand. What is the role?" It's assuming that the students know what you're talking about and can participate intensely in that process.

Matt: I can agree with a lot of what was said, and it seems as though the questions are set up in a way that's open-ended, where there's no right or wrong answers, but it allows readers to share their personal interaction with the text. I think that what is more important here when we think about our level of students is that the structure of what we did as far as setting up a community of learners. We had the opportunity to read independently. Then we wrote. Then we shared in small group. Then we went to the large group. Then we went back to independence, and that allowed, I think, really a safe atmosphere for people to share that personal reaction that they had.

Before discussing these excerpts as examples of inquiry, it is worth noting how clearly the facilitator influenced the discussion. Facilitators make or break inquiry discussions by the ways they conduct themselves, the roles they play, and the kinds of follow-up questions they ask to keep discussions focused and moving forward. The participants, for example, understand that the facilitator "didn't summarize or paraphrase" or "validate what the respondents were saying," behaviors that could easily have led to more talk and evaluation of comments by the facilitator than from the participants. Instead, "He was bringing us back" to the question, and the questions "assume that the audience has a level of intelligence and expertise to be able to participate in the process, as opposed to being talked to in the process."

The questions posed for these discussions were carefully designed to invite adults to figure out underlying assumptions of the author and her text and to use reading, writing, and talking as interrelated processes to create interpretations. We chose the text for its puzzlement and wonder and for its complexities and ambiguities (ACT, 2006). And although we posed these questions for our learners, they could just as easily have been posed by the learners or taken from other lessons or texts. It is not a question of who asks the question but of whether the question is the right one for these learners in this context.

Inquiry is also a stance or an attitude toward learning and learners. The participants seem to understand that when they comment on the facilitator's role and the conduct of the discussion, it is "as much about being open to wonderment and puzzlement, and trying to construct and test explanations of the phenomena that evoked those feelings, as it is about mastering any particular body of information, although the facets of inquiry are ultimately interdependent" (Wells, 1999, p. 63). In order for learners, whether adults or adolescents, to inquire into a text or a sequence of texts, they must clearly see the problems being posed and they must be engaged—the puzzlement and wonder that Wells refers to.

Moffett (1968) and Postman and Damon (1967), in separate but congruent textbooks, were part of the first wave of American ELA teacher educators who promoted pedagogies that invited middle and high school students to inquire into texts and language in ways that helped them understand literature and language study as systems. Their curricula, basically nonauthoritarian but sequenced and somewhat scripted, invited students to take active roles as apprentices in literature and language study. When students used these curricula to question ideas and texts with references to other texts and engaged in varied and critical responses to texts and to each other, they judged their sequences of activities as successful (Postman & Damon, 1967; Moffett, 1968). Learning the content was not an end point, although students did learn content, but only as a means for further inquiry and knowledge.

In the system of nested layers of inquiries in DL ELA, as in the Moffett and Postman curricula, learners, whether adults or adolescents, realize over time that complex and difficult texts do not provide them with apparent right answers and that their teachers will not provide them with one right answer to an authentic inquiry. Instead, the goal of inquiry is the development of habits that foster enjoyment and persistence in seeking understanding.

ENCOURAGING DL ENGLISH LANGUAGE ARTS STUDY

Inquiry learning asks a deep level of literate engagement of teachers and students as they explore, defend, and elaborate their thinking about texts, concepts, language, and their learning. This kind of instruction is quite different from what goes on in typical ELA classrooms (Applebee, 1993) that follow a pattern of instruction referred to as I-R-E (initiate-respond-evaluate). In such classrooms (Marshall, 1989; Cazden, 1986; Mehan, 1979), one-way discussions predicated on teacher questions, students' responses, and teacher evaluation is often interspersed with lectures and individual seatwork. From a cognitive perspective, I-R-E instruction emphasizes information transmission and rote learning—the kinds of learning that support students, ironically, on high-stakes multiple-choice tests. I-R-E instruction in ELA is often part of the dominant skills approach that focuses on details of language, word and sentence structure, vocabulary, and rules and templates for composition. Literature instruction in such a skills approach centers students on such things as reading texts chapter by chapter, followed by detailed comprehension questions, with little or no work on interpretive tasks that reach across ideas from the whole text. I-R-E and skills-based instruction offer limited (if any) opportunities for students to problem-solve readings of difficult texts, develop ideas across multiple texts, and engage in interpretive discussions and writings. I-R-E instruction represents the status quo in the English curriculum (Applebee, 1993; Applebee, Langer, Nystrand, & Gamoran, 2003; Nystrand & Gamoran, 1991, 1992; Nystrand, Gamoran, Kachur, & Prendergast, 1997; Marshall, 1989), and few teachers are prepared for ELA inquiry instruction because their own experiences as learners has been otherwise. Their preparation as teachers also likely echoed I-R-E instruction rather than the methods of inquiry used in DL ELA with challenging texts.

Over the past two decades of curriculum development in reading and ELA, textbooks and school districts have attempted to create equity in reading and literature study by gearing reading selections and assignments to low expectations. A common failing in the profession is the simplifying of reading materials to make them accessible to all students instead of supplying teachers and students with the tools they need to grapple with challenging texts. The teaching apparatus attached to these selections in textbooks has also been watered down (Woodward & Elliott, 1990), often by breaking selections into smaller, excerpted parts; posing only low-level comprehension questions for students (Applebee, 1993; Beck & McKeown, 1991, 1992, 1994); and the common practice of glossing all challenging concepts and vocabulary. In essence, this simplification of selections in textbooks and school curricula has taken challenging texts off the table for many students. Consequently they have not learned the hard work of reading and rereading, close reading, and building cases for interpretations derived from complex texts.

Yet a recent ACT report (2006), *Reading Between the Lines: What the ACT Reveals About College Readiness in Reading,* found that "the ability to read complex texts is the clearest differentiator between those ready for college-level reading and those not" (pp. 16–17). The report presents data indicating that many students, even those successful in gaining admission to major universities, are underprepared for handling complex texts. Moreover, state standards rarely address the issues of reading and writing about complex texts, and teachers receive little or no preparation to design curricular units that teach students to read, write about, and learn from purposely sequenced rigorous texts. The ACT report describes six features of texts that define rigorous reading selections:

1. Relationships—Interactions among ideas or characters in the text are subtle, involved, or deeply embedded.

2. Richness—The text possesses a sizable amount of highly sophisticated information conveyed through data or literary devices.

3. Structure—The text is organized in ways that are elaborate and sometimes unconventional.

4. Style—The author's tone and use of language are often intricate.

5. Vocabulary—The author's choice of words is demanding and highly context dependent.

6. Purpose—The author's intent in writing the text is implicit and sometimes ambiguous. (p. 17)

In addition to a call for strengthening reading instruction in all subjects by incorporating rigorous texts with these attributes into the curriculum, the authors of the report recognize that teachers are not prepared to design instruction and curriculum with rigorous texts. Instruction for teachers to help them help their students with challenging texts has been mixed at best over the past twenty-five years (Mayher, 1989; Powell, Farrar, & Cohen, 1985; Purves, 1991; Scholes, 1998). So has the opportunity to apprentice to rigorous curricula that takes students deep into interpretive work with and across texts (Sosniak & Perlman, 1990; Woodward & Elliot, 1990), although there is evidence that when beginning teachers study and engage with a rigorous, purposefully sequenced curriculum such as Pacesetter, they extend their understandings of both content and more sophisticated pedagogies (Grossman & Thompson, 2004). Consequently, the ACT authors call for systematic, long-term "guidance and support" for teachers through professional development, so that they can learn how to design lessons and curricula for students with challenging texts. This is what we do.

Encouraging DL ELA instruction and its methods of inquiry in the classroom is a knotty problem. For ELA inquiry teaching and learning to take hold, teachers, like students, must have (1) opportunities to learn core concepts and habits of thinking in ELA; (2) a rigorous curriculum that "mirrors the work of the discipline" in its tasks, texts, and talk and that positions learners as apprentices; (3) opportunities to engage in meta-understandings of their learning through reflection on their studies; (4) a community that enables socializing intelligence by encouraging risk taking, help seeking, question asking, problem solving, and reflective analysis; and (5) their work assessed through multiple forms of informal and formal assessments that gauge their "grasp of content area concepts; their habits of inquiring, investigating, problem solving, and talking," as well as "their learning processes and their interests" (McConachie, Resnick, & Hall, 2003, pp. 5–6).

THE DISCIPLINARY LITERACY ELA PROJECT

At the heart of DL ELA inquiry learning, students engage in substantive problem solving and collaborative work, including discussions of and writings about challenging literature through oral and written exchanges of ideas. In our DL ELA project, such exchanges are predicated on the teachers' strategic uses of the ELA tools, which we present later in this section, that scaffold students from comprehension to higher-order interpretive questions and ill-structured tasks (Simon, 1973) for which there are multiple possible solutions that position students to form new knowledge in their responses. In such exchanges, students, taught to warrant their understandings and interpretations with textual evidence, are encouraged to explore ideas from multiple perspectives and debate the efficacy of their ideas, warrants, and perspectives with each other.

Our project, then, aims to help teachers develop their abilities to understand, design, and use rigorous inquiry curricula with lessons within units that move students from comprehension to higher-order thinking skills in reading and writing with complex, sequenced texts. One way we do this is by introducing participants to ELA units of study developed for students. These units are designed around nominal themes or concepts, such as the relationship between writing and identity, so that students can study, for instance, each text as a case for a particular perspective on a theme or concept. They can also study one text through the concepts or ideas presented in others. As well as encouraging coherent study across multiple texts, each unit takes students deep into individual texts, so that they are scaffolded through tasks that move from comprehension to higher-order thinking such as interpretation. Working from well-developed models of ELA instruction for college freshmen (Bartholomae & Petrosky, 2002) and from iterations of those models for high school students (McConachie, Petrosky, Plasse, Hall, & Parshall, 2004; Mihalakis, Seitz, McConachie, Petrosky, Hall, & Carpenter, 2006a, 2006b; Petrosky, 2006; McConachie et al., 2006), we developed a set of purposely sequenced and scaffolded ELA lesson and unit design features (Petrosky, 2006) that apprentice learners to patterned, cyclical habits of thinking for the individual texts they study and their studies across multiple texts.

ELA Lesson and Unit Design Features

Many of the tasks represented by the ELA Lesson and unit design features require rereading as a key method for dealing with difficult texts. Learners are always asked to reread for particular purposes or with particular questions in mind. The number of times students are asked to reread a single text depends on its difficulty, the students and their needs, and the goals of the unit.

We suggest generally that learners apprentice to the tasks of the ELA lesson and unit design features by composing individual quick writes in reader-writer notebooks to get their thinking on paper and to learn to think on paper through relatively unconstrained writings. We follow the quick writes with discussions of them in pairs or trios and frequently ask these small groups to chart and then display their discussions, so that others in the group see them. Once everyone has had an opportunity to study the charts, we conduct whole-group discussions of the task or question, with the teacher charting the group's responses.

These rituals and routines—using reader-writer notebooks for quick writes, rereading, sharing one's quick-write thinking with two or three peers, charting, studying others' responses, and participating in large group discussions—support learners' work with the design features in a number of ways. They help create nonthreatening environments for intellectual work that allows learners to see and hear how others have approached and thought about the tasks or questions. They scaffold students through the tasks or questions by requesting initial thinking in the form of quick writes where the goal is to get their thoughts down without regard to language conventions. Learners thus develop the habit of discovering what is on their minds when they think and then write quickly. Discussions with pairs or trios create accountability to the task at hand and to the group through intellectual intimacy that allows students to share their thinking in a semiprivate situation before taking it public with a larger group, where it can be debated and tracked through teacher charting.

These are the key ELA lesson and unit design features:

- A *nominal theme* or a genre study that focuses a unit of study on big ideas (for example, miseducation or writing and identity) that reaches across all of the texts in the unit

- Purposely sequenced *rigorous texts* appropriate for the students, the theme, and inquiry studies
- *Overarching questions* that present the big ideas as inquiry questions to reach across and connect all of the texts under study (including the students' writing)
- *Comprehension and sorting questions* that allow students to get the gist of a text while sorting out characters and settings
- *Difficulty questions* that help students unravel the difficulties of texts as appropriate at the whole-discourse and sentence levels
- *Identifying significance* tasks that ask students to locate significant moments in a text and explain why those moments are significant to the text
- *Guiding questions* to pose interpretive tasks that take students deep into discussions of and writings about the individual texts
- *Writing tasks* to invite students to write about texts and to write like the texts (in the style of the selection and in imitation of an author's sentences and grammatical structures)
- *Step-back tasks* regularly paced after key pieces of work (comprehension questions, identifying difficulty or significance, and so on) that ask students to study their learning by analyzing what and how they learned
- *Retrospective assignments* for capstone work with each text that encourage students to (1) rethink and revise papers on the unit's big ideas or overarching questions as they progress through a unit and (2) revisit their studies of their learning by analyzing what they learned and how they learned
- *Formative and summative assessments* that focus on the habits of thinking and big ideas that the students studied and used in the unit

The presence and frequency of each of the ELA lesson and unit design features vary within every unit. Although all units have certain features that organize and drive the intellectual work, such as a nominal theme, overarching questions, and retrospective assignments, students may not always read each text to consider moments they consider significant to the text. Since the ELA design features represent scaffolded tasks, their use with individual texts in a unit depends on whether the scaffolding is needed given the nature of the texts, learners, and goals of the unit.

Unit Architectures

As a transitional device into unit design, we coined the term *unit architectures* in DL ELA to represent graphic outlines of curricular structures that enable the development of coherent lessons and units built around interrelated sequences of texts and assignments. Unit architectures are one-page visual representations of ELA units that allow unit developers to graphically and conceptually display the design features for the units they develop. They make it possible to see on one sheet the overall sequence of work that will occur over the length of the unit, as well as the specific work for each text. An architecture mirrors the inquiry structures of ELA by organizing key design features and texts as a model of a sequence of "practices through which knowledge is generated" (Popkewitz, 2004, p. 27), extrapolated from, and taught. An architecture centers a set of purposely sequenced texts around a key academic concept and displays the ELA lesson and unit design features that enable teaching and learning over a unit of instruction. It is the big picture for a unit presented as one-page graphic. Figure 6.1 presents a unit architecture for a response to literature unit that invited learners to study texts through three lenses: gender, elements of literature, and reader response.

Notice that the three overarching questions in the unit architecture reach across the three texts and that for each individual text, there is work in comprehension, identifying and explaining significant moments, writing about interpretive questions, writing imitatively as an apprentice to selected sentences, culminating formal written assignments, and retrospective assignments that prompt learners to reconsider the three overarching questions each time they read another text. The work represented in the architecture can be done by learners in combinations of quick writes to prepare for discussions, pair or trio sharing of quick writes, charting, whole-group discussions, and formal writing assignments that can be taken through revisions and editing.

Naming the Design Features

Naming and making the ELA lesson and unit design features visible is important, although it is not common practice in ELA curriculum design. We have learned that naming and making the design features visible allows us to translate habits of thinking (ways of reading, writing, talking) into activities and assignments with a clarity that is not possible without them. The naming and visibility also bring the scaffolding of assignments and activities into clear focus for instructors and learners, since we encourage instructors to post architectures in their classrooms

Figure 6.1
Unit Architecture for a Multi-lens Response to Literature Unit

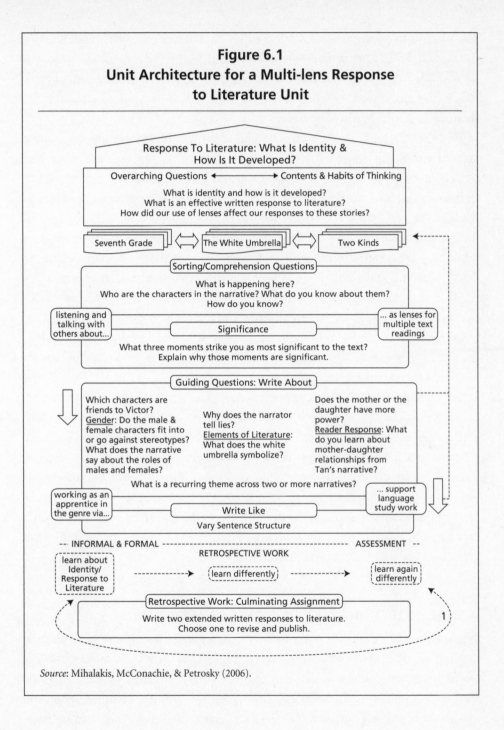

Response To Literature: What Is Identity & How Is It Developed?

Overarching Questions ◄───────► Contents & Habits of Thinking

What is identity and how is it developed?
What is an effective written response to literature?
How did our use of lenses affect our responses to these stories?

Seventh Grade ⟷ The White Umbrella ⟷ Two Kinds

Sorting/Comprehension Questions

What is happening here?
Who are the characters in the narrative? What do you know about them?
How do you know?

listening and talking with others about... ──── **Significance** ──── ... as lenses for multiple text readings

What three moments strike you as most significant to the text?
Explain why those moments are significant.

Guiding Questions: Write About

Which characters are friends to Victor?
Gender: Do the male & female characters fit into or go against stereotypes? What does the narrative say about the roles of males and females?

Why does the narrator tell lies?
Elements of Literature: What does the white umbrella symbolize?

Does the mother or the daughter have more power?
Reader Response: What do you learn about mother-daughter relationships from Tan's narrative?

What is a recurring theme across two or more narratives?

working as an apprentice in the genre via... ──── **Write Like** ──── ... support language study work

Vary Sentence Structure

-- INFORMAL & FORMAL -------------------------------- ASSESSMENT --

RETROSPECTIVE WORK

learn about Identity/ Response to Literature ----► learn differently ----► learn again differently

Retrospective Work: Culminating Assignment

Write two extended written responses to literature.
Choose one to revise and publish.

1

Source: Mihalakis, McConachie, & Petrosky (2006).

and refer to the design features when orienting students to their ongoing work in the unit. Finally, naming and making design features visible allows us to put them on the table, so to speak, so that others can understand the intellectual work they represent, engage in discussions and critiques of them, and use or transform them in their own lessons and units.

Because teaching is a patterned language—conversations among people around commonly shared subjects that are themselves represented by various objects of study such as texts—design features help create patterns or structure in instruction. Such conversations in DL are designed to apprentice students to the kinds of intellectual work being done in the disciplines. We would go one step further and argue that teachers work from patterns represented as design features when they create lessons and units, whether they are aware of them as such or not. In reading and writing workshops that feature genre or author studies as the foci of their curricula (Atwell, 1998), for instance, the design features have to do with such things as the establishment of genre or author class libraries for independent reading and writing, invitations to students to write in the genre of the works they are reading, comprehension discussions, minilessons on aspects of craft, writers' conferences, and so on.

Design features allow us to create tasks and activities that present students with scaffolded intellectual studies that take them deeper and deeper into individual texts. They also make it possible to create tasks and activities that position students to work across multiple texts, partly because they are patterned. Design features and the conceptual architectures that present them as units of study have been used by our district partners to represent thematic, genre, author, literary response, and cultural studies. The design features themselves appear to be flexible enough to be moved around in lessons and units and scaffolded in different ways given the needs of students and instruction.

A SNAPSHOT OF INQUIRY IN AN ELA CLASSROOM

We now turn to a case of an ELA inquiry classroom. This snapshot takes us into the first arc of lessons in the unit (see Figure 6.1) to provide a sense of how a teacher and her students work with the first story, "Seventh Grade," by Gary Soto (1990), on comprehension questions, identifying and explaining significant moments, creating interpretations and discussing them, writing responses to literature, and, finally, studying the story through a gender lens. The classroom from which this case is derived is a middle school classroom in a large urban West Coast district with high numbers of English language learners. The case is not meant to be comprehensive in any way but to provide a glimpse into the work a teacher did with her students around the ELA lesson and unit design features with inquiry rituals and routines.

The Case

Jan Kollen, a ten-year teaching veteran at Jade View Middle School, and her seventh-grade students are beginning a twenty-lesson response-to-literature unit designed to deepen students' understandings of identity, short stories, and different kinds of responses to literature.

Students spend their time in Ms. Kollen's class reading, writing, thinking, and talking in specific patterned ways about a sequence of short stories, as well as model responses to literature. Over the next four weeks, students will read and discuss three short stories, study models of response to literature, and write both short and extended responses to these stories. These patterned ways of working foster their developing understandings of the overarching inquiries of the unit to expand their literary knowledge, deepen their engagement with their reading, and assist their creation of sophisticated, written responses to literature.

The First Arc of Instruction: Checking Prior Knowledge

As students enter the room, they immediately notice and comment on the new overarching inquiries and the unit architecture posted on large chart paper in front of the room. Students can be heard reading the questions aloud to themselves or to one another as they retrieve their reader-writer notebooks and settle into their seats. When class begins, Ms. Kollen asks one student, Marcus, to read the following overarching inquires aloud:

- What is identity, and how is it developed?
- What are the characteristics of an effective written response to literature?
- How did your uses of literary lenses affect your responses to these short stories?

Since students are familiar with units that have been built with overarching inquiries, Ms. Kollen asks students to say what they think they will be working on over the course of the unit instead of telling them this information. Various students quickly call out "identity" and "response to literature" but are stumped with the new concept of literary lenses. She asks students to hypothesize what literary lenses might be, charting their initial understandings so they can be revisited and revised as students gain more information. This brief discussion provides a starting point for students' learning and an assessment of what they already know or think about literary lenses.

Ms. Kollen explains to students that they also will be working on developing methods they can use to become better readers of literary texts. Instead of preteaching generic reading strategies, Ms. Kollen and her students will model and discuss some of their own habits of reading over the course of the unit.

Then Ms. Kollen asks students to consider what they already know about identity and how it is developed—the first overarching inquiry. Students open their reader-writer notebooks—a notebook they have kept throughout the year to try out and record their thoughts, ideas, and new learning—and begin writing what they know about identity and how it develops by writing paragraphs, creating concept maps, or jotting lists. Ms. Kollen walks around the room as students are writing to get a sense of their prior knowledge on the topic. After a few minutes of writing time, she invites students to share their ideas with a partner before inviting them to share with the class. During the whole-class share, she lists their ideas on large wall charts that will be revisited, revised, and amended as the unit progresses and students deepen and change their understandings about identity through the stories they read and discuss.

Students also spend time during this period writing in their notebooks about what they do when reading a short story, concentrating on what they do to keep focused and what they do when they do not understand what they're reading. One student writes, "I try not to listen to side conversations, not watching or listening to television, and not drifting away to other things. . . . When I don't understand what I'm reading I continue to read until I understand it and if I still don't understand it then I either ask someone or come back to it later."

Students share their writing in groups of two and three initially, talking among themselves, giving Ms. Kollen the opportunity to circulate around the room to quickly assess their habits of reading and use that information to decide her instructional focus for their first read/think aloud. Kollen notices that very few students mention that they reread or ask themselves the comprehension questions about the text, so she decides that she will introduce them to these methods in their first arc of lessons.

Comprehension   Ms. Kollen introduces students to the first short story, "Seventh Grade," by Gary Soto. This selection is purposely placed first in the unit, as it is the shortest and least complex of the three stories students will read in terms of the relationships between the characters, vocabulary, and style; it is also one that is closest to students' own experiences. Ms. Kollen writes the comprehension questions on the board:

- What is happening here?
- Who are the characters?
- What do you know about them? How do you know?

These questions will guide students' first reading of the story. Ms. Kollen explains that the purpose of this first reading is to get the gist of the text by sorting out the characters, sequence of events, and setting; she also tells students that she will begin reading this text aloud and will stop once or twice to have students discuss the answers to the comprehension questions orally. As she reads aloud, students are following along with her, and when she stops to ask the comprehension questions, many students raise their hands to answer. Ms. Kollen had determined previously to stop at the end of a plot section so as not to diminish the story's dramatic unfolding of events. Each stop is only long enough to listen to responses and let students clear up any misunderstandings. After reading the first few pages, she turns the reading over to students to finish the last third independently, reminding them to stop periodically to check their understanding by answering the comprehension questions themselves.

When students have finished reading, they compose quick writes to answer the comprehension questions in their notebooks before discussing their quick writes in pairs. As students are writing and sharing, Ms. Kollen circulates around the room to assess students' comprehension of the story, taking note of what individuals and groups of students misunderstood or found difficult to comprehend. Then she facilitates a whole-group discussion of the comprehension questions, reminding students to use evidence from the text to support their responses. Most students remember to use evidence since this is an established way of working in Ms. Kollen's classroom; however, occasionally a student offers an unsupported response, and Ms. Kollen asks the student to return to the text to cite evidence. When moments of disagreement or misunderstanding surface, especially those that arise from a misreading of the text, Ms. Kollen asks students to return to the text to reread relevant sections and then reconsider their response given their rereading.

After the whole-group discussion, Ms. Kollen asks students to reflect on their reading by composing another quick write about how stopping periodically while reading to answer the comprehension questions helped their understanding of the text. This habit allows students to begin to manage their own learning and provides Ms. Kollen the opportunity to hear how students did with this new reading method. After writing for a few minutes, the class has a whole-group discussion. Maria, the student who said she normally continues reading when she does not understand, says, "Stopping to answer the questions helped me understand the story better because I got to learn more about the characters and what was happening in the story in steps." Another student, Kenny, says, "I think that it helped stopping to answer the questions because what was happening was easier to get. This is different from the way I read. I just read all the way and don't stop or ask myself what's going on."

Significant Moments   Now that students understand the gist of the story, they are ready to deepen their inquiry into it by rereading to locate moments they consider significant to the story and explain why they consider those moments significant. With this act of locating and explaining moments (which can be a phrase, sentence, paragraph, or something else), students begin to consider what they think is important in the text. Ms. Kollen models a significant moment and explanation of her own before asking students to do this individually in their reader-writer notebooks. She reminds them that there are two important aspects of this: deciding on the moments that they think are significant to the story and their explanations of why they think those moments are significant. Students take about fifteen minutes to reread the story and complete the task. They select a range of moments; however, most moments identify a key character trait, event, or theme in the text, as is evident in Table 6.1. Even when students choose the same moment, as they frequently do, their explanations vary, allowing everyone to understand that there can be multiple paths into reading and understanding the story.

Interpretation   After discussing significant moments in pairs and with the whole group, students move to interpretive work that asks them to reread the story again, this time to respond to another question about it. The question posed

Table 6.1
**Student Samples of Significant Moments
in Seventh Grade**

Significant Moment	Explanation
"Bonjour," Victor whispered. He wondered if Teresa heard him.	"This is important because it shows that Victor wants to impress Teresa but he's not sure of himself. He whispered the French word because he didn't feel brave enough to say it out loud. Victor has likes, but he's shy."
On the way to his homeroom, Victor tried a scowl. He felt foolish until out of the corner of his eye, he saw a girl looking at him.	"This sentence shows that Victor is not a leader because he is a follower because even though he thought that a scowl was foolish, he tried it to see if it worked."
Teresa asked him if he would help her with French. "Sure anytime," Victor said. "I won't be bothering you, will I?" "Oh no, I like being bothered."	"This is important because it shows that Victor really likes Teresa so he pretends to know French. That shows he changed his identity for Teresa."

for this third reading asks students to delve deeper into the text to come up with an interpretation of the ideas using evidence from the story to support it. Students are ready to do this interpretive work because their previous readings, writings, and discussions of the story have prepared them. They know too, from work with other stories, that interpretive questions have multiple, varied answers that can be supported with evidence from that text and that they have to come up with the answer and the passages from the text that they think support it. The question that Ms. Kollen writes on the board is, "Who is a friend to Victor?"

After seeing the question, students get back into the story, rereading and skimming sections, then composing quick writes in their notebooks to get their thoughts on paper before taking a few minutes to share with a partner. This pair talk allows students to try out their thinking with one other person in a fairly safe way before going public with the whole group; it also allows Ms. Kollen to hear students' responses and gauge how they are doing with supporting their interpretations with evidence from the text. If Ms. Kollen had more time, she would ask each pair to chart their thinking by listing the major points of their interpretations, along with quick summaries of the parts of the story that support it. She likes to have them present these charts to the class, so that each student practices explaining his or her interpretation, but she does not have time for that today, so she opens the discussion to the whole group.

During this discussion, students debate their interpretations, often reading out loud from the text, while Ms. Kollen facilitates by holding students accountable to the accepted methods of discussion for her class. She reminds students to back up their interpretations with evidence from the text and presses students to explain how the evidence supports their interpretations. She does not actively participate in the discussion by offering her own interpretation or validating students' responses because she knows these behaviors will limit students' inquiry and talk. She does, however, take notes to track the students' interpretations for herself so that she can refer back to who said what and to point out agreements and disagreements to keep the discussion focused and moving. Her notes also help her later when she reflects on how individual students are progressing in their ability to develop and support interpretations of texts.

A key moment in the discussion comes when one student, Mariana, asks, "But what is a friend? I mean, what does it mean to be a friend? It seems like we need to talk about that if we're going to get anywhere saying who is a friend to Victor because everyone says a different idea it seems."

Another student agrees with Mariana by saying, "Yeah, we have to define what it means to be a friend! Just like we had to say what power was when we answered the question for that other story."

A boy sitting next to Mariana says, "We need a friend chart!"

Other students murmur agreement and begin to start talking among themselves about what it means to be a friend. Ms. Kollen lets them talk while she hurriedly lists the characteristics she hears them talking about on a chart in the front of the room. The discussion lasts for about twenty minutes as students turn to debates over whether certain characters, especially Teresa, act like friends or are merely being friendly or nice, and whether Mr. Bueller, a teacher who allows Victor to lie in class, can be a friend to Victor, who is his student. "Would a friend allow someone to lie?" a student asks.

At the end of the discussion, Ms. Kollen reads from the tracked interpretations to recap what students discussed. She is careful not to gloss or explain away their differences, nor does she try to pull it all together into a consensus. Then she gives students the opportunity to share what they learned by engaging in the discussion. A couple of students say they learned that there is a difference between being friends with someone and being a friend to someone. Others share that they reconsidered certain characters, a few say they changed their minds about whether certain characters are friends to Victor after the friends' discussion, and some state that they thought they should have begun by talking about what a friend is.

Ms. Kollen asks students to share how they felt they did as a class. Most believe they did a good job since she rarely had to step in to remind them to use evidence and since they talked to each other without raising their hands—two aspects of the inquiry-based discussion they have been working on. However, one student said there were at least six people who did not say anything and that getting everyone to talk should be one of their goals for the next discussion.

Creating Written Responses

To begin addressing the second overarching inquiry, "What are the characteristics of an effective written response to literature?" and to build on the work students just did, Ms. Kollen asks students to review their notebook entries for their interpretative responses to the question, "Who is a friend to Victor?" With Ms. Kollen's guidance, they review their interpretations, evidence, and explanations from the class wall charts to prepare to work together to complete a shared writing of a response to literature. Writing together as a group apprentices students to the habits of thinking and some of the ways of working that writers use when they write responses to literature.

As with the discussion, Ms. Kollen does not do the thinking for the students. Instead, she facilitates the writing in key ways. One way is by guiding students through the steps in writing a response to literature and bringing their awareness to the steps by naming them—for example, analyzing the question, rereading the text, gathering evidence, grouping and sorting the evidence, coming up with an interpretation, and explaining the ways evidence supports the interpretation. The purpose is to give students a model of how to write a response, so that they have practice engaging in the task for when they are asked to do so independently in later lessons. The other way that she facilitates the writing is by asking key questions that writers ask as they create responses to literature. Some of these questions include, "What is the question asking? What evidence do we have to answer the question? Is the evidence accurate and appropriate? Is it adequate? What big ideas emerge from the question?" She reminds the students that they are not writing the definitive answer to the question, "Who is a friend to Victor?" She is guiding them, she tells them, through the process of writing their responses for others who have not listened to their discussion or thought very much about the question, although they can assume that the readers of their responses will have read the story.

When the class is finished creating their responses, she asks them to step back and describe the process they went through to create it. Together the class comes up with the following list:

- Figure out the question and what you have to do.
- Find sentences and passages from the story that relate to the question.
- Take notes.
- Come up with big ideas (conclusions) from the story that answer the question.
- Write assertion (thesis) statements—what you have to prove.
- Connect text evidence with your assertion (thesis).
- Draft a response—include assertion, evidence, and explanations.
- Revise and edit draft.

After discussing the process, students reread the response the group created, as well as another response Ms. Kollen shares that was written by a student from another group using the same question. Using these two responses as the basis, Ms. Kollen asks them, "So what are the characteristics of an effective written response to literature?" Students call out the characteristics while she lists them on chart paper. This chart, along with others created for the unit, are posted, revisited, and amended as the unit progresses. At this point, the characteristics of an effective written response they are able to name are:

- Clearly stated assertion
- Gives evidence from the story and explains how it relates to the assertion
- Shows under-the-surface understandings of the story
- Has good organization
- Uses correct grammar, spelling, and punctuation

This chart, along with summarizing the students' thinking, provides students with clear expectations of the characteristics of an effective response. It also gives Ms. Kollen an informal assessment of what the students understand about responses at this point in the unit; she will use the information garnered from this assessment as she plans future lessons around writing responses to literature. Over the course of the unit, students will be asked to write multiple short and extended responses to literature, and this chart, which will become more specific and developed as the unit progresses, will provide a guide for students as they construct their responses.

Gender Study: Using a Literary Lens

Now that the students are familiar with "Seventh Grade" from all their work with the story, Ms. Kollen introduces the concept of literary lenses. Literary lenses are prevalent in ELA, yet often students are introduced to only one lens—the elements of literature—without ever knowing that this is just one way of thinking about texts. This unit introduces students to three literary lenses and asks students to consider how using different lenses affects their responses to stories. Using "Cinderella," Ms. Kollen models how to do a gender reading by analyzing the characters of Cinderella and Prince Charming. She writes a short list of questions on chart paper that they can use to analyze characters through the gender lens:

- What do women get to do? Men?
- Who gets to be smart? Beautiful?
- Who gets to speak? Who is silent or mostly silent?
- Who acts with authority? Who doesn't?
- Who gets to do interesting things? Who doesn't?

Then she and the students together analyze the characters of Cinderella and Prince Charming before she asks students to step back and think about the evidence they have gathered for both characters, in much the same way they did to create their written responses. She writes the big inquiry question on the board: "What does this fairy tale say about the roles of females and males?" Students offer a range of responses from, "If you're pretty, guys will fall in love with you" to "Men only care about looks," and "Marriage is the end goal and a cure for unhappiness." Now that Ms. Kollen sees that students understand how to do a beginning gender reading of a text, she asks them to work with a partner to do a gender reading of "Seventh Grade" by analyzing the key male and female characters using the questions on the chart. As the students work, Ms. Kollen circulates around the room to offer assistance and support when needed. She also uses this opportunity to assess students' level of understanding and consider whether she needs to reteach key concepts before she moves on to the next part of the lesson.

After students have completed their work with their partners, Ms. Kollen asks them to individually write a response in their notebooks to the question, "What does 'Seventh Grade' say about the roles of females and males?" Before they begin, she quickly surveys the students by asking them what resources in the room they might use to help them write. Students point to the posted charts for creating a response and for analyzing gender. Ms. Kollen will ask students to turn in this response, and she will use it as an assessment of what they understand about writing responses to literature and about doing a gender reading of a text. As with other assessments, the information will guide her future lessons.

Reflections on Gender Readings

As is the case with most key work that students do, at the close of the work on gender readings, Ms. Kollen asks them to step back and reflect on what they learned by doing this gender reading. One student writes, "What I learned is that although there has been stereotypes set for both men and women, they might or might not work. . . . Reading through a gender lens helped me identify stereotyped ideas about men and women. . . . Writers form many character identities by following stereotypes." Another student writes:

> Doing a gender reading helped me understand the story more because we got under the surface stuff the author was trying to tell us. For example, when I first read the story I did not pay attention to the under the surface stuff that was going on in the story like the gender stereotyping. . . . So I think that the gender chart really did change my understanding of the story but in a real positive way.

The class completes this arc of lessons by returning to the concept of identity and how it can develop in stories. They revise and add to the chart they created in response to the first overarching inquiry on the first day of the unit. Then they continue their studies with the more complex texts that are arranged to be progressively further from students' own experiences.

DISCIPLINARY LITERACY PRINCIPLES IN ACTION

The case of Ms. Kollen's class shows the DL principles in action in a middle school classroom. We now reflect on Ms. Kollen's classroom through the lens of the five DL principles.

Principle 1: Knowledge and Thinking Must Go Hand in Hand

In Ms. Kollen's classroom, content learning and process learning were not treated as separate areas for instruction. Instead, Ms. Kollen organized instruction so that students learned about key ideas, concepts, and questions of the discipline by engaging in the work of the discipline.

Students began their learning about the concept of identity and how it is developed by reading, rereading, writing, and talking about "Seventh Grade," a text that deals with issues of identity and identity construction. Students learned about a method for becoming more proficient readers by using that method and then reflecting on how it increased their comprehension. They learned about and used methods for developing oral and written responses to literature, such as understanding the question being asked, finding moments in the text that related to the question, and developing an interpretation in response to the question and supporting it with evidence. They did this by reading, interpreting, analyzing, discussing, and writing about "Seventh Grade" multiple times with scaffolded and sequenced questions. Finally, they learned about reading literature through different lenses by using one lens, gender, to do a reading of "Seventh Grade," and then reflecting on how that changed their understanding of the text.

Ms. Kollen did not make a choice about whether to teach content or process. Instead, she married content and process learning, which resulted in students' doing the intellectual work of understanding key ideas and concepts in the discipline.

Principle 2: Learning Is Apprenticeship

Ms. Kollen's students were apprenticed to ways of reading, writing, and talking in English language arts by doing the work of the discipline. Ms. Kollen presented students with authentic learning activities and tasks that mirror the work of the discipline, and she supported students to engage in those tasks by designing scaffolded and sequenced reading, writing, and speaking assignments. Students engaged in multiple readings of a text using genuine questions to guide each reading. They read to get the gist of the text using the questions, "What is happening here? Who are the characters? What do we know about them? How do we know?" They read to interpret the text using the question, "Who is a friend to Victor?" And they read to analyze the text through a gender lens using the question, "What does 'Seventh Grade' say about the roles of females and males?" Following each reading, students wrote to learn and then shared their writing in small and large groups. They also crafted and defended multiple literary arguments orally and in writing and analyzed a text using a literary lens. At multiple times in the lessons, students discussed their interpretations of the text as an English language arts community, working through the interpretations, trying them on for size, and rejecting those for which evidence could not be garnered.

Principle 3: Teachers as Mentors of Apprentices

Students were able to work as apprentices because Ms. Kollen provided them with questions and tasks that require active engagement and put the necessary scaffolds in place to assist the students to function with increasing independence. Ms. Kollen modeled aspects of reading and writing such as stopping periodically when reading to monitor comprehension and choosing and explaining moments that are significant to the text. She also guided students through the process of writing a response to literature by first writing with the class and then sharing a response with them that was written by another student before asking students to use those experiences to identify and examine elements of a response to literature. When apprenticing students to do a gender reading of the text, Ms. Kollen used direct instruction to teach students the questions that can guide a gender reading before assisting them to do a gender reading of "Cinderella." Then she asked students to do a gender reading of "Seventh Grade," a more difficult text, with a partner before asking students to individually compose a response to literature on their gender analysis. The variety of instructional approaches Ms. Kollen used worked to assist students' learning in order to help them become increasingly independent learners.

Principle 4: Classroom Culture Socializes Intelligence

Ms. Kollen's classroom provided a safe and supportive learning environment for students in which they felt comfortable expressing their ideas, questions, understandings, and misunderstandings. Students engaged in multiple text-based discussions where the focus was not on restating "correct" interpretations but on students' developing and sharing their own interpretations using the established ways of working in the discipline. Ms. Kollen treated the students as capable thinkers and thus was able to hand discussions over to them and step in only as needed. This was especially evident in the discussion in which students addressed the question, "Who is a friend to Victor?" Ms. Kollen might have begun the lesson by having students define the qualities of a friend, knowing this would help them in their discussion of the question. Instead, she allowed students to work through this on their own, trusting their ability to use their reasoning skills to come up with this as a group. Had no one suggested defining the qualities of a friend, Ms. Kollen might have intervened with this suggestion and used this moment to talk about the importance of carefully analyzing the question at hand.

Ms. Kollen created a community in which the students were active participants in their own learning, reflecting on their own learning, using each other as resources, taking control of discussions, and evaluating and setting goals for themselves.

Principle 5: Instruction and Assessment Drive Each Other

Each time students were asked to respond to a question or complete a task, Ms. Kollen was circulating around the room, reading students' quick writes, listening in on their pair or trio discussions, or recording what students were saying during whole-group discussions. She used these occasions to assess students' understanding of the content and habits of thinking and used those assessments to plan follow-up instruction. This became clear early in the class when Ms. Kollen asked students to write about what they do when reading to keep focused and what they do when they do not understand what they are reading. Ms. Kollen had thought through various methods to introduce to students to help them become better readers of literary texts, but it was not until she heard what students already do that she decided on the instructional focus for the lesson. Assessing students' current practices allowed her to tailor her instruction to their needs.

In addition, Ms. Kollen knew before she started teaching the unit what the culminating assessment would be. Over the course of the unit, she would be asking students to write multiple responses to literature with her guidance and with the help of their peers. As the culminating assessment, she was going to ask students to write two responses to literature individually on questions they did not discuss as a class and then choose one of those two responses to revise and publish. She listed this assessment on the unit architecture that students saw the first day of the unit. Knowing the assessment allowed Ms. Kollen to make sure that the learning opportunities she provided would help students acquire the necessary knowledge and skills in order to be successful on that assessment. She planned these learning opportunities to include multiple opportunities for students to write responses to literature with others and individually, to get feedback on their writing from their peers and from herself, to see various models of effective responses to literature and analyze those responses in terms of what makes them effective, and to reflect on the methods they used to create and support their responses. This preparation began when Ms. Kollen engaged students in writing a response to literature as a group and then asked the students to step back and talk about the steps they went through to create a response to literature before asking students to write another response individually.

Students benefit from knowing the culminating assignment early in a unit. The assignment gives them a road map of what is to come and the opportunity to take an active part in their own learning. It allows them to see the relevance of the instruction and how it prepares them for active engagement in their final assessment.

In DL classrooms, instruction and assessment are two sides of the same coin. We work with teachers to view everything that students do as a source of information into students' learning and thinking and then to use that information to guide instruction. Every question students respond to orally or in writing is an opportunity for teachers to assess what students understand and consider what to do next given where students are. That means that informal assessments are ubiquitous, and they take many forms: quick writes, small and large group discussions, observations of students as they work to complete a task, one-on-one conferences, and others.

Rather than waiting until the end of a unit to see what students understand by their performance on a unit test or culminating writing assignment, teachers in DL classrooms monitor students' understanding as they progress through a unit by analyzing data from various informal assessments and then making adjustments on the spot. We work with teachers to think through their lessons in advance to anticipate possible student difficulties with particular texts or tasks and plan ways to address those difficulties given the nature of students' responses and what those responses may reveal about students' learning. While the unit architecture is a road map of the intellectual work students will engage in as they progress through a unit, we work with teachers to consider ways they can continually monitor and adjust instruction through reteaching, providing additional scaffolding, conferring with students one on one or in groups, and otherwise assisting students given how each student is progressing in understanding key concepts and habits of thinking.

In addition to the myriad informal assessments that occur in DL classrooms, teachers design multiple formal assessments, including those that are embedded in the units and those that come toward the end of a unit and provide summative data. The assessments, consistent with authentic, inquiry-based tasks that reflect the intellectual work students have been engaged in, mirror the work of the discipline and ask students to extend their learning rather than just display it.

In the unit from which the classroom case in this chapter is derived, students' first formal assessment was to write an individual response to literature on the second text, "The White Umbrella," in response to the question, "What does 'The White Umbrella' say about the roles of females and males?" This formal assessment reflects the work students engaged in with "Seventh Grade" in which they created both written and oral responses to literature on other inquiry-based questions such as "Who is a friend to Victor?" and "What does 'Seventh Grade' say about the roles of females and males?" In addition, students practiced using the accepted ways of writing and defending a response to literature, which include developing interpretations, supporting them with evidence from the text, and explaining the evidence as it relates to the interpretations. This formal assessment extended students' learning in that it asked them to do similar work—write a response to literature through a gender lens—with a different and more difficult text.

To ensure successful engagement with the embedded and summative formal assessments, we work with teachers to ensure that students are given multiple opportunities to understand the criteria for success. This might happen as it did in Ms. Kollen's classroom, where students wrote and read a model of response to literature and then stepped back to consider the characteristics that make a response to literature effective. As students work on their formal assessments, they are given opportunities to plan, draft, and revise their work with peer and teacher feedback that is focused on helping students' advance their learning and meet the criteria for success.

PRINCIPALS' SUPPORT

We don't want to give the impression that Ms. Kollen's inquiry teaching came easily or quickly to her and her students. Nor do we wish to give the impression that it was a solitary accomplishment for her. The process for teachers of moving from their initial professional learning with us to developing and teaching their own inquiry lessons and units is long and complex. Teachers cannot do it without support from each other and their principals.

Disciplinary literacy ELA classrooms look and sound quite different from traditional classrooms where the teachers do most of the talking or the pattern of talk is I-R-E. Principals need to understand these differences in order to support the work. That means they need to have knowledge about and understanding of the ELA lesson and unit design features and unit architecture and the rituals and routines that support student content learning and apprenticeship into the discipline. Equally important is principals' understanding that student learning can be assessed in multiple ways.

We engage principals in a number of professional development sessions in which they participate as learners in inquiry lessons and then metacognitively reflect on the content and pedagogy of their learning and the multiple opportunities for assessment. This exercise allows them to begin to understand the features of effective inquiry teaching and learning and consider the implications for teachers, students, and themselves. After engaging principals as learners in inquiry lessons, we introduce them to the DL observation protocol and an ELA content observation tool. The protocol and tool further assist principals in understanding inquiry teaching and learning by giving them guidance on what to look for in ELA classrooms and how to have an instructional conversation with teachers. Engaging in lessons and using the DL observation protocol and content tools are two important components in helping principals support teachers in their work.

Principals must also appreciate that just as learning is not a solitary endeavor for students, it is not a solitary endeavor for teachers either. Teachers need time to work with their building colleagues to plan lessons, analyze student work, observe other classes, and continue their studies of inquiry teaching and learning. Consequently, principals must be flexible with scheduling to allow such building-level communities of practice. Without ongoing opportunities to learn and engage in deep examination of practice together, change is unlikely to be sustainable. Finally, principals need to understand that change takes time and is often accompanied by false starts and missteps. They need to communicate this understanding to their teachers so that teachers know they are supported and encouraged to take risks by trying new things.

CONCLUSION

This chapter presented a thick overview of the DL ELA project—its foundations and its implications for teaching—through a brief and partial case of one teacher and her students over a week's instruction. We touched on issues of professional development and leadership, but there is much more to say about professional development and leadership that prepares teachers for this kind of inquiry teaching and for their own creation of units for use in their classrooms and schools. Chapter Seven presents a fuller description of how DL leadership and professional learning assist the improvement in practice of curriculum writers, teachers, coaches, and administrators.

The process of moving to inquiry-based instruction is complex and entails long-term commitments from everyone who participates in the project. But it is a necessary movement in order to ensure that students have opportunities to think and use knowledge in creative and critical way to solve problems, develop and defend interpretations to literature, and write their own texts in ways that apprentice them to the disciplines of English language arts.

Embedding Disciplinary Literacy

Leadership and Professional Learning

Stephanie M. McConachie
Rosita E. Apodaca

"Why invest in disciplinary literacy?" is one of the first questions that district and school leaders will have to answer. If they are about to commit substantial time to DL practice, it needs to produce value-added instruction with improved student learning. In Chapter Two we addressed, "Why DL?" in two ways. First, we presented the disciplinary literacy (DL) model of teaching and learning on the diagonal, which linked increased content learning to the use of the right habits of thinking. Then, we described the DL design principles (see also Appendix A) to explicate what students do to learn better and what teachers do to support their improved learning. Now with Figure 7.1, we answer the question in terms of benefits to students. All educators need to answer this question. Leaders especially need a powerful way to communicate the benefits and big ideas of DL practices to those they lead and to key constituencies in their communities.

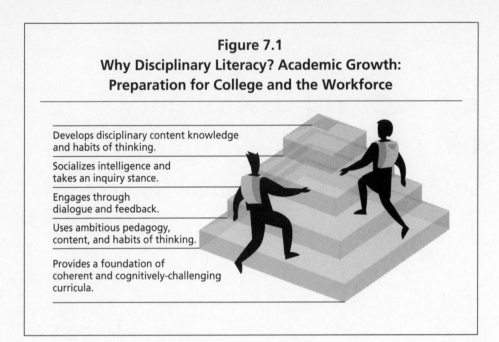

Figure 7.1
Why Disciplinary Literacy? Academic Growth:
Preparation for College and the Workforce

Develops disciplinary content knowledge and habits of thinking.

Socializes intelligence and takes an inquiry stance.

Engages through dialogue and feedback.

Uses ambitious pedagogy, content, and habits of thinking.

Provides a foundation of coherent and cognitively-challenging curricula.

The major goal of DL is students' academic growth to prepare them for college and the workforce. Students deserve the opportunity, along with the responsibility, to succeed academically and use what they know and can do to live fuller lives. We use David Conley's (2007) operational definition of *college ready*:

> [The] level of preparation a student needs in order to enroll and succeed—without remediation—in a credit-bearing general education course at a postsecondary institution that offers a baccalaureate degree or transfer to a baccalaureate program. "Succeed" is defined as completing entry-level courses at a level of understanding and proficiency that makes it possible for the student to consider taking the next course in the sequence or the next level of course in the subject area. [p. 5]

Preparation for the workforce in a global economy requires understanding how to solve complex subject matter problems using contextualized thinking and communication skills that parallel the demands of college preparatory learning. Figure 7.1 lists in sequence, from bottom to top, attributes of DL that support this preparation. The attributes encompass the ideas of the DL design principles. They are written, however, to highlight the academic, intellectual, and social benefits to students. The three attributes of curriculum, pedagogy, and dialogue realize the fourth attribute of socializing intelligence and an inquiry stance. All contribute to the fifth attribute of students' developing disciplinary content knowledge and the habits of thinking necessary for college and the work force. When DL systemic practice is implemented well in a school, students have repeated experiences across their academic courses with rigorous curricula, dialogue, and feedback. Whether students are in a history, geometry, biology, or an English literature course, they can expect specific talk and pedagogical routines to become their habits of thinking and practice, enabling them to focus directly on ideas and conceptual understandings. Their classroom learning communities socialize intelligence and invite an inquiry stance class by class throughout the school day.

Believing in the value of dialogue, socializing intelligence, and so on (see Figure 7.1 for a complete list of these attributes) for students does not make it any easier to reconcile those beliefs against the weight of the status quo and the turmoil of change. A principal from a high-performing urban high school reflects on her teachers' initial resistance to DL and what changed their minds:

> At first we thought DL was intrusive to the work we were doing. In fact, some teachers thought that teachers and principals from other schools should come see us teach since we thought we did quite well. Over a couple of semesters, however, after trying the approaches with students in classrooms, we began to see for ourselves how DL materials and tools could improve our work. What I learned from this is that change is not the way to position this effort. Improvement is the way in which we finally responded to it. In fact, the resisters are now DL advocates. It is driving our improvement as we embrace its shared structures, content tools, and the common language for our work.

Teachers had to make sense of the DL approaches and tools by seeing them in action. Then they could begin to engage in DL practice. Working for reform, like inquiry learning, is a social process that benefits from steady facilitation and supportive invitations with enough time to revisit old beliefs and redirect effort. Giving educators information about the effects of their practice without giving them ways to improve is insufficient. Nor is it simply enough to give educators access to new knowledge and skill that has the potential to increase student learning. Providing educators with the means to improve their practice in order to change the effects of their practice is, in fact, knowing the right thing to do. This has a greater probability of raising achievement, even in high-performing schools (Elmore, 2008).

In this excerpt, another high school administrator highlights "Why DL?" for students and teachers:

> Experiencing the lesson is a necessary part of growing DL. The observations—the pre-lesson conference and post-conference—are a huge part. The observations build collaboration and understanding. If the teachers find one aspect useful to a teacher, you garner buy-in. It's difficult to get buy-in in high-performing schools, but DL opens up a spectrum of where they could go—not just maintaining but pushing forward. There is a whole team of ninth-grade ELA [English language arts] teachers making this their own and talking it up to the other grade-level teams.

She goes on to give reasons that her faculty should invest its time in DL:

> Lessons are rigorous but very inviting to students, because the lessons provide various entry points into the content. DL provides equity by giving students who do not normally have access to rigor, a way to interact with cognitively demanding work. For me, that was huge. It got kids that normally may not experience that rigorous type lesson engaged in a very rigorous one—content-wise and task-wise.

Two ideas emerge here. First, inviting students into their learning by providing multiple entry points is important. With the right setup and task, each student will draw from what he or she knows to engage with cognitively demanding work. Second, achieving equity in learning opportunities requires us to consider each student's intellectual life in a school. Embedding DL routines and relevant, challenging tasks into lessons are fundamental components of making equity and excellence attainable for every student. Even in a designated high-performing school, every student is not experiencing rigorous-type lessons. The administrator has taken up the challenge of engaging those who are only "maintaining"—the ones not being asked or shown how to increase their learning with rigorous, relevant lessons.

CHAPTER OVERVIEW

DL systemic practice fosters the kind of teaching and learning that David Conley describes in his book, *College Knowledge: What It Really Takes for Students to Succeed and What We Can Do to Get Them Ready* (2008):

> A high school program of instruction that prepares students for college success requires intentionality and a certain commonality of purpose. The program must be geared toward a clear goal: a level of intellectual and skill development that connects seamlessly with what will be expected of students in college. Therefore, the faculty must have a vision of what a well-educated student looks like after four years of study at their school. This vision of a well-educated student can serve to guide the structure of the academic program and ensure that educational experiences over the four years are intentional and additive from the student's perspective....Few schools have attempted to create this sort of integrated, coherent, intellectually definable and defensible articulation of how a successful student would think, act, and learn after completing the school's program of instruction. [p. 102]

District and school leaders learn to use the DL framework, support materials, professional learning modules, and content tools to develop the kind of coherent instructional program that Conley describes. This chapter explains what we have learned from districts where we work and, if we were to make a proposal for a systemic way of implementing DL practice in schools and districts, what we would do. This chapter explains our proposal for systemic enactment.

BUILDING THE DISTRICT VISION AND ORGANIZATION

Once district and school leaders invest in DL, they learn about forming learning organizations that build and sustain communities of practice (Wenger, 1998a; McLaughlin & Talbert, 2006). Together with several district leaders, Lauren Resnick, Institute for Learning director, coined the phrase *nested learning communities* (Resnick & Hall, 1998) to describe learning organizations, where

> not only students but also education professionals are learners. Teachers, principals, and central-office administrators form communities of adult learners who are focused on improving their practice and

becoming increasingly expert as conductors of learning communities in the classroom, the school, and the district. . . . The purpose of *nested learning communities* is to enhance the knowledge and instructional base of all education professionals—teachers, principals, and administrators alike—by making student learning the dominant focus of daily activities. [p. 109]

When Resnick and the Institute for Learning fellows introduced nested learning communities to partner districts a decade ago, the idea was relatively new. She drew examples from the medical and legal professions to help educators understand that change could not occur without an ongoing learning, inquiring orientation from all participants. The use of instructional and organizational tools helps school administrators make cultural shifts to ongoing learning in the service of improving student learning, but the tools do not work well in closed, noninnovative environments. School improvement happens sooner and better in organizations that encourage effort, risk, talk, and collegial problem solving, including critique. Leadership operates through rich interactions that develop social and intellectual capital. Elmore (2008) argues for the necessity of high social capital in schools in order to achieve high intellectual capital: "The problem of how to create and deploy knowledge in the leadership of improvement is a classic problem of social capital. The knowledge itself doesn't reside in the individuals; it resides in the relationships among individuals engaged in the practice. What a teacher or principal 'knows' has no value, except insofar as it can be used to create or enhance knowledge and skill in others" (p. 60).

Nested learning communities make it possible to establish conditions for success. From this fundamental idea of the centrality of improving student learning by improving everyone's instructional base of knowledge comes the inherent responsibility to support each person's and role group's learning with actions up and down the system. District leaders begin support for DL by living this central idea of nested learning communities. The work begins with frank dialogue among district administrators, principals, and teacher leaders about the need to learn and apply learning in schools with openness and commitment to trying out new routines and practices and replacing those that are less effective. For DL, all leaders become accountable for starting and completing implementation with fidelity. In the midst of pressure to use quick fixes and programs that look easy and offer simple recipe-like solutions, it makes a significant difference when superintendents and other district leaders learn and interact shoulder to shoulder with principals about how to lead DL systemic practice. As part of setting the stage for the work ahead, district leaders explain that the success of the project emerges over time, and not in just one or two semesters. In the words of a superintendent of a large urban district implementing DL systemic practice, "This is a marathon that we're running, not a sprint. And you've got to build the capacity for that, and you've got to be able to sustain and go to scale with that.... I think I have a very strong intellectual team committed to deep thinking, but also dedicated to staying the course of the marathon" (Apodaca, 2007).

DL systemic practice cannot be implemented well or fully without strategic district leadership. To say that there are challenges to implementing major systemic practices across four core content areas in multiple middle and high schools simultaneously does not begin to capture the complexity and immensity of the task. Three major actions require strategic district leadership. First is inspiring and building a case for why to institute DL and how it will benefit the community to improve the education and academic growth of its young people. The vision has to have enough substance to breed excellence and learning, not compliance. The ideas in Figure 7.1 represent the basis of a district's vision for well-educated students. Next, the vision requires amplification through clear expectations and accountability. Clear expectations begin with identifying district needs. For instance, which secondary schools would benefit the most from implementing DL systemic practice? What are the requirements for their involvement? Will there be an application and interview process? Or given the importance of college and workforce preparation, should all of the district's secondary schools be involved? If only some of the schools will be involved, have leaders ensured that the selected schools enroll students from a diverse demographic and achievement range? If selected schools are limited to those that are high performing or low performing, DL practice can be inaccurately perceived as a treatment for a certain type of student. What intellectual and resource capacity does the district have, or is it willing to recruit or resource in support of this effort? Who will lead the work centrally, and what resources have been allocated? What plan is being established to acculturate professional personnel into DL systemic practice? What assessment and evaluation system will be used to gauge progress?

Clear expectations and accountability include knowing how to identify and act on behaviors that weaken, stall, or derail DL implementation. For instance, allowing the same nonproductive teaching and learning practices to continue masked by new vocabulary fosters teacher cynicism and disbelief about the school's commitment to DL instructional changes. Modifying the DL tools, using only some of them, or not learning how to use them well can become normalized if this situation is not monitored and addressed. The tools carry the theory; using tools that are not aligned to DL can create dissonance and incoherence for teachers and students. When leaders arrange professional learning or purchase new materials that contradict DL instructional coherence, the nonalignment needs to be addressed. A prime example of this is an across-the-curriculum use of generic templates and reading strategies regardless of the disciplinary tasks or texts students are working to complete and understand. When leaders promote a generic one-size-fits-all practice, teachers, especially those who have led the change and understand the implications for students' learning, lose their exuberance and creativity regarding instructional reform and begin to work under the radar. Since implementers will be assessing their improvement against the indicators of DL by content area (see the DL principles in Appendix A), it is more productive and coherent to learn and use the tools designed from those indicators. Part of building accountability requires district leaders to listen and join conversations with their school leaders when issues related to change arise. Conversations that include, "But we already do this," or "These are significant practices but not for our students" or "not for those students," difficult though they are to hear, are starting points of conversation and should be used as opportunities to increase involvement and offer alternatives to foster the necessary learning orientation.

The third area of strategic leadership is clarifying how DL systemic practice will be situated in relationship to existing curricular and instructional practices and other major reform strategies. Specifically, how will DL practices be aligned with other district professional learning, practices, programs, and initiatives? To identify and align all of the programs and initiatives reaching into the schools, curriculum leaders have to work jointly with line administrators, the supervisors of principals. To fulfill the focused alignment toward intellectual and instructional coherence in the schools, district leaders need to step into their principals' and teachers' shoes in order to visualize the power of aligned practices in a school learning community. Then they need to visualize a day or week of competing programmatic demands devouring the valuable time of principals and teachers. The joint work of all role groups has resulted in clear guidelines for alignment.

And in some situations, leaders combined departmental budgets and calendars to achieve the intended instructional coherence.

DL SYSTEMIC LEADERSHIP IN ACTION

In a medium-sized urban district beginning DL systemic practice, the chief academic officer began with establishing shared expectations through ongoing, supported dialogues. She organized bimonthly meetings for the district's content leaders and executive directors who supervise principals focused on DL systemic practice. With input from this newly formed community, she introduced structured dialogues to enable team members to puzzle out specific problems of practice for secondary teaching and learning. The meeting structure afforded team members a place and a group to reflect with persistence and depth on the impact of professional learning and to plan the next steps. If the science director was assessing the effects of a past professional development session, he was not alone, but part of this community. If the executive director was planning an upcoming principals' meeting and school visit, it was not occurring in a vacuum.

After the first semester of learning about DL with principals and school lead teams in a large urban district, the district leader set up a structure of guiding coalitions for the principals she supervises. A guiding coalition is a team with "strong position power, broad expertise, and high credibility that can make change happen" (Kotter, 1996, p. 66). The idea, borrowed from John P. Kotter of the Harvard Business School, mirrors other ideas about the importance of a strong team leading a major project such as DL systemic practice to successful realization.

As the supervisor of a large number of schools, the district leader began using guiding coalitions in order to establish meaningful distributed leadership and to build her principals' capacity to lead DL systemic practice in their schools (I. Durant, personal communication, February 8, 2009). The work was established using two tiers of involvement. For tier 1, the supervisor selected a small group of principals to be principal leaders. This group, known as the guiding coalition principals, studied DL practice with her in an ongoing professional learning community. In that first year, the principals, with the supervisor present, also began to observe each other's work to extend DL professional learning into their schools. As part of these observations, they received feedback from their colleagues and supervisor.

In the second tier of work, each guiding coalition principal facilitated three principals in a learning community called a quad that mirrored the practices of the central guiding coalition. The guiding coalition principals led the quads without remuneration, strong evidence of their belief in the viability of this approach. The supervisor carefully formed the quads so that each new principal was in a learning community with three experienced ones. Just as the central group had done, these quads studied DL topics together, observed the work in each other's schools, and gave feedback to each other on the work's progress. To provide the feedback, they used The Learning Walk* routine, which will be described later in this chapter.

The supervisor of principals selected the focus of the work based on discussions with the guiding coalition principals and several questions. First, where were the biggest gaps in student achievement? Second, what content area did the majority of principals need to know more about in order to improve conversations with teachers about instruction? Third, were district content experts available to support the necessary in-depth discussions of content and pedagogical content knowledge? Specifically, these were the focal areas of their work:

- Improve our understanding of mathematics' instruction
- Learning to observe math teaching and provide feedback
- Learning to plan and converse with teachers about mathematics
- Learning to develop and implement professional development in their schools based on teacher and student data (including classroom observation data)

The guiding coalition principals met with their supervisor monthly and were required to arrange their quad meetings around this central schedule. On occasion, the supervisor attended the quad meetings, but as an observer only. After making observations, she met with the guiding coalition principal to discuss ways to move the work deeper, holding the meetings in the principal's office where each would be more at ease. She treated monitoring and assessing progress in learning communities and in classrooms as a major responsibility. Consequently, she organized a regular schedule for formative feedback to principals. At the time of our interview with the supervisor, she had not observed teacher professional development work, but it is something she will be doing in the coming months. Evaluation of the work is done annually, and principals know explicitly what is

*The Learning Walk® is a registered servicemark of the University of Pittsburgh.

required to earn a high designation on the district's principal evaluation, since the work is directly tied to their formal evaluation.

BUILDING THE SCHOOL ORGANIZATION FOR DL

With the support of the district, each principal prepares to build his or her school organization for DL by forming or repurposing an existing group to become the school's guiding coalition. Coalition members need to have the ability, interest, credibility, and position power to lead the implementation of DL systemic practices. Usually each school's guiding coalition includes the principal, assistant principals, teacher leaders, coaches, and department chairs. Those selected typically represent administrative leadership and content leadership. Kotter (1996) cautions against having too many managers versus leaders in coalitions. In our case, it is the mix of content teaching expertise and broad organizational understanding (school administrators and content experts) that is more likely to foster creative, innovative ideas.

With the guiding coalition (some schools call these cabinets, others name them the leadership team, and so on) as a resource, the principal will have the intellectual and social resources to develop better plans, models, launches, and responses to actions than if he or she had done this work alone. The guiding coalition members are responsible for building their school organizations so that DL practices and routines can be learned and applied in the four academic areas. Therefore, the principal will need to ensure that the coalition, once formed, is positioned in the school in a straightforward manner so that DL structures, tools, and materials can be used to advantage.

The members of the coalition, the school's first wave of learners of DL practices, will join guiding coalitions from other district schools at three-day institutes. At their training, the coalition learns as a team and becomes clear about what is and is not DL systemic practice. They draft an initial plan for their school that builds from a vision of DL to establish purposes, resources, and outcomes for growth in each academic area. This group will consider how DL will be at the core of the school's instructional program. When competing demands, programs, or overall conflicting practices threaten implementation of DL, this group will navigate these waters. It is inevitable that challenges to the coalition's work will surface. DL practices in most secondary schools are perceived as a break from the past and in conflict with existing norms of categorizing learners by ability and course-level work. To counter these changes, educators may try to adopt DL practices without changing existing practice or undertaking learning to acquire new knowledge and skills. Sometimes those just beginning to learn DL practices try to have the press of implementation fit into their existing paradigm for responding to reform initiatives: "This too shall pass" or applying the "flavor of the month" metaphor. One central administrator related her experience leading DL implementation when she moved from district to school leadership:

> When you come to the campus level, everybody is urging "just tell me what to do." In other words they want kind of a lockstep—these are the steps, and this is DL. It is really the experience of living it and going through the lessons and having a deeper understanding of what is involved and how the pieces fit together. There is actually a continuum, and you can step in and out of that continuum of experience, but it's really necessary to experience the whole thing at some point in time. So that was really hard to convey on the campus because they really wanted something that was like a recipe. Give me the steps, let me complete it, and then I can check it off my list and move on. And really for me, DL is more of a continuum, and it gives you different entry points in which you do different activities for different purposes, but yet it reaches all ability levels. It always gives you that fallback that you can reach all ability levels and have them engage in really rigorous lessons.

Absent a strong district accountability system, it is the school's guiding coalition that determines how best to handle DL implementation tensions. In addition to the ones already mentioned, tensions may include pulling away from lesson observations for a few months given the state accountability system, responding to faculty members' use of non-DL tools and pedagogical routines, and implementing effective ways to orient a new principal to the school's DL goals. In the face of high turnover of teachers and principals, coalition members across a district and in each school are not only responsible for teaching new teachers about DL; they become the district's institutional memory. They are the resources that understand the underlying principles for the instructional actions and routines. They make it possible to sustain an initiative such as DL despite changing personnel year by year.

Table 7.1 shows three stages of a school's DL implementation. The school's guiding coalition uses the listed domains of effective leadership of DL implementation to organize and guide the work. The guiding coalition and the school community make sense of what it means to work (commit to achieve a shared vision with clear goals that focus on quality teaching and learning), know (commit to develop a profound understanding of the disciplines and the competence to accomplish the desired results), and lead (commit to principled leadership that is genuinely shared with others in the school and is supported with adequate time and resources). These beliefs develop over time and through repeated experiences. In addition, a school community accomplishes the major activities, establishes the structures, and achieves the learning and improvements of its current stage before moving to the next. Schools vary in their rate of progress depending on several variables, including recruitment and the available resources of time, expertise, and commitment. In brief, here are summary statements of the domains for effective leadership of DL implementation:

- *Building the vision and organization* includes the organizational actions and structures that build and manage the culture necessary to establish DL as a systemic improvement practice in a school.

- *Understanding and implementing the practice: Content knowledge, pedagogical content knowledge, and habits of practice* address the instructional core of teaching and learning. A practice is the "collections of patterned actions, based on a body of knowledge, skills, and habits of mind that can be objectively defined, taught and learned" (Elmore, 2008, p. 44). The pedagogy, learning, tools, routines, and organizational practices depicted in each of the content chapters exemplify what is learned and applied from this domain.

- *Observing and giving feedback* refers to the ideas and actions necessary to build a school community's capacity to enact ongoing observations with effective feedback to improve practice. Enacting this domain contributes to ongoing cycles of study, application, reflection, and assessment on the quality and performance of implementation.

Table 7.1

Progression of DL Implementation Organized by a School's Guiding Coalition

	Preparation	Stage 1	Stage 2
Building the vision and organization	• Secure resources. • Establish the campus guiding coalition. • Delineate roles and responsibilities. • Establish norms, lines of communication, and calendar of activities for implementation. • Prepare for school professional learning communities (PLCs). • Plan DL professional learning and launch meeting.	• Communicate vision to school. • Launch DL professional learning. • Make the calendar of activities public, and set up a monitoring system for implementation goals. • Make roles and responsibilities public. • Develop a schoolwide PLC plan and begin implementation. • Toward end of this stage, reflect on work and plan stage 2, including calendar of activities. • Engage new principals and teachers in the practice.	• Monitor PLCs and data from observations and make adjustments. • Revisit and refresh vision with all staff. • Toward end of this stage, reflect on work and plan stage 3, including calendar of activities. • Engage new principals and teachers in the practice.
Understanding and implementing the practice: Content knowledge, pedagogical content knowledge, and habits of practice	• Determine vision, goals, and scope of work. • Engage as learners in DL lessons from two to four academic areas. • Develop a beginning understanding of the what and why of DL, including differences and similarities in key tasks, text, and talk in four disciplines. • Study PLC process using a handbook. • Learn how to use one content tool in each academic area.	• Coalition continues to develop its understanding of DL pedagogy, tools, and systemic practice. • Teachers engage in DL lessons to understand the what and why of DL in their academic area. • Principal joins other district principals to study DL leadership, including organizational routines, distributed leadership, and how to deploy knowledge, skills, and habits of practice in school to improve teaching and learning.	• DL implementation plans are based on district and school needs, observations, and other pertinent data. • Teachers learn and use DL content tools to select or develop tasks, texts, and in their planned and enacted lessons. • Coalition with district content leaders learns how to assess curricula using DL tools.

Observing and giving feedback	• Develop a shared understanding of the value of classroom observations accompanied by quality feedback. • Review how the observation protocol can be used to improve practice and build community with principals and teachers.	• District's coalition principals and assistant principals observe each other's classrooms and schools in designated disciplines to give each other feedback on level and quality of implementation. • Coalition teacher leaders observe each other's classrooms to give each other feedback on the practice. • Coalition leaders work with an external expert facilitator on classroom observation process.	• District's coalition principals and assistant principals continue visiting each other's schools as outlined in stage 2. • Coalition's teacher leaders observe and are observed teaching using lessons with DL essential features. Principals and other teachers are invited into observations and debriefs. • External expert facilitator observes and assesses facilitation of observations and debriefs.
Developing and providing professional development	• School's guiding coalition supported by external expert facilitators. • Design the launch institute. • Review the school's DL plan. • Engage in DL training as outlined in above cells of this table. • Plan, practice, and reflect on facilitation of professional learning.	• Coalition teacher leaders engage teachers in PLCs using DL lessons, modules, and practices. • Principals plan with teacher leaders, observe them teaching DL lessons, and ensure that they hold PLCs to study DL practices and tools. • Principal and assistant principals join different PLCs to learn and to assess collaborative work. • District leaders join different PLCs as learners, occasional cofacilitators, and leaders to assess progress and quality of support for teachers. • External expert facilitators and district leaders review and coach improved content of PLC plans.	• Coalition leaders continue to implement the DL plan. • Principals continue their planning with teachers, observing classrooms, and begin to use a DL instructional leadership tool to observe and guide instructional conversations. • Principals, assistant principals, and district leaders continue their involvement in PLCs as outlined in stage 2. • External expert facilitators and district leaders continue to coach improved content of PLC implementation.
Evaluating implementation and performance	• Have a clear understanding of how fidelity to program implementation will be tied to evaluation of performance. • Develop and communicate means of evaluation.	• External expert facilitator confers with supervisors of guiding coalition leaders on progress of implementation. • District supervisors of guiding coalition leaders observe the work and confer with each leader to evaluate implementation and plan appropriate support and interventions.	• External expert facilitator confers with supervisors of guiding coalition leaders. • District supervisors of guiding coalition leaders observe the work and confer with each leader to evaluate fidelity to implementation and plan appropriate support and interventions.

Note: PLC = professional learning community.

- *Developing and providing professional development* fosters nested learning communities through multiple learning opportunities embedded in authentic tasks of practice for different role groups. The professional learning assists intellectual and instructional coherence through its curricular and content examples, stable content tools, cycles of action (study, apply, reflect, and assess), and learning structures (sessions, professional learning communities, one-on-one conferring, instructional conversations, observations).

- *Evaluating implementation and performance* includes setting up internal accountability systems that embody the scope and intent of the implementation. Administrators and others participate in evaluating quality and performance. There is collaborative, regular monitoring supported by the necessary understandings and actions to adjust plans and strategies in response both to progress and stalemates.

UNDERSTANDING AND IMPLEMENTING THE PRACTICE

In the preparation stage of DL implementation, assistant principals, the principal, and other members of the guiding coalition begin to learn the key ideas and pedagogical routines of the four disciplines well enough so that they can identify similarities and differences in driving questions and pedagogical practice. External expert facilitators lead initial professional learning to support principals and guiding coalition members. In addition to these sessions, supervisors of principals form professional learning communities (PLCs) for secondary principals to deepen school leadership understanding of DL instruction and implementation. The following excerpt from an external evaluation from DL provides a glimpse into the work of a large urban district's PLC for principals:

> Principals began to delve into issues regarding instruction, such as how to define "rigor," and ensuing discussions and shared readings developed individuals' knowledge of DL-like instruction and ideas for their instructional leadership. This work also developed shared conceptions of, and commitment to, the district's instructional reform goals.... Meetings of DL-PLC school principals focused more intensively on learning around content-specific notions of rigor.... One principal described that, in addition to reading articles and having conversations about their practices: "We are DL-practice-specific." As an example, he told us: "We actually worked through an English

lesson and we went through the process that the teachers go through. And so we read a passage and we had questions and we talked about it. And so we sort of had a snapshot of a DL lesson as if we were the student. And so we had that sort of exposure. And so then we took that and talked about the components of the lesson to say, 'Okay, these are the types of things that we should be seeing in the classroom.'"
[Talbert, David, & Lin, 2008, pp. 29–30]

Well-designed and well-run principal-level PLCs require a skilled DL facilitator who may be the principal's supervisor, another administrator, or an external DL leader. The PLC curriculum and means of collegial interaction will need to build school leaders' skills and habits of practice to lead and co-lead observation and feedback on DL practices well enough to promote critical examination of disciplinary practices.

Teachers or coach content leaders, in addition to developing increased content and pedagogical knowledge, also learn how to be skilled facilitators of content-based, ongoing PLCs for the academic area they lead. The principal and teacher PLCs draw on ideas of communities of practice, developed by Etienne Wenger (1998b). Below are Wenger's descriptions of the dimensions:

> What is it about? *Its joint enterprise as understood and continually renegotiated by its members.*
>
> How does it function? *Mutual engagement that binds members together.*
>
> What capability has it produced? *The shared repertoire of communal resources (routines, artifacts, vocabulary, styles, etc.) that members have developed over time.* [p. 2]

In the DL-PLC work, teachers and administrators strive to realize these three dimensions. The explanations and examples that follow provide illustrations of each:

- *What is it about?* PLC members engage in joint work by academic area to accomplish improvements in teaching and learning and to understand the larger purpose of their work. In other words, they have a shared belief that all students can achieve to high standards and a shared mission to prepare students for college, the workforce, and life. To do this, they build and manage their knowledge of practice toward intellectual and instructional coherence.

They do this by reading the research on effective teaching methods; learn to select and use content tools; studying the features and routines of lessons; analyzing and developing units, curricula, and courses; and conducting deep examinations of intended and enacted practice.

- *Mutual engagement*: They work collaboratively, using cycles of inquiry to study, apply, reflect, and assess. They sustain their learning about teaching and learning by working toward collective definitions of resources and needs; using shared content tools; observing and being observed teaching, coaching, and mentoring; and providing each other with evidentiary feedback.

- *What capability has it produced?* They create a shared language, shared expectations, accountability for their practice, and intentional student outcomes year by year. The work produces a shared repertoire of student work samples, improved lessons and units, clearly stated understandings of their school and academic area's intellectual coherence, high levels of content knowledge and pedagogical practice, understanding of their students' learning of that content, and improved student learning.

The content teacher leaders will be the first group to try out DL lessons, routines, and practices with students. It is also in their classrooms that coalition members practice observing and developing feedback on lessons using DL content tools. The coalition members initially lead as learners of an improved instructional core of content, teaching, and student learning of that content. Their knowledge of the instructional core validates their later collective role as the school's clearinghouse for what is going on in the school with teachers, students, and external facilitators of DL. With the principal, they establish instructional priorities and determine fidelity checks on DL implementation with external facilitators.

DL implementation challenges a principal to assume a pivotal role in his school's instructional improvements. If principals delegate a key function such as offering in-depth feedback to teachers, they are not fulfilling a central responsibility. They are delegating away the means to offer relevant support to a teacher. Schools that use DL well must have a principal and assistant principals who play a key role in advancing the work. When principals are knowledgeable about DL practice, what they have to say after classroom observations has advanced the work. This does not preclude teachers giving other teachers feedback or department chairs giving feedback, but it cannot exclude the principal. Conversely, there are times that actions by less knowledgeable principals have caused unintended consequences that have stalled or stopped DL progress. Principals are listened to by teachers and set a tone and expectations for performance. Few teachers will openly work in ways that contradict the principal.

Actions That Support Principals' Instructional Leadership

Given the reality of principals' fast-paced, multiple encounters with many departments, events, and personnel in the course of each hour, day, and month throughout the academic year, how can they be expected to remember professional learning that occurred a month or more ago? DL content tools and learning examples have to be concise and modified from teachers' content tools so they include only what is necessary for a successful instructional observation and conference. In the future, one can envision access to handheld technology so a principal can hit a series of buttons that reorient him or her to professional learning of a month ago. So when the learning becomes immediately useful at the time of an observation, for example, a principal presses a set of buttons to call up a video from a content area or a description of a pedagogical routine relevant to the class he or she will be entering. In the interim, principals use video and binders of professional learning materials to refresh their learning before lesson observations and instructional conversations. There is no magic bullet for purposeful principal learning and actions. DL implementation requires a series of formats to support building genuine ownership on the principals' part, especially for those who lead comprehensive high schools. Their role is not minds-off delegation but minds-on engagement to build a nested learning organization with networks of communication on the improvement work and supportive supervisory practice.

Figure 7.2 shows estimates of how much time will be spent on each domain by year of implementation. Initially, district and school leaders spend a substantial amount of time building the vision and the organization and learning the practice—the first two listed domains. If time is well spent, it will result in higher social and intellectual capital that will make later observations and feedback opportunities more natural and productive because they will occur within stronger, more academically coherent and innovative organizations.

Scheduling Teacher Professional Learning Communities and Observations

District and school leaders have arrived at solutions for scheduling teacher PLCs and observations in multiple ways. Some have been able to maneuver the master schedule so a department or half a department of two grade levels has a shared

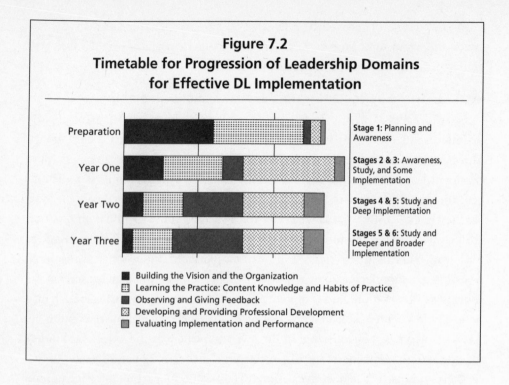

Figure 7.2
Timetable for Progression of Leadership Domains for Effective DL Implementation

Preparation — Stage 1: Planning and Awareness

Year One — Stages 2 & 3: Awareness, Study, and Some Implementation

Year Two — Stages 4 & 5: Study and Deep Implementation

Year Three — Stages 5 & 6: Study and Deeper and Broader Implementation

■ Building the Vision and the Organization
▦ Learning the Practice: Content Knowledge and Habits of Practice
▪ Observing and Giving Feedback
▨ Developing and Providing Professional Development
▦ Evaluating Implementation and Performance

period in which to meet. Others have garnered extra minutes weekly from start and end times of the school day in order to bank time for a weekly PLC drawn from the added minutes of individual planning periods the other four days of the week.

These changes do not happen immediately in a school and may not take place until the second year of engagement in DL work. When the guiding coalition, with other teachers and district leaders, sees the need to rethink the schedule and is unhappy because practices are not benefiting students, actions inevitably are taken. For example, in an advanced DL district, the superintendent and the supervisor of principals were engaged and knowledgeable enough after a year of participation in the DL reform that they succeeded in securing twenty late-start days per school year for PLC meetings. Leaders took action after realizing that the existing practice of teachers meeting after school and on Saturdays, even if remunerated, would not elevate student learning quickly enough. The reality of having trained DL district and school teacher leaders who wanted and knew how to lead PLC groups using DL tools and materials became the catalyst for leadership action. When key leaders and stakeholders realized the benefits of focused time within the school day and diverted major resources to this arrangement, they found the time for this significant work. Setting aside time for DL learning and practice is difficult at best even when it is designated for that purpose by a board of education. Finding time on a regular basis to study and do the DL work is a critical indicator of progress, commitment, and alignment for DL implementation.

TOOLS TO SUSTAIN DL IN SCHOOLS AND CLASSROOMS

How does a reform persist in the face of changing leaders, teacher turnover, and the press of competing demands at the secondary level? Coburn's research (2003) offers a perspective that includes explicit attention to how the knowledge and authority for the reform is transferred from external sources to teachers who use what they learned to make consequential change in classrooms. The five identified leadership domains offer a road map only. Instantiating use of content and pedagogical content tools requires turning professional learning and initial applications of tools into internalized habits of professional practice.

For the purposes of this chapter, we limit our discussion to tools that guide processes and routines to achieve high-quality instruction. These are the pedagogical content tools included in earlier chapters as well as the study and organizational protocols that we reference in this chapter (see Appendix C for a list of representative DL tools.) Together, they support DL practices and routines in professional learning sessions, PLCs, and enacted lessons.

Figure 7.3 shows the nest of instructional tools that learners use at various levels of DL learning. The DL design principles and the principles of learning (described in Chapter Two) form the overall framework within which the other tools and protocols nest.

The instructional tools carry the theory and research in their design and use. In essence, each tool, whether it is the DL design principles or a content-specific one, such as, for DL mathematics, "thinking through a lesson: the key to successfully implementing high-level tasks," is meant to extend social and intellectual capabilities (Smith, Bill, & Hughes, 2008; Hughes & Smith, 2004). If the key function of this mathematics tool, for example, is to enable the active analysis of levels of cognitive demand and complexity, the tool works to assess math tasks and lessons regardless of the particular mathematics course. The content tools provoke sustained conversations and reflection on practice within and across role groups and tasks. They are a driving force for the cultural shift into tool-mediated actions by teachers.

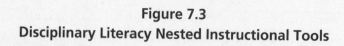

Figure 7.3
Disciplinary Literacy Nested Instructional Tools

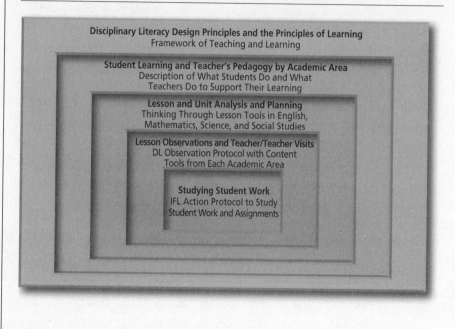

Disciplinary Literacy Design Principles and the Principles of Learning
Framework of Teaching and Learning

Student Learning and Teacher's Pedagogy by Academic Area
Description of What Students Do and What
Teachers Do to Support Their Learning

Lesson and Unit Analysis and Planning
Thinking Through Lesson Tools in English,
Mathematics, Science, and Social Studies

Lesson Observations and Teacher/Teacher Visits
DL Observation Protocol with Content
Tools from Each Academic Area

Studying Student Work
IFL Action Protocol to Study
Student Work and Assignments

OBSERVATION AND FEEDBACK ROUTINE

The leadership domain of observation and feedback supports the routine of lesson observations. Resnick and Spillane (2006) provide insight into the significance of routines in transforming instructional practice. They use the phrase *kernel routine* to describe how routines seed and propagate new forms of practice in schools. The idea is to introduce a routine that is highly specified and supported by well-defined tools and strategies and therefore can be implemented quickly at a reasonable level of quality under the guidance of the principal. The routine has to be visibly focused on teaching and learning and responsive to established standards of accountability in the school. Kernel routines serve two core goals: they anchor school practice in teaching and student learning, and they connect and weave together other organizational routines in the school to more fully focus the organization's attention on instruction and learning rather than on institutional compliance.

To open up instructional practice to examination, administrators and teachers use "lesson observations and teacher/teacher visits," a kernel routine, facilitated by the DL observation protocol (see Appendix B). It is not a stand-alone protocol but is used with a content tool to ground observations in the specifics of the tasks, text, and talk of the academic area being observed. The protocol guides how to observe a lesson and how to be observed teaching a lesson. Unlike formal teacher evaluations conducted by principals and assistant principals, this observation provides formative assessment data useful for promoting deep examination and reflection on practice for the teacher and the observers alike. The data are in the form of evidence-based descriptions and thought-provoking questions from the observing group to the observed teacher with no summative ratings or judgments. The observations are meant to foster reflection on practice by the observed teacher and those who joined the teacher on the observation and reflection. The protocol with content tool puts in place routines for examining practice with colleagues. At the center of the observation is the teacher, who determines the focus of the observation based on what she or he is trying to accomplish with the DL tools, materials, and approaches. This teacher leader comments on the change she saw in observations:

> There was a shift from a focus on teachers' to students' learning when we started to use the protocol. The questions and the way that the protocol is organized has you looking at instruction through the lens of what the teachers want you to focus on which is really helpful. It gives you a context for your observation. More importantly from the protocol, the evidentiary statements are particularly important for talking about it. You have something in front of you that is an actual—this is what actually happened—and allows you to ask questions that are rooted in student learning.

The observation protocol was originally developed as a risk-controlled way for teachers to begin observing others' practice and allowing others, including principals, to observe their practice. The DL protocol's design adheres to the design assumptions of The Learning Walk tool (Goldman, Johnston, Micheaux, & IFL Fellows, 2001; Institute for Learning, 2008) used by principals, district administrators, and teachers. Both tools support classroom visits tied to teachers' professional learning. Like the DL protocol, The Learning Walk tool was designed by the Institute for Learning to assist teachers and school administrators in observing classrooms and collecting evidence about how students learn and teachers teach and the impact of the teacher's work on student learning. Unlike the DL protocol, The Learning Walk visits are for shorter periods of time than a whole class period, have some procedural differences, and offer more varieties of classroom observations. A newer version of The Learning Walk tool (Apodaca, 2008) mirrors the DL protocol and is used by administrators for shorter observations and observations of multiple room visits during one class period. By visiting several rooms, educators can look for patterns and trends.

Both tools are designed to inform teachers and other school leaders about the instructional core, which represents the critical work of teaching and learning that goes on in classrooms. According to Elmore, there are basically only three ways to increase learning and performance: increase the knowledge and skill of teachers, somehow affect content, and alter the relationship of the student to the teacher and the content (Elmore, n.d.; Childress, Elmore, & Grossman, 2006). In order to increase student learning and achievement, teachers and other school leaders must continuously improve the instructional core. The observations are done through the eyes and voices of students and provide teachers face-to-face feedback that has the potential to change practice in an area that teachers themselves specify prior to the observation.

Before use, the tools require training with video and a practice session that employs an appropriate DL content tool. Teacher and administrator observers practice and receive feedback on the quality of their descriptive statements and questions related to the observed lesson. When a judgmental, summative evaluative statement is made, such as, "The teacher's main discussion question was excellent," the facilitator guides the participant to revisit the question to note what was judgmental about it. Then he or she asks the participant to rephrase the observation as a descriptive statement, such as, "Two-thirds of the students talked to each other about the question, 'Who is a friend to Victor?' during the large group discussion. Most offered different answers using text-based reasons."

The following provides an example of how one teacher used DL tools and routines to further her understanding of DL practice. Ms. Thompson, whose science class and lesson were described in Chapter Five, has been engaged in studying DL science for two years and is exploring implementation of DL more deeply in her classroom. Her district has made a commitment to school-based PLCs, allowing her time to meet with colleagues to reflect on their practices. The

PLC group has been engaged in studying DL science practices at the district level through large group professional development and has been building on those experiences through their small group study.

After a semester of monthly two-hour PLC meetings, Ms. Thompson takes the next step of inviting science colleagues into her classroom in order to prompt reflection on her teaching and theirs through a DL science observation. She is working to have students develop evidence-based scientific explanations and asks the group to focus their observations around the probing questions she will use to guide students toward improving their explanations. Specifically, she asks them, "How well do my questions increase students' ownership of their explanations? How well do my questions facilitate students' ability to cognitively wrestle with their explanations?" While Ms. Thompson is the primary person taking a reflective stance on her practice, the group is also invited to reflect on their common learning and teaching. This shifts the responsibility and intellectual resources from an isolated teacher to a community of learners. After the experience, a teacher described her vision of the observation through a sports metaphor: "When you are on a basketball team, you may focus on a specific skill such as lay-ups. You ask your teammates to watch you do lay-ups to help you do them better. As they are watching and giving you feedback, they also get better at their lay-ups. The same thing happens when you invite a team into your classroom to do a DL observation. Your teammates help you improve on a teaching area, and in the process they learn about their practices too."

In the following excerpt, a principal reflects on how the observation protocol increased ownership of instructional improvement from only school principals to teachers and principals:

> The DL observation protocol made those visits safe and gave them a structure. Having teachers visit one another meant that no longer was just the administrative team walking through classrooms or observing a lesson, but teachers were as well. That did two things: I stopped (or my assistant principals stopped) being the only brokers of information. I began hearing follow-up conversations in the teachers' workroom or in the hallway, "How did you do that?" "I tweaked my lesson or I rewrote or I thought about it in a different way." So it spawned teacher-to-teacher dialogue about instruction in ways that nothing else we had tried had done.

The second thing it did was the de-privatization of instruction. We couldn't hide behind myths that that is a good teacher or that's just my opinion. As they incorporated the DL model of why that was good instruction, it brought the principles of learning to life for them. They began talking about why they made instructional decisions based on research and best practice. It allowed someone like Christine [a teacher leader and department chair] to come to me and say, "It's no longer okay for my colleague across the hall to teach the way she has been teaching."

"Well, that's true. What do you want me to do?"

She responded, "I am going to practice what I'm going to say with you—but I don't want you to say it."

That was a huge shift from someone saying, "It's the administrator's job to tackle instructional issues." While there is still a role for a principal in the process, teacher leaders are willing to have those difficult conversations with their colleagues.

In this school, the core content teams organized their own schedules of observations so each teacher was observed once by departmental colleagues and observed other teachers twice each semester. Each observation followed the protocol of a previsit meeting where the teacher described what he or she would be implementing from the DL tools and routines, stated goals of the lesson, and provided a focus question to observers. Following the observation, there was a postlesson discussion for all participants facilitated by the content's teacher leader.

Figure 7.3 shows the relationship of the tools to one another. This is not a one-way road map. The tools are used within patterned structures of participation that may begin with one sequence but can change later as participants gain understanding and ownership of the tools and processes and are better able to self-direct their learning. The broadest-patterned structure includes the cycle of study-apply-reflect-and-assess that moves the use of tools from sessions to smaller PLCs to classrooms and then back into the sessions or PLCs.

By the final level, teachers use a protocol to study student work samples, comparing the level of performance to district or state standards and the assignment's written expectations. At first, teachers use student work samples provided by the expert external facilitator. By the second round, teachers analyze their own or colleagues' student work samples and assignments.

DEVELOPING AND PROVIDING PROFESSIONAL LEARNING

Sustained professional development is a complicated matter that involves nested communities of learners in a district, as well as various kinds and levels of support for teachers, administrators, and central office staff. At the heart of professional development, adults become learners who experience disciplinary literacy lessons and modules, or mini-units, and engage in the kinds of learning they will bring to their students. A key part of this process asks learners to step back from their engagement to reflect on their learning. Here, a district leader reflects on the impact of his district's DL professional learning:

> I believe in the opportunity for teachers to come together to talk about their content and the pedagogy. The professional development in our district has become better. Especially in our DL schools, it is truly centered on their content, and the pedagogy and the ongoing assessment is part of that also. For example, teachers thinking constantly about, "What question can I ask or how can I redirect the thinking so that they better understand the concept?" ... It is great work, but we look forward to DL becoming almost second nature to our district so that it is something naturally ingrained into our professional development and in all of our conversations."

District and school leaders must value sustained and robust opportunities to study and practice full, extended examples of teaching and learning that they can emulate, replicate, examine, modify, and transfer to curriculum and instruction (Talbert & David, 2007; Talbert et al., 2008; David & Green, 2007a & b). These conclusions about leaders' perspectives align with the findings of larger-scale professional development studies and policy papers (Coburn & Russell, 2008; Correnti, 2008; Penuel, Fishman, Yamaguchi, & Gallaher, 2007). That is, teachers are influenced to change instructional practice by working with fully developed lessons and tools situated within curricula and courses, not generic strategies and methods that are presented in decontextualized ways.

Cognitive Apprenticeship

DL professional learning builds from a model of cognitive apprenticeship. "Cognitive apprenticeship," write Collins, Brown, and Newman (1989), "is an instructional method for teaching an acceptable way of understanding and doing tasks, solving problems, and dealing with problematic situations" (p. 69). The structures, routines, and use of tool-mediated actions fostered in each of the academic areas form the basis of this practice-based means of professional development: "The key to cognitive apprenticeship is that models [teachers] demonstrate and explain how they deal with ill-defined, complex, and risky problems and give the learners an opportunity to approximate this behavior under risk-controlled conditions" (Brandt, Farmer, & Buckmaster, 1993, p. 75).

Learning as Apprenticeship for Students

As part of adult learners' first year in the DL project, they study the principles of learning, in particular, learning as apprenticeship (Resnick, Hall, & IFL Fellows, 2003). The following text describes features of learning as apprenticeship for students:

> *Modeling and observation.* Apprentices spend a significant amount of time observing masters or more advanced apprentices at work. From this observation, mediated by conversations in which critical features of the work or product are pointed out and processes are analyzed, they learn to discriminate good from poor practice, and acceptable from unacceptable outcomes.
>
> *Active practice.* This is the heart of apprenticeship, where most learning comes from actually working at a task or project, rather than learning from a removed position about how it is done. As apprentices to teachers, visiting experts, and sometimes their more advanced peers, students practice learning by developing products and performances under controlled conditions in and beyond the classroom.
>
> *Scaffolding.* Apprenticeship learning models do not require that beginners do the entire job that they are learning by themselves. Instead, products are created jointly, apprentices doing the part they can, masters or more advanced apprentices doing the more demanding parts. The more experienced person, in other words, provides a form of scaffolding for the work of the beginner. As student apprentices begin to develop competence in a content area—and the self-management skills that develop alongside expertise—teachers gradually reduce the amount of supportive scaffolding they provide and students must make more and more decisions for themselves.

Coaching. Successful apprenticeship also depends on the availability of a coach—a supportive expert who observes and comments on the apprentice's efforts, who challenges and suggests modified ways of working. Student apprentices are coached by their teachers, more advanced peers, and visiting experts.

Guided reflection. Successful learning, like successful teaching and other professional practice, must be a reflective process, one in which individuals are continually considering, evaluating, and improving on their own work. This reflective capacity and disposition needs to be cultivated during the apprenticeship period. It is not just a matter of time for reflection—although that is crucial—but also the opportunity to engage in a reflective process with a community of others. [pp. 26–30]

Learning as Apprenticeship for Educators

This section discusses the features of learning as apprenticeship for adult learners.

Modeling and Observation   In modeling and observation, the professional developer enacts the full activity so that learners as observers can develop a mental model or picture of what to do. In DL professional learning, there are two levels to the modeling. First, the teacher as model is enacting an aspect of the lesson for adult learners and then stepping back to guide discussion of the instruction. So there could be thinking aloud to reveal tricks of the trade for learners and then thinking aloud to reveal tricks of the trade instructionally.

It is critical during professional learning to discuss with educators if, when, for whom, and how much of a model is needed. In DL mathematics, for example, a misplaced model lowers the task's cognitive challenge by eliminating the critical thinking of mathematical activity learners need to do to approximate ways of thinking and working as mathematicians. Modeling is helpful to assist and advance learning when it is placed in the sequence of the lesson at the time and to the degree that learners need it to advance their understanding (Brandt et al., 1993). The inverse is also true. Modeling stops engagement in grappling with a problem if it takes away the challenge of meaning making necessary to construct knowledge. The math content chapter, for example, begins with a non-DL classroom example of procedures for solving a math problem being copied onto the chalkboard as modeled solutions. These models reduced learners to copying solutions.

One challenge to using modeling examples is assessing the level of complexity needed for adult learners to be genuinely engaged in learning anew, knowing that the same model needs to be relevant to their secondary students not yet expert in the content area under study. However, it is worth taking on the challenge since working in these lesson-specific ways makes it more likely that teachers' approximations will be successful later in their classrooms (Brandt et al., 1993; David & Greene, 2007b).

Active Practice   As Resnick et al. (2003) noted in the description of learning as apprenticeship, active practice "is the heart of apprenticeship." One of the challenges in professional learning is reserving time for teachers and teacher leaders to practice as part of sessions so that the DL facilitator can be part of the necessary feedback loop. In DL, learning problems from the disciplines and the pedagogical scaffolding that adult learners use during practice are designed to mirror the kinds of assistance that practitioners of the discipline would be able to access from experienced and capable people working in that discipline. The scaffolding assists learners in procedural knowledge, that is, how to do something. Procedural knowledge is equivalent to DL's application of habits of thinking. Learners are guided to use the habits of thinking that they think will help them reach deeper and better conceptual understanding of the declarative or content-learning problems under study. The scaffolding includes structures and procedures and the interactional unfolding of learning activities (Bruner, 1977; Smagorinsky, 2008). The structure and the interactions are designed to assist learners' growing understanding of core concepts and development of habits of thinking, including skills of the discipline. As learners progress, the scaffolding (that is, the structures and interactional unfolding) is gradually removed to encourage and allow learners to self-direct and manage their own learning.

In PLCs, teachers practice refining lesson planning guided by DL tools. For example, English studies teacher leaders facilitate examination of student texts for inclusion and sequencing in units. The tool, DL criteria of text selection, serves as a scaffold for the process. It guides the discussion to issues of text complexity and relevance and brings fresh perspective on the importance of careful sequencing of readings to set up lessons that require retrospective work of one text and across texts. Careful analysis of the lessons' texts raises expectations for the quality of the lessons and has made the standards more relevant according to several teacher leaders. They relate high school teachers' impressions: "We're always being told that the content standards are in the lessons, but now we're asking where, how?" Working from the ELA design features, which require aligning the content of overarching questions to the unit's texts and lesson tasks, helped teachers connect the learning purpose of the standards to the ideas and structures taught from the student texts. As one teacher leader stated, "What content, skills, and habits of thinking are you working on in this lesson right now? To make the academic purpose intentional and transparent is one of the purposes of DL."

Learning as apprenticeship supports differentiated instruction. Novice adult learners in the learning community, who have had little or no experience in these kinds of conversations or who may have limited pedagogical content knowledge, have the support of guided practice, a structured lesson or task, and fellow learners with whom to practice. More advanced learners have access to the total model, making it possible for them to accelerate their learning or for the teacher to guide them into more difficult aspects of the modeled performance. The natural differentiation acknowledges that most learning occurs when the teacher's role has been diminished as each learner takes charge of what he or she is making sense of or producing.

As adult learners work within DL, especially after engaging in the observational protocol with core content tools, they shift their role from that of content expert and source of all knowledge to that of colearner, resource person, and coach. Stouch draws on Merriam and Caffarella's analogy from sports: "A coach shares methods, approaches, and strategies for learning—the game plan—as well as the specific plays. While expert knowledge (the specific plays) is still of great value, the coaching is what makes it possible for learners to go out and play successfully, learning throughout their lifetimes" (cited by Stouch, 1993, p. 66). The role of teachers implementing DL lessons and using content-specific tools shifts from keeper and dispenser of knowledge to master inquirer who challenges, assists, and coaches learners.

Coaching Professional development builds learning how to learn into the sessions and school practice for teacher leaders and coaches engaged in the DL project. Given the realities of funding in districts, it is rare for middle and high schools to have full-time coaches in each of the four academic areas. Instead, districts arrange for talented teachers, some of them also department chairs, to have reduced teaching loads so that they can also work as disciplinary coaches and members of the school's guiding coalition. They become the voice of the content expert at strategic planning meetings and the trained facilitators of teacher-based PLCs and other professional learning experiences. If a department chair is not selected, it is necessary to include the department chair in the training to ensure that a key departmental and school spokesperson is fully knowledgeable about aligning established departmental policies and procedures with DL student and teacher needs.

Figure 7.4 shows the coaching structures that are part of DL systemic practice (Staub & Bickel, 2003; Bill, 2007; Staub, West, & Bickel, 2003).

Guided Reflection   During the guided reflection phase of learning as apprenticeship in DL sessions, the DL facilitator and learners discuss what has been learned, how it was learned, and when and where the learning could be used. It is also a time for the adult learners to step back from the lessons and, as

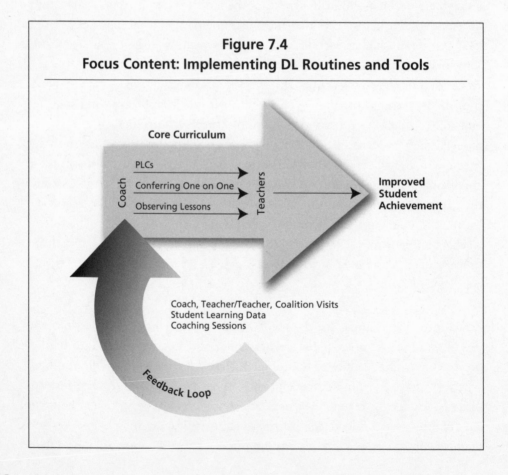

Figure 7.4
Focus Content: Implementing DL Routines and Tools

Core Curriculum

PLCs
Conferring One on One
Observing Lessons

Coach

Teachers

Improved Student Achievement

Coach, Teacher/Teacher, Coalition Visits
Student Learning Data
Coaching Sessions

Feedback Loop

teachers, consider how the learning applies to their own teaching practice. A key aspect of this reflective process is developing the disposition that teaching and learning are worth examining. Adult learners learn what to notice while developing the habit of practice of how to notice by slowing down to examine critical attributes of practice. For example, learners answered the following reflective questions after developing their first draft of an inquiry-based English studies unit:

> What did you notice when you compared the questions on the unit architecture? Which questions did you mark as ones that will maintain cognitive demand and require students to do independent thinking? Why those questions? What do you notice about the questions you did not mark? Then … what did you learn or what insights did you gain from comparing the questions? How might you use this as you continue to develop the unit? [Petrosky, McConachie, Mihalakis, 2007, p. 34].

CONCLUSION

In DL, external facilitators and instructional leaders guide teachers to reflect on their practice with a trained eye. Artifacts of practice that depict the work of teaching (such as student work samples, teacher assignments, a lesson or unit plan, or a video of an enacted lesson) are used as "sites for critique, inquiry, and investigation. Teachers have the opportunity to develop knowledge central to teaching by engaging in activities that are at the heart of a teacher's daily work" (Smith, 2001, p. 2). Teachers who integrate DL practice into their own practice become its advocates. And they take this stance because of the positive changes that they see in students and their professional community. In the words of one teacher leader:

> I think that the students in general have become part of the process. The students are involved in the talk, the rubric process, the grading process. They help with what is expected of them through developing criteria, and so I think the students have become more active in the classroom instead of being passive. The DL tools, the principles of learning, make everyone in the process more active, not only the

process but also the content. We are not just given information, but we are all part of developing understanding together.

In our PLCs, we work together to improve our practices, to make our group a stronger group. We talk together; teachers talk to each other, helping each other improve their practice, helping each other learn. If you use DL practice, the students become a group helping each other learn. They literally become a PLC. They do. They start to sound just like our group sounds when all are working together. Same thing happens with adults that happens with students—both have aha moments.

Implementing DL systemic practice involves creating a complex web of interactions with multiple role groups working together: first, in unison to build the vision and reality of a school's intellectual coherence, and then by academic area to revitalize each discipline's intellectual coherence with students.

Disciplinary Literacy Design Principles by Core Academic Area

HISTORY/SOCIAL STUDIES

1. Knowledge and thinking must go hand in hand: Students learn core concepts and habits of thinking within each discipline as defined by standards and content requirements.

What Are Students Doing as Learners?	How Are Teachers Supporting Students' Learning?
Students:	*Teachers:*
Regularly engage in historical inquiry, tackling themes, concepts, and content by reading and analyzing multiple sources, both primary and secondary.	Select texts and documents that will engage students in genuine historical analysis and interpretation.
Learn and use skills of historical analysis supported by evidence through reasoning, writing, and talk.	Weave specific ways of working through each unit of study such as use of evidence to support reasoning, analysis, and synthesis of multiple sources.
Engage in understanding historical events, people, systems, and movements as historical phenomena situated in specific time and place.	Coach students to use these habits with increasing complexity and ability over time.

2. Learning is apprenticeship: Learning activities, curricula, tasks, text, and talk apprentice students within the discipline.

What Are Students Doing as Learners?	How Are Teachers Supporting Students' Learning?
Students:	*Teachers:*
Share their interpretations of historical documents and events and challenge others' interpretations by making use of evidence and asking questions to ensure their own understanding.	Guide students through analysis and interpretation, providing opportunities for ongoing, authentic historical inquiry through reading, talk, formal. and informal writing.
Learn by "doing" history through engagement in ongoing, authentic historical inquiries.	Select materials and plan tasks and discussions to support student learning of concepts, processes, and habits of thinking specified by learning standards in history and current historical scholarship.
	Design opportunities for students to discuss, elaborate, and build on each other's ideas.

3. Teachers as mentors of apprentices: Teachers apprentice students by giving them opportunities to engage in rigorous disciplinary literacy activity and providing scaffolding through inquiry, direct instruction, models, and coaching.

What Are Students Doing as Learners?	How Are Teachers Supporting Students' Learning?
Students:	*Teachers:*
Work with peers and with the teacher to construct meaning of texts (written, visual, statistical), present interpretations, and defend those interpretations.	Use various instructional approaches and pedagogical scaffolds to teach historical concepts, processes, and habits of thinking.
Refine and extend their historical knowledge through ongoing study of multiple texts and revisiting guiding concepts and inquiries.	Model reading, interpretation, and analysis of multiple genres of texts, making explicit the ways of working that lead to the development of historical interpretations.

4. Classroom culture socializes intelligence: Intelligence is socialized through community, class learning culture, and instructional routines.

What Are Students Doing as Learners?	How Are Teachers Supporting Students' Learning?
Students:	*Teachers:*
Regularly participate in debating, discussing, explaining, and analyzing historical problems and issues in pairs, small groups, and as a whole class.	Create a community within the classroom where students can safely share their emerging ideas and interpretations, build from one another's ideas, and work together to figure out historical problems and questions.
Understand and value learning from one another and from the teacher, emphasizing the importance of gathering multiple interpretations.	Enable students to safely engage with difficult text, supporting them to build from fragile understanding to robust knowledge.
	Treat all students as smart and capable learners who are expected to contribute to class work and discussion.

5. Instruction and assessment drive each other: Instruction is assessment driven, and assessment is instruction driven.

What Are Students Doing as Learners?	How Are Teachers Supporting Students' Learning?
Students:	*Teachers:*
Receive formative feedback from the teacher on their progress and process of creating historical interpretations.	Research and assess student understanding of historical content, concepts, and interpretations by analyzing students' use of inquiry strategies, reading, writing, and reasoning strategies.
Reflect on what they have learned (content) and how they have learned (habits of thinking) and how their thinking on both have changed.	Use multiple forms of formal, informal, and formative assessment data to guide instruction.

MATHEMATICS

1. Knowledge and thinking must go hand in hand: Students learn core concepts and habits of thinking within each discipline as defined by standards and content requirements.

What Are Students Doing as Learners?	How Are Teachers Supporting Students Learning?
Students:	*Teachers:*
Regularly engage in solving cognitively challenging mathematical tasks that require them to think and reason about key mathematical concepts or strategies for solving problems.	Establish a routine by which students work with others to explore mathematical ideas, make and test conjectures, and provide justifications to support their claims.
Apply and adapt a range of problem-solving strategies (for example, looking for patterns, working backward, guessing and checking, solving a simpler problem, trying a special case).	Press students to both talk and listen— note connections between new and previously understood concepts, suggest ways of representing those concepts, share their understanding of mathematical concepts.
Create and test mathematical conjectures and form generalizations that allow them to build and connect mathematical concepts and make sense of mathematical procedures.	Coach students to use a range of tools for making sense of mathematics, including language and materials (for example, manipulatives, calculators and different representations).

2. Learning is apprenticeship: Learning activities, curricula, tasks, text, and talk apprentice students within the discipline.

What Are Students Doing as Learners?	How Are Teachers Supporting Students Learning?
Students:	*Teachers:*
Engage in a series of related tasks using different strategies and representations and examine the mathematical content illuminated by each with the goal of deepening their understanding of key mathematical ideas.	Select and sequence a set of related tasks focused on the same mathematical ideas, and reflect on the connections between them and the use of one problem to solve another problem.
Engage in learning activities that allow them to deepen their own understanding by discussing their thinking with others, making sense of problem-solving methods, and posing and responding to questions and challenges.	Encourage students to use and make connections between multiple representations (pictures, written symbols, oral language, real-world situations, manipulative models) with the goal of explicitly writing and talking about the meaning of mathematical concepts.
	Promote writing to learn by establishing norms, assisting learners to note their problem-solving pathways and to track their learning, and establishing metacognitive reflection and articulation as a regular pattern in learning.

3. Teachers as mentors of apprentices: Teachers apprentice students by giving them opportunities to engage in rigorous disciplinary literacy activity and providing scaffolding through inquiry, direct instruction, models, and coaching.

What Are Students Doing as Learners?	How Are Teachers Supporting Students Learning?
Students:	*Teachers:*
Work with peers to analyze a task and figure out what the task is asking them to do and the approach that is best to use.	Consistently model the problem-solving process, using reflective prompts as a means of guiding the problem-solving process.
Reference and explore the use of different problem-solving strategies and representations, and discuss the differences.	Reflect aloud for students on the relationship among tasks, consider how the tasks are similar and how they are different, and ask students how they might use what they have learned from solving one problem to solve another problem.
Note patterns and relationships, make conjectures, and discuss ways of proving conjectures.	Model for students writing and reflecting on the problem-solving process, mathematical understanding, and errors.

4. Classroom culture socializes intelligence: Intelligence is socialized through community, class learning culture, and instructional routines.

What Are Students Doing as Learners?	How Are Teachers Supporting Students Learning?
Students:	*Teachers:*
Know that they are responsible for justifying and proving their claims.	Create a respectful community within the classroom where students are active participants in creating, sharing, discussing, debating, and analyzing their solutions to mathematical tasks.
Understand that they have the right and responsibility to ask questions and seek resources to advance their learning or to gain additional clarification.	Provide time, and encourage students to reflect on why one method is more efficient than another to form mathematical conjectures and generalizations and to provide justifications for their claims.
Know that they are responsible for helping others understand their thinking and for understanding the thinking of their peers.	

5. Instruction and assessment drive each other: Instruction is assessment driven, and assessment is instruction driven.

What Are Students Doing as Learners?	How Are Teachers Supporting Students Learning?
Students:	*Teachers:*
Keep track of their understanding of mathematical ideas and problem-solving strategies, what misconceptions they have resolved, and what ideas and processes they are still unclear about.	Regularly assess students' understanding of mathematical concepts, problem-solving strategies, and skills as they engage in tasks.
Note connections that they have made between strategies and concepts.	Provide feedback to students by asking questions that prompt students to consider or construct different problem-solving strategies or to form mathematical generalizations.
Receive specific written and verbal feedback on their use of representations to develop understanding of concepts, connections between representations, written mathematical reasoning, and problem-solving processes, as well as mathematical accuracy.	Measure students' understanding of concepts and skills by how their work is advancing.
	Use multiple forms of formal, informal, and formative assessment data to guide instruction.

SCIENCE

1. Knowledge and thinking must go hand in hand: Students learn core concepts and habits of thinking within each discipline as defined by standards and content requirements.

What Are Students Doing as Learners?	How Are Teachers Supporting Students Learning?
Students:	*Teachers:*
Develop habits of thinking in science as they simultaneously learn core science content and the processes of science through inquiry-based learning experiences.	Select and enact arcs of lessons that build on students' learning from previous years and prepare students for the next-level science courses.
Develop understandings about and abilities to do science as they develop and answer scientifically oriented questions, analyze data, develop evidence-based explanations, consider possible alternate explanations, and compare their explanations with current scientific knowledge.	Use a variety of combinations of inquiry-based strategies (for example, generating scientifically oriented questions or using questions provided by others or the materials, developing evidence-based explanations from provided data sets or from data collected by students, designing and conducting experiments) that develop students' abilities to use scientific habits of thinking as they learn core science content.
Communicate and justify their explanations to others and through the process assess their own understanding and reflect on how and what they have learned.	Ensure that students both talk and listen—share their understanding about scientific concepts, note connections between new and previously understood concepts, suggest ways of representing those concepts, discuss methods for investigating problems, respond to questions posed by their peers, make sense of other students' explanations, and ask questions of others to ensure their own understanding.

2. Learning is apprenticeship: Learning activities, curricula, tasks, text, and talk apprentice students within the discipline.

What Are Students Doing as Learners?	How Are Teachers Supporting Students Learning?
Students:	*Teachers:*
Engage in learning activities that allow, encourage, and support them to cognitively wrestle with authentic scientific tasks (for example, studying and reporting findings on a lake system, collecting and analyzing data on projectiles) while using and making sense of foundational concepts in science (for example, living systems interact with their environment and are interdependent with other systems).	Guide and facilitate the learning of science content through an inquiry-based approach that allows students to engage in the practices of science; in other words, do not take away students' opportunity to cognitively wrestle with foundational concepts and science processes.
Have regular opportunities to demonstrate their competency in scientific reasoning and practices (for example, safe and effective use of laboratory equipment, ability to generate a scientifically oriented question) and understandings of science content through development and enactment of authentic science products and performances.	Provide multiple opportunities to demonstrate competency through various authentic science products and performances, including, but not limited to, written scientific explanations, science notebooks, class discussions, and conducting experiments.
Reflect on and communicate their thinking about what they are doing in science, and communicate about it to others while holding each other accountable to the evidence and pushing for sound reasoning, thus emulating the practice of the scientific community.	Guide students to use evidence-based explanations as a means of refining and communicating their understanding and to push the thinking of their peers.

3. Teachers as mentors of apprentices: Teachers apprentice students by giving them opportunities to engage in rigorous disciplinary literacy activity and providing scaffolding through inquiry, direct instruction, models, and coaching.

What Are Students Doing as Learners?	How Are Teachers Supporting Students Learning?
Students:	*Teachers:*
Engage in the work of science at the hand of the teacher as a master scientist and mentor, reflecting on the teacher's practices as a model learner of science—shifting the role of teacher as source of information to that of mentor.	Guide and facilitate learning as a mentor, and make instructional plans to allow students to work as apprentices, serving as models rather than as sources of information.
Are supported with a variety of strategies and tools (for example, Accountable Talk, evidence-based explanation tool) to scaffold student learning as they move from apprentice toward master (as defined by the standards).	Encourage students to cognitively struggle (do the thinking) with science, requiring students to analyze data, draw conclusions from the data, develop evidence-based explanations, consider alternate explanations, and communicate and justify those explanations.
Work with peers and the teacher to advance their understandings of science and abilities to perform scientific process and skills (that is, scientific inquiry).	Challenge students to accept and share responsibility for their own learning to move along the path from apprentice to mastery (that is, being scientifically literate adults).

4. Classroom culture socializes intelligence: Intelligence is socialized through community, class learning culture, and instructional routines.

What Are Students Doing as Learners?	How Are Teachers Supporting Students Learning?
Students:	*Teachers:*
Function as a scientific community: striving to understand and address scientifically oriented questions, considering data and scientific ideas to develop evidence-based explanations, struggling with possible alternate explanations as they elicit scientific reasoning from all members of the community (all students).	Design and manage a safe (physically and emotionally) learning environment that provides students with time and resources necessary for learning science, recognizing and responding to student diversity, and encouraging all students to participate fully in learning science
Not only communicate their explanations, but provide feedback to each other as they revise their explanations to refine their own understandings of the content and develop common understandings in the class.	Provide differentiation through scaffolding techniques (amount of support provided to the student) rather than in reducing the cognitive demand of the task (the scaffolding allows students to struggle with the content and skills but supports them to achieve mastery, eventually without the scaffolds).
Are helped to respect and work to understand varying cultural perspectives and multiple approaches, including that they understand and value writing and talking with others about scientific questions and their explanations.	Encourage all students to take responsibility for the learning of all members of the community; nurture collaboration among students; structure and facilitate ongoing formal and informal discussion based on a shared understanding of rules of scientific discourse (demand respect for diverse ideas, skills, and experiences of all students).

5. Instruction and assessment drive each other: Instruction is assessment driven, and assessment is instruction driven.

What Are Students Doing as Learners?	How Are Teachers Supporting Students Learning?
Students:	*Teachers:*
Produce a set of quality work products (for example, lab reports, written explanations, visual and oral representations) through which they can articulate their understanding of scientific ideas and processes.	Provide students with clear expectations and use multiple and ongoing methods to systematically gather data about student understanding and ability (for example, observe student performance using lab equipment, evaluate student written explanations, review lab notebooks, process quizzes, monitor class discussions), and use these data to provide specific written and verbal feedback and allow opportunities for self and peer assessment to ensure that students acquire concepts and skills.
Have multiple opportunities to demonstrate their understandings and competencies and are assessed on what they have the opportunity to learn.	Use student assessment data, observations of teaching, and interactions with colleagues to reflect on student achievement in light of instructional practices to improve teaching and learning.
Are able to assess their own learning and the learning of their peers along with the teacher, based on clearly articulated expectations and learning goals.	Modify the lesson or arc, in activities, pace, or depth, based on assessment of student understanding and performance, such that all students have multiple opportunities (for example, revision of drafts) to achieve the learning goals or more deeply develop their understanding.

ENGLISH LANGUAGE ARTS

1. Knowledge and thinking must go hand in hand: Students learn core concepts and habits of thinking within each discipline as defined by standards and content requirements.

What Are Students Doing as Learners?	How Are Teachers Supporting Students Learning?
Students:	*Teachers:*
Engage in literary inquiry, developing oral and written interpretations and arguments related to a unit's texts, nominal themes, and overarching questions.	Develop and use nominal themes, culminating projects, and overarching questions to drive a unit's intellectual work that derive from the ideas in texts, learners, and identified content and habits of thinking.
Learn about and use different lenses for responding to text (cultural, historical, literary elements, gender, reader response).	Develop and use sequenced arcs of lessons that guide students to progress from reading comprehension to critical thinking in reading, writing, and talking.
Learn and use methods (for fiction, nonfiction, poetry, and exposition) that other authors use to gather, organize, and present their sources and arguments.	Engage students in inquiry work that prompts them to revise their understandings of key concepts at various moments in units.

2. Learning is apprenticeship: Learning activities, curricula, tasks, text, and talk apprentice students within the discipline.

What Are Students Doing as Learners?	How Are Teachers Supporting Students Learning?
Students:	*Teachers:*
Use pedagogical routines, such as quick writes, pair and trio work, second and third readings, identifying and explaining difficult and significant moments in texts, writing about and writing like texts, and shared inquiry discussions to learn more about the content, ideas, and structures of texts with increasing complexity and ability over time.	Coach and guide students to use the pedagogical rituals and routines to read, write about, and create complex texts.
Talk and listen. They share their responses to texts, share their methods for comprehending and interpreting texts, respond to peers' comments and questions, make sense of others' interpretations, and ask questions of others to ensure their own understanding.	Coach and guide students to problem-solve collaboratively, promote writing to learn, assist learners to make thinking visible, provide routines for note taking and tracking learning, establish norms for discussion and writing, and establish metacognitive reflection and articulation as regular patterns in learning.
Work from writing assignments that apprentice them to the intellectual work of literacy projects that regularly engage readers and writers outside of school.	Guide students to engage in discussions through the use of genuine inquiries about complex texts, follow-up questions, requests for clarification and elaboration, and assisting connection making between stated ideas and ideas in texts, and bringing students back to the guiding questions.

3. Teachers as mentors of apprentices: Teachers apprentice students by giving them opportunities to engage in rigorous disciplinary literacy activity and providing scaffolding through inquiry, direct instruction, models, and coaching.

What Are Students Doing as Learners?	How Are Teachers Supporting Students Learning?
Students:	*Teachers:*
Read, write about, and compose texts similar to a unit's core text or with texts they select.	Model, as necessary, aspects of reading and writing such as comprehension of the text, drawing inferences, and identifying and examining structural elements of a genre or author's arguments and methods so that students can read and write in that genre.
As necessary, use models and other support from peers and teacher to learn from others' reading and writing.	Assist students' awareness of the writing or reading difficulties and problems they are encountering and how they are resolving them.
Select and use the appropriate tools, learning techniques, and approaches to comprehend, interpret, and write with increasing independence, accuracy, and proficiency.	Use and model a repertoire of tools, resources, techniques, strategies, and skills to assist students to take on more responsibility for their learning and to become more expert readers and writers.

4. Classroom culture socializes intelligence: Intelligence is socialized through community, class learning culture, and instructional routines.

What Are Students Doing as Learners?	How Are Teachers Supporting Students Learning?
Students:	*Teachers:*
Are part of inquiry discussions where the emphasis is on the students' interpretations and socialization into the intellectual routines of the discussion. Part of the socialization is to value and understand that the written record of their reading and writing can help them in talking with others and in developing their own thinking and future writing.	Create a community where students are central participants in creating, sharing, and discussing complex and relevant ideas about literature, language, and their lives.
	Set up a print-rich environment, displays of student work, and provide examples of literacy in school and out.
Know that they have the right and responsibility to ask questions, justify their own responses with evidence from texts, and challenge other's ideas as well as the teacher's ideas.	Create a safe, engaging, and productive work environment, including arranging the student working groups, tables, and desks for discussion.
	Group students in pairs or trios so that novice English learners can work with more fluent English speakers.

5. Instruction and assessment drive each other: Instruction is assessment driven, and assessment is instruction driven.

What Are Students Doing as Learners?	How Are Teachers Supporting Students Learning?
Students:	*Teachers:*
Create quality work products and receive specific feedback on their progress in reading and interpreting texts and on their written work during conferring times with their teacher and peers.	Develop quality writing assignments with clear goals.
Revisit and rework texts, others' and their own, from retrospective questions and assignments.	Regularly confer with students to assist and advance their learning by giving specific, constructive feedback on their written work and initial and revisited comprehension, interpretation, and analysis of texts.
Track their learning, and reflect on what they are learning and how they learned it; use these self-assessments and reflections to adjust their learning goals.	Assess feedback by how it assists students' participation and performance.
	Use informal and formal assessments to plan, guide, monitor, and change instruction.

Disciplinary Literacy Observation Protocol

OVERVIEW

The purpose of a DL observation protocol is to provide a structure to conduct productive observations that advance DL practices in the district. The protocol is used in conjunction with a variety of DL tools that provide foci through which to observe classroom instruction.

The reasons for conducting a DL observation include providing a focus for reflecting on a teacher's practice, creating a common vision of high-quality instruction, and opening up practice to both honor teacher work and to establish accountability for the effectiveness of teacher professional development.

A DL observation differs from The Learning Walk protocol, which might have a broader focus than a DL observation, including emphases other than DL; however, both protocols include the process of making noticings and wonderings.

In support of these purposes, a DL observation has the following features:

- It is grounded in a commitment to an effort-based concept of intelligence and education.

- It uses the lens of the disciplinary literacy design principles (which are grounded in the Principles of Learning) and other content-specific tools.

- It is focused on student learning as much as on teaching.

- It is always part of a recursive professional development cycle.

- It is evidence based rather than judgmental.

- It may last for up to the entire class period.

PREPARING FOR THE OBSERVATION

An observation is best situated in the context of ongoing professional development. So when setting up observations, consider the following questions: What has been the focus of professional development, and, as a result, what should we be looking for in the classroom(s)? How might we explore aspects of this professional development through classroom observations? Which tools will serve as our focus as we study practices?

Prior to the day of the observation, distribute the following to all participants:

- The focus for the observation and the tool
- Pertinent lesson details called for by the tool and focus question
- Reminder of expectations (for example, reading the materials in advance, reviewing relevant materials, and responding to task questions)
- If visiting multiple classrooms, provide information about any coplanning that occurred around the common lesson or how the classes connect, or on what patterns we should focus our attention
- Details about time and location

CONDUCTING THE OBSERVATION

Stage 1: Preobservation Meeting

The participants meet prior to the observation. The discussion of the preobservation might include the teacher(s) responding to the following:

- What are the learning goals for the lesson?
- Where is this lesson situated within the arc of lessons?
- What is your focus question, and how is the focus question related to the content tool?
- What might we see and hear from students during the lesson related to the focus question?

Stage 2: Classroom Observation

Participants then move into the classroom for observation, trying to be as unobtrusive as possible. Participants observe and take notes to be prepared to share evidence-based observations and wonderings related to the identified focus and lens.

Stage 3: Postobservation Feedback Meeting

Participants organize their notes to make decisions about the most pertinent noticings and wonderings related to the focus question. They reconvene for a discussion, making sure all noticings and wonderings are evidence based and relate to the focus and lens. Teacher may choose to respond to feedback and ask questions.

REFLECTING ON THE PROCESS AND NEXT STEPS

Stepping back, participants reflect on this situation and consider how they can use what they learned to inform their own practice. The group considers potential next steps to advance their professional learning. Some questions to consider as part of this reflection are:

- What was your biggest insight today? What new ideas or practices did you learn today? Why were they significant?

- What thoughts do you have about your past practice based on today's new learning? What do you want to do differently in the future?

- What do you want to learn more about in order to implement the learning back in your school?

- How would you like to continue your learning? Where should the group learning go next?

- What questions, comments, or suggestions do you have?

Selected Disciplinary Literacy Tools

Foundational Tools	Purpose
Professional learning communities (PLCs) handbook	Defines professional learning communities conceptually and provides guidelines for PLCs. Includes tools to support instructional goals and cycles of study, application, reflection, and assessment
Principles of learning (POLs)	Research-based framework of practices that invite effort and support rigor for all students
POL of Accountable Talk moves and functions	States teacher moves for student talk to improve learning with function of each move and examples by academic area
Teaching and learning on the diagonal	Calls for teaching and learning "on the diagonal": using content-specific habits of thinking to develop understanding of the conceptual content of each discipline
DL design principles	Describe critical aspects of instruction, including knowledge domains, applying critical thinking to specific discipline problems, learning and teaching as apprenticeship, effort-based environments to socialize intelligence, and the integral nature of assessment to instruction

Continued

Foundational Tools	Purpose
DL observation protocol with appropriate content tool	The protocol guides how to observe a lesson and how to be observed teaching a lesson; the content tool grounds the observation in specifics of the tasks, text, and talk of the academic area being observed
Institute for Learning action protocol for studying student work samples	Focuses study of student work samples on how well the work meets standards or an assignment's written expectations

Content-Specific Tools	Purpose of Tool
English language arts (ELA)	
DL design principles in ELA	Identify quality instruction in English language arts
Pedagogical rituals and routines	Patterned actions used with authentic tasks and texts through collaboration, coaching, the sharing of solutions, multiple occasions for practice, and the articulation of reflections
ELA lesson/unit design features (Petrosky, 2006)	Organize and drive the intellectual work of lessons and the unit
Unit architecture	Graphic outline of a curricular structure that enables the development of coherent lessons and units built around interrelated sequences of texts and tasks
Criteria of text selection	Means of assessing student texts for instructional, cultural, social, and intellectual relevance and rigor
Thinking through an arc of lessons	Assists in planning and analyzing lessons

Content-Specific Tools	Purpose of Tool
Mathematics	
DL design principles in mathematics	Identify quality instruction in mathematics
The mathematics tasks framework (Stein & Smith, 1998)	Identifies the three implementation phases of high-level tasks
The math task analysis guide (Stein, Smith, Henningsen, Silver, 2000)	Characteristics of low- and high-level tasks that are used as the basis of selecting or analyzing tasks (Stein et al., 2000)
Factors associated with maintenance and decline of high-level demands (Stein & Smith, 1998)	Factors in lessons that contribute to the decline or maintenance of cognitive demand of high-level tasks during instruction (Stein & Smith, 1998)
Thinking through a lesson protocol (Smith, Bill, & Hughes, 2008)	Assists in planning and analyzing lessons (Smith et al., 1998)
Science	
DL design principles in science	Identify quality instruction in science
Five essential features of inquiry	Delineate how to use inquiry in science in appropriate and sophisticated ways
Writing evidence-based explanations	Illustrates how to write scientific explanations from claims and evidence
Thinking through a lesson protocol	Assists in planning and analyzing lessons
Conceptual navigation chart and graphic organizer	Allows analysis of conceptual cohesiveness in curricula
Planning and facilitating high-quality professional development	Guide the planning and facilitation of high-quality professional development for professional development providers within the district

Continued

Content-Specific Tools	Purpose of Tool
Social studies/history	
DL design principles in social studies/history	Identify quality instruction in social studies/history
Analyzing the architecture of a lesson	Supports analyses of instructional and conceptual design of lessons
Unit planning guide	Supports development of inquiry-driven units in social studies/history
Thinking through a unit of instruction	Assists in planning and analyzing lessons
Planning and facilitating high-quality professional development	Guides planning and facilitation of high-quality professional development
Defining rigor in history/social studies	Uses national standards to define and enact rigor in history/social studies lessons and units

REFERENCES

Chapter One

Biancarosa, C., & Snow, C. E. (2006). *Reading next—A vision for action and research in middle and high school literacy: A report to Carnegie Corporation of New York* (2nd ed.). Washington, DC: Alliance for Excellent Education.

Brown, J. S., Collins, A., & Duguid, P. (1989). Situated cognition and the culture of learning. *Educational Researcher, 18*(1), 32–41.

Coburn, C. E. (2003). Rethinking scale: Moving beyond numbers to deep and lasting change. *Educational Researcher, 32*(6), 3–12.

David, J. L., & Greene, D. (2007, October). *Improving English language arts instruction in Los Angeles High Schools: An evaluation of the Institute for Learning-LAUSD ELA Pilot Program.* Palo Alto, CA: Bay Area Research Group.

David, J. L., & Greene, D. (2008, February). *Improving mathematics instruction in Los Angeles High Schools: Follow up to the evaluation of the PRISMA Pilot Program.* Palo Alto, CA: Bay Area Research Group.

Deshler, D., Palinscar, A., Biancarosa, G., & Nair, M. (2007). *Informed choices for struggling adolescent readers.* Newark, DE: International Reading Association.

Godley, A. J., Carpenter, B. D., & Werner, C. A. (2007). "I'll speak in proper slang": Language ideologies in a daily editing activity. *Reading Research Quarterly, 42*(1), 100–131.

Graham, S., & Perin, D. (2007). *Writing next: Effective strategies to improve writing of adolescents in middle and high schools* Washington, DC: Alliance for Excellent Education.

Grigg, W., Donahue, P., & Dion, G. (2007). *The nation's report card: 12th-grade reading and mathematics 2005* (NCES 2007–468). Washington, DC: U.S. Department of Education, National Center for Education Statistics.

Hess, F. M. (2008). *Still at risk: What students don't know, even now*. Washington, DC: Common Core

Kauffman, D., Johnson, S. M., Kardos, S. M., Liu, E., & Peske, H. G. (2002). "Lost at sea": New teachers' experiences with curriculum and assessment. *Teachers College Record, 104*(2), 273–300.

Langer, J. A. (2002). *Effective English instruction*. Urbana, IL: National Council of Teachers of English.

Lee, C. D. (2001, Spring). Is October Brown Chinese? A cultural modeling system for underachieving students. *American Educational Research Journal, 38*(1), 97–141.

Lee, C. D. (2008). The centrality of culture to the scientific study of learning and development: How an ecological framework in education research facilitates civic responsibility. *Educational Researcher, 37*(5), 267–279.

Leinhardt, G. (1992, April). What research on learning tells us about teaching. *Educational Leadership, 49*(7), 20–25.

McConachie, S., Hall, M. W., Resnick, L. B., Ravi, A. K., Bill, V. L., Bintz, J., et al. (2006). Task, text, and talk: Literacy for all subjects. *Educational Leadership, 64*(2), 8–14.

McConachie, S., Resnick, L. B., & Hall, M. W. (2003). *The case for disciplinary literacy*. Unpublished manuscript, University of Pittsburgh, Institute for Learning, Learning Research and Development Center.

Moje, E. B., Overby, M., Tysvaer, N., & Morris, K. (2008). The complex world of adolescent literacy: Myths, motivations, and mysteries. *Harvard Educational Review, 78*(1), 1–44.

Mullis, I.V.S., Martin, M. O., Gonzalez, E. J., & Chrostowski, S. J. (2004). *Findings from IEA's Trends in International Mathematics and Science Study at the fourth and eighth grades*. Chestnut Hill, MA: TIMSS and PIRLS International Study Center, Boston College.

National Center on Education and the Economy. (2007). *Tough choices or tough times: The report of the New Commission on the Skills of the American Workforce*. Washington, DC: Author.

National Council of Teachers of Mathematics. (2000). *Curriculum and evaluation standards for school mathematics*. Reston, VA: Author.

National Research Council. (1996). *National science education standards*. Washington, DC: National Academy Press.

National Research Council. (2000). *Inquiry and the national science education standards*. Washington, DC: National Academy Press.

O'Brien, D., Stewart, R. A., & Moje, E. B. (1995). Why content literacy is difficult to infuse into the secondary school: Complexities of curriculum, pedagogy, and school culture. *Reading Research Quarterly, 30*(3), 442–463.

Perle, M., Grigg, W., & Donahue, P. (2005). *The nation's report card: Reading 2005* Washington, DC: U.S. Department of Education, National Center for Education Statistics.

Petrosky, A. R. (2006). Inquiry teaching and learning in an environment shaped by behavioral standards and high stake testing. In W. Sawyer & B. Doecke (Eds.), *Only connect: English teaching and democracy*. Kent Town, South Australia: Wakefield Press.

Schleppegrell, M. J. (2004). *The language of schooling: A functional linguistic perspective*. Mahwah, NJ: Erlbaum.

Shanahan, T., & Shanahan, C. (2008) Teaching disciplinary literacy to adolescents: Rethinking content literacy. *Harvard Educational Review, 78*(1), 40–59.

Slavin, R. E., Cheung, A., Groff, C., & Lake, C. (2008). Effective reading programs for middle and high schools: A best-evidence synthesis. *Reading Research Quarterly, 43*(3), 290–312.

Stein, M. K., Smith, M. S., Henningsen, M. A., & Silver, E. A. (2000). *Implementing standards-based mathematics instruction: A casebook for professional development*. New York: Teachers College Press.

Talbert, J., & David, J. (2007, August) *Evaluation of Austin Independent School District disciplinary literacy professional learning communities*. Stanford, CA: Hewlett Foundation.

Talbert, J., David, J., & Lin, W. (2008, September). *Evaluation of the Disciplinary Literacy-Professional Learning Community (DL-PLC) Initiative in Austin Independent School District*. Stanford, CA: Hewlett Foundation.

Vacca, R. T., & Vacca, J. L. (1993). *Content area reading* (4th ed.) New York: Harper-Collins.

Chapter Two

Applebee, A. N., Langer, J. A., Nystrand, M., & Gamoran, A. (2003). Discussion-based approaches to developing understanding: Classroom instruction and student performance in middle and high school English. *American Educational Research Journal, 40*(3), 685–730.

Ball, C. C., Dice, L., & Bartholomae, D. (1990). Telling secrets: Student readers and disciplinary authorities. In R. Beach & S. Hynds (Eds.), *Advances in discourse processes: Developing discourse practices in adolescence and adulthood* (pp. 134–165). New York: Guilford Press.

Banks, J. A., & Members of the LIFE Diversity Consensus Panel. (2007). *Learning in and out of school in diverse environments*. Seattle: LIFE Center and the Center for Multicultural Education, University of Washington.

Biancarosa, C., & Snow, C. E. (2006). *Reading next—A vision for action and research in middle and high school literacy: A report to Carnegie Corporation of New York* (2nd ed.). Washington, DC: Alliance for Excellent Education.

Boyer, P. (1996). Cognitive constraints on cultural representations: Natural ontologies and religious ideas. In L. A. Hirschfeld & S. A. Gelman (Eds.), *Mapping the mind: Domain specificity in cognition and culture*. Cambridge: Cambridge University Press.

Bransford, J., Brown, A. L., & Cocking, R. (Eds.). (1999). *How people learn: Brain, mind, experience, and school*. Washington, DC: National Academy Press.

Collins, A., Brown, J. S. & Newman, S. E. (1989). Cognitive apprenticeship: Teaching the crafts of reading, writing, and mathematics. In L. B. Rensick (Ed.), *Knowing, learning, and instruction: Essays in honor of Robert Glaser* (pp. 453–494). Mahwah, NJ: Erlbaum.

Delpit, L. (1995). *Other people's children*. New York: New Press.

Dewey, J. (1938). *Experience in education*. Indianapolis, IN: Kappa Delta Pi Publishing.

Fillmore, L. W., & Snow, C. E. (2000). *What teachers need to know about language*. Washington, DC: U.S. Department of Education.

Geisler, C. (1994). *Academic literacy and the nature of expertise: Reading, writing, and knowing in academic philosophy*. Mahwah, NJ: Erlbaum.

Goos, M. (2004). Learning mathematics in a classroom community of inquiry. *Research in Mathematics Education, 35*(4), 258–291.

Grossman, P. L., & Stodolsky, S. S. (1995). Content as context: The role of school subjects in secondary school teaching. *Educational Researcher, 24*(8), 5–23.

Heath, S. B. (1983). *Ways with words*. Cambridge: Cambridge University Press.

Hirschfeld, L. A., & Gelman, S. A. (1994). Towards a topography of mind: An introduction to domain specificity. In L. A. Hirschfeld & S. A. Gelman (Eds.), *Mapping the mind: Domain specificity in cognition and culture*. Cambridge: Cambridge University Press.

Lave, J., & Wenger, E. (1991). *Situated learning: Legitimate peripheral participation*. Cambridge: Cambridge University Press.

Leinhardt, G. (1992, April). What research on learning tells us about teaching. *Educational Leadership, 49*(7), 20–25.

Leinhardt, G. (1993). Instructional explanations in history and mathematics. In W. Kintsch (Ed.), *Proceedings of the Fifteenth Annual Conference of the Cognitive Science Society* (pp. 5–16). Mahwah, NJ: Erlbaum.

Leinhardt, G., & Young, K. M. (1998). Writing from primary source documents: A way of knowing in history. *Written Communication, 15*(1), 25–68.

Leonardo, Z. (2004). Disciplinary knowledge and quality education [Theme issue]. *Educational Researcher, 33*(5).

Michaels, S., O'Connor, M. C., Hall, M. W., & Resnick, L. B. (2002). *Accountable Talk: Classroom conversation that works* (Version 2.1). [Online resource]. Pittsburgh, PA: University of Pittsburgh.

Moffett, J. (1987). *Teaching the universe of discourse*. Portsmouth, NH: Boynton/Cook.

Moje, E. B., Overby, M., Tysvaer, N., & Morris, K. (2008). The complex world of adolescent literacy: Myths, motivations, and mysteries. *Harvard Educational Review, 78*(1), 1–44.

Nystrand, M. (2006). Research on the role of classroom discourse as it affects reading comprehension. *Research in the Teaching of English, 40*(4), 392–412.

Petrosky, A. (2004, November 26). *Positioning teachers: The standards movement, high stakes tests and alternative inquiry-based professional development in disciplinary literacy*. Keynote address at the Australian Association of Researchers in Education Annual Meeting, Melbourne, Australia.

Petrosky, A. R. (2006). Inquiry teaching and learning in an environment shaped by behavioral standards and high stake testing. In W. Sawyer & B. Doecke (Eds.), *Only connect: English teaching and democracy*. Kent Town, South Australia: Wakefield Press.

Resnick, D. P., & Resnick, L. B. (1989). Varieties of literacy. In A. E. Barnes & P. N. Stearns (Eds.), *Social history and issues in human consciousness: Some interdisciplinary connections* (pp. 171–196). New York: New York University Press.

Resnick, L. B. (1990). Literacy in school and out. *Daedalus, 119*(2), 169–185.

Resnick, L. B., Hall, M. W., & the Fellows of the Institute for Learning. (2003). *Principles of learning: Study tools for educators* (Version 3.0). [Online resource]. Pittsburgh, PA: University of Pittsburgh.

Resnick, L. B., & Nelson-LeGall, S. (1997). Socializing intelligence. In L. Smith, J. Dockrell, & P. Tomlinson (Eds.), *Piaget, Vygotsky and beyond* (pp. 145–158). London: Routledge.

Resnick, L. B., Saljo, R., Pontecorvo, C., & Burge, B. (1997). *Discourse, tools, and reasoning: Situated cognition and technologically supported environments*. Berlin: Springer-Verlag.

Scarcella, R. (2003). *Academic English: A conceptual framework*. (Tech. Rep. 2003–1). Santa Barbara: Linguistic Minority Research Institute, University of California.

Schwab, J. J. (1978). Education and the structure of the disciplines. In I. Westbury & N. J. Wilkof (Eds.), *Science, curriculum, and liberal education: Selected essays* (pp. 229–272). Chicago: University of Chicago Press.

Shanahan, T., & Shanahan, C. (2008). Teaching disciplinary literacy to adolescents: Rethinking content literacy. *Harvard Educational Review, 78*(1), 40–59.

Short, D. J., & Fitzsimmons, S. (2007). *Double the work: Challenges and solutions to acquiring language and academic literacy for adolescent English language learners*. New York: Carnegie Corporation.

Talbert, J., & David, J. (2007). *Evaluation of Austin Independent School District disciplinary literacy professional learning communities*. Stanford, CA: Hewlett.

Tharp, R. G., & Gallimore, R. (1998). *Rousing minds to life: Teaching, learning and schooling in social context*. Cambridge: Cambridge University Press.

Willingham, D. T. (2007, Summer). Critical thinking: Why is it so hard to teach? *American Educator*, 8–19.

Wineburg, S. (1991). On the reading of historical texts: Notes on the breach between school and academy. *American Educational Research Journal, 28*, 495–519.

Chapter Three

Bain, R. B. (2000). Into the breach: Using research and theory to shape history instruction. In P. N. Stearns, P. Sexias, & S. Wineburg (Eds.), *Knowing, teaching and learning history* (pp. 331–352). New York: New York University Press.

Bodnar, J. (1985). The *transplanted: A history of immigrants in urban America*. Bloomington: Indiana University Press.

Boix-Mansilla, V. (2000). Historical understanding: Beyond the past and into the present. In P. N. Stearns, P. Sexias, & S. Wineburg (Eds.), *Knowing, teaching and learning history* (pp. 390–418). New York: New York University Press.

Couvares, F. G., Saxton, M., Grob, G. N., & Billias, G. A. (Eds.). (2000). *Interpretations of American history: Patterns and perspectives*. New York: Free Press.

Gerstle, G. (2001). *American crucible: Race and nation in the 20th century*. Princeton, NJ: Princeton University Press.

Handlin, O. (1973). *The uprooted*. Boston: Little Brown.

Holt, T. (1990). *Thinking historically: Narrative, imagination, and understanding*. New York: College Entrance Examination Board.

Leinhardt, G. (2000). Lessons on teaching and learning history from Paul's pen. In P. N. Stearns, P. Sexias, & S. Wineburg (Eds.), *Knowing, teaching and learning history* (pp. 223–245). New York: New York University Press.

Leinhardt, G., & Young, K. M. (1996). Two texts, three readers: Distance and expertise in reading history. *Cognition and Instruction, 14*(4), 441–486.

Levine, L. W. (1996). *The opening of the American mind: Canons, culture and history*. Boston: Beacon Press.

Morrison, J., & Zabusky, C .F. (Eds.). (1980). *American mosaic: The immigrant experience in the words of those who lived it*. New York: Dutton.

Payne, C. (1998). Debating the civil rights movement: The view from the trenches. In S. F. Lawson & C. Payne (Eds.), *Debating the civil rights movement, 1945–1968* (pp. 99–136, 167). Lanham, MD: Rowman & Littlefield.

Takaki, R. (1993). *A different mirror: A history of multicultural America*. New York: Little, Brown.

Wineburg, S. (1991). On the reading of historical texts: Notes on the breach between school and academy. *American Educational Research Journal, 28,* 495–519.

Wineburg, S. (1994). The cognitive representation of historical texts. In G. Leinhardt, I. L. Beck, & C. Stainton (Eds.), *Teaching and learning in history* (pp. 85–135). Mahwah, NJ: Erlbaum.

Chapter Four

American Association for the Advancement of Science. (1993). *Benchmarks on-line, 2: The nature of mathematics.* Retrieved July 1, 2009, from http://www.project2061.org/publications/bsl/online/index.php?chapter=2&txtRef=&txtURIOld=%2Fpublications%2Fbsl%2Fonline%2Fch2%2Fch2.htm#C.

Boaler, J., & Humphreys, C. (2005). Connecting mathematical ideas: Middle school video cases to support teaching and learning. *Educational Researcher, 8*(1), 32–42.

Brown, J. S., Collins, A., & Duguid, P. (1989). Situated cognition and the culture of learning. *Educational Researcher 18*(1), 32–42.

Bruner, J. (1986). *Actual minds, possible worlds.* Cambridge, MA: Harvard University Press.

Charles, R. (2005). Big ideas and understandings as the foundation for elementary and middle school mathematics. *Journal of Mathematics Education Leadership, 8*(1), 9–24.

Collins, A., Brown, J. S., & Holum, A. (1991, Winter). Cognitive apprenticeship: Making thinking visible. *American Educator,* 1–18.

Cuoco, A., Goldenberg, E. P., & Mark, J. (1996). Habits of mind: An organizing principle for mathematics curricula. *Journal of Mathematical Behavior, 15,* 375–402.

Davis, E. (2003). Prompting middle school science students for productive reflection: Generic and directed prompts. *Journal of the Learning Sciences, 12*(1), 91–142.

English, L. D., & Warren, E. (1999). Introducing the variable through pattern exploration. In B. Moses (Ed.), *Algebraic thinking, grades K–12: Readings from NCTM's school-based journals and other publications* (pp. 141–145). Reston, VA: National Council of Teachers of Mathematics.

Ge, X., & Land, S. (2004). A conceptual framework for scaffolding ill-structured problem-solving processes using question prompts and peer interactions. *Educational Technology Research and Development, 52*(2), 1042–1629.

Geisler, C. (1994). *Academic literacy and the nature of expertise: Reading, writing, and knowing in academic philosophy.* Mahwah, NJ: Erlbaum.

Goos, M. (2004). Learning mathematics in a classroom community of inquiry. *Journal for Research in Mathematics Education, 35*(4), 258–291.

Henningsen, M. A. (2000). *Engaging middle school students with cognitively challenging mathematical tasks: Classroom factors that influence students' high-level thinking, reasoning, and communication during consecutive lessons.* Unpublished doctoral dissertation, University of Pittsburgh.

Leahy, S., Lyon, C., Thompson, M., & Wiliam, D. (2005). Classroom assessment: Minute by minute, day by day. *Educational Leadership, 63*(3), 19–24.

Leinhardt, G. (1992). What research on learning tells us about teaching. *Educational Leadership, 49*(7), 20–25.

Mehan, H. (1979). *Learning lessons: Social organization in the classroom.* Cambridge, MA: Harvard University Press.

Michaels, S., O'Connor, M.C., Hall, M. W., & Resnick, L. B. (2002). E-book. In *Accountable Talk: Classroom conversation that works* (Version 2.1). [Online resource]. Pittsburgh, PA: University of Pittsburgh.

National Center for Education Statistics. (1999). *The Third International Mathematics and Science Study.* Washington, DC: author.

National Council of Teachers of Mathematics. (2008). *Illuminations.* Retrieved August 23, 2008, from http://illuminations.nctm.org/Lessons.aspx.

Pellegrino, J. W. (2006). *Rethinking and redesigning curriculum, instruction and assessment: What contemporary research and theory suggests.* Retrieved August 23, 2008, from http://www.skillscommission.org/pdf/commissioned_papers/Rethinking%20and%20Redesigning.pdf.

Resnick, L. B., & Nelson-LeGall, S. (1997). Socializing intelligence. In L. Smith, J. Dockrell, & P. Tomlinson (Eds.), *Piaget, Vygotsky and beyond* (pp. 145–158). London: Routledge.

Rogoff, B. (1990). *Apprenticeship in thinking: Cognitive development in social context.* New York: Oxford University Press.

Rosenshine, B., Meister, C., & Chapman, S. (1996). Teaching students to generate questions: A review of the intervention studies. *Review of Educational Research, 66*(2), 181–221.

Shepard, L. A. (2008). Formative assessment: Caveat emptor. In C. A. Dwyer (Ed.), *The future of assessment: Shaping teaching and learning* (pp. 279–303). New York: Taylor & Francis.

Silver, E. A., Kilpatrick, J., & Schlesinger, B. (1995). *Thinking through mathematics: Fostering inquiry and communication in mathematics class.* New York: College Board.

Smith, M. S., Bill, V., & Hughes, E. K. (2008). Thinking through a lesson: Successfully implementing high-level tasks. *Mathematics Teaching in the Middle School, 14*(3), 132–138.

Smith, M. S., Hughes, E. K., Engle, R. A., & Stein, M. K. (2009). Orchestrating discussions of challenging tasks: Keeping your eye on the mathematics to be learned. *Mathematics Teaching in the Middle School, 14*(9), 548.

Stein, M. K., Smith, M. S., Henningsen, M. A., & Silver, E. A. (2000). *Implementing standards-based mathematics instruction: A casebook for professional development.* New York: Teachers College Press, and Reston, VA: National Council of Teachers of Mathematics.

Stigler, J. W., & Hiebert, J. (1999). *The teaching gap: Best ideas from the world's teachers for improving education in the classroom.* New York: Free Press.

Stylianides, G. J., & Silver, E. A. (2004). Reasoning and proving in school mathematics curricula: An analytic framework for investigating the opportunities offered to students. In D. E. McDougall & J A. Ross (Eds.), *Proceedings of the 26th Annual Meeting of the North American Chapter of the International Group for the Psychology of Mathematics Education* (Vol. 2, pp. 611–619). Toronto: Ontario Institute for Studies in Education, University of Toronto.

van Oers, B. (2001). Educational forms of initiation in mathematical culture. *Educational Studies in Mathematics, 46,* 59–85.

Vygotsky, L. S. (1978). *Mind in society: The development of higher psychological processes.* Cambridge, MA: Harvard University Press.

White, B., & Frederiksen, J. (1998). Inquiry, modeling, and metacognition: Making science accessible to all students. *Cognition and Instruction, 16*(1), 3–118.

Willingham, D. T. (2007, Summer). Critical thinking: Why is it so hard to teach? *American Educator,* 8–19.

Zimmerman, B. J., & Schunk, D. H. (2001). *Self-regulated learning and academic achievement: Theoretical perspectives.* Mahwah, NJ: Erlbaum.

Chapter Five

American Association for the Advancement of Science. (1989). *Science for all Americans: Education for a changing future.* New York: Oxford University Press.

American Association for the Advancement of Science. (1993). *Benchmarks for science literacy.* New York: Oxford University Press.

Banilower, E., Cohen, K., Pasley, J., & Weiss, I. (2008). *Effective science instruction: What does research tell us?* Portsmouth, NH: RMC Research Corporation, Center on Instruction.

Bell, P., & Linn, M. (2000). Scientific arguments as learning artifacts: Designing for learning from the Web with KIE. *International Journal of Science Education, 22*(8), 797–817.

BSCS. (2006). *BSCS Biology: A human approach* (3rd ed.). Dubuque, IA: Kendall/Hunt Publishing

BSCS. (2007, January). *Sustaining global competitiveness: A decade of action for K–12 science and technology education.* Bethesda, MD: Office of Science Education, National Institutes of Health.

Bybee, R. W. (Ed.). (2002). *Learning science and the science of learning.* Arlington, VA: NSTA Press

Chicago Museum of Science and Industry. (2008, March 20). *The state of science in America.*

Chinn, C. A., & Brewer, W. F. (2001). Models of data: A theory of how people evaluate data. *Cognition and Instruction, 19*, 323–393.

Coburn, C. E., & Russell, J. L. (2008, September). District policy and teachers' social networks. *Educational Evaluation and Policy Analysis, 30*, 203–235.

Committee on Science, Engineering, and Public Policy. (2007). *Rising above the gathering storm: Energizing and employing America for a brighter economic future.* Washington, DC: National Academy Press.

Driver, R., Squires, A., Rushworth, P., & Wood-Robinson, V. (2006). *Making sense of secondary science: Research into children's ideas.* New York: Routledge

Educational Services Incorporated. (1966). *Behavior of mealworms. Teacher's guide. Elementary science study.* New York: McGraw-Hill.

Jiménez-Aleixandre, M. P., Rodríguez, A. B., & Duschl, R. A. (2000). "Doing the lesson" or "doing science": Argument in high school genetics. *Science Education, 84*, 757–792.

Kuhn, D. (1993). Science as argument: Implications for teaching and learning scientific thinking. *Science Education, 77*, 319–338.

Kuhn, L., & Reiser, B. (2005). *Students constructing and defending evidence-based scientific explanations.* Paper presented at the National Association of Research in Science Teaching, Dallas, TX.

McNeill, K. L., & Krajcik, J. (2006, April). *Supporting students' construction of scientific explanation through generic versus context-specific written scaffolds.* Paper presented at the annual meeting of the American Educational Research Association, San Francisco.

McNeill, K. L., Lizotte, D. J., Krajcik, J., & Marx, R. W. (2006). Supporting students' construction of scientific explanations by fading scaffolds in instructional materials. *Journal of the Learning Sciences, 15*(2), 153–191.

Michaels, S., O'Connor, M. C., Hall, M. W., & Resnick, L. B. (2002). *Accountable Talk: Classroom conversation that works* (Version 2.1). [Online resource]. Pittsburgh, PA: University of Pittsburgh

National Commission on Excellence in Education. (1983). *A nation at risk: The imperative for educational reform. A report to the nation and the Secretary of Education United States Department of Education.* Washington, DC: Author.

National Research Council. (1996). *National science education standards.* Washington, DC: National Academies Press.

National Research Council. (1999). *How people learn: Brain, mind, experience, and school.* Washington, DC: National Academies Press.

National Research Council. (2000). *Inquiry and the national science education standards.* Washington, DC: National Academies Press.

National Research Council. (2005). *How students learn: Science in the classroom.* Washington, DC: National Academies Press.

National Research Council. (2006). *America's lab report: Investigations in high school science. Committee on High School Science Laboratories: Role and vision.* Washington, DC: National Academies Press.

Newton, P., Driver, R., & Osborne, J. (1999). The place of argumentation in the pedagogy of school science. *International Journal of Science Education, 21*(5), 553–576.

Resnick, L. B., Hall, M. W., & the Fellows of the Institute for Learning. (2003). *Principles of learning: Study tools for educators* (Version 3.0). [Online resource]. Pittsburgh, PA: University of Pittsburgh.

Rhoton, J., & Shane, P. (Eds.). (2006). *Teaching science in the 21st century.* Arlington, VA: NSTA Press.

Sandoval, W. A., & Reiser, B. J. (2004). Explanation-driven inquiry: Integrating conceptual and epistemic scaffolds for scientific inquiry. *Science Education, 88,* 345–372.

Schneps, M. H., & Sadler, P. M. (2003). *A private universe: Minds of our own.* [DVD]. Cambridge, MA: Harvard-Smithsonian Center for Astrophysics.

Chapter Six

ACT. (2006). *Reading between the lines: What the ACT reveals about college readiness in reading.* Retrieved September 15, 2006, from http://www.act.org/path/policy/pdf/reading_report.pdf.

Anzaldúa, G. (1987). *Borderlands/la frontera: The new mestiza.* San Francisco: Aunt Lute Books.

Applebee, A. N. (1993). *Literature in the secondary schools: Studies of curriculum and instruction in the United States.* Urbana, IL: National Council of Teachers of English.

Applebee, A. N., Langer, J. A., Nystrand, M., & Gamoran, A. (2003). Discussion-based approaches to developing understanding: Classroom instruction and student performance in middle and high school English. *American Educational Research Journal, 40*(3), 685–730.

Atwell, N. (1998). *In the middle: Writing, reading, and learning with adolescents.* Portsmouth, NH: Boynton/Cook.

Bartholomae, D., & Petrosky, A. R. (2002). *Ways of reading* (6th ed.). Boston: Bedford/ St. Martin's Press.

Beck, I. L., & McKeown, M. G. (1991). Substantive and methodological considerations for productive textbook analysis. In J. P. Shaver (Ed.), *Handbook of research in social studies teaching and learning* (pp. 496–512). New York: Macmillan.

Beck, I. L., & McKeown, M. G. (1992). Young students' social studies learning: Going for depth. In M. J. Drehere & W. H. Slater (Eds.), *Elementary school literacy: Critical issues* (pp. 133–156). Norwood, MA: Christopher-Gordon.

Beck, I. L., & McKeown, M. G. (1994). Outcomes of history instruction: Paste-up accounts. In J. F. Voss & M. Carrettero (Eds.), *Cognitive and instructional processes in history and the social sciences.* Mahwah, NJ: Erlbaum.

Cazden, C. (1986). Classroom discourse. In M. Wittrock (Ed.), *Handbook of research on teaching* (3rd ed., pp. 432–463). New York: Macmillan, for the American Educational Research Association.

Dewey, J. (1938). *Experience and education.* Indianapolis, IN: Kappa Delta Pi Publishing.

Grossman, P., & Thompson, C. (2004). *Curriculum materials: Scaffolds for new teacher learning?* Seattle Center for the Study of Teaching and Policy: University of Washington.

Marshall, J. D. (1989). *Patterns of discourse in classroom discussions of literature.* Albany: State University of New York at Albany, Center for the Learning and Teaching of Literature.

Mayher, J. S. (1989). *Theoretical practice in language education.* Portsmouth, NH: Boynton/Cook.

McConachie, S., Hall, M. W., Resnick, L., Ravi, A. K., Bill, V. L., Bintz, J., et al. (2006). Task, text, and talk: Literacy for all subjects. *Educational Leadership, 64*(2), 8–14.

McConachie, S., Petrosky, A., Plasse, L., Hall, M. W., & Parshall, C. (2004). *Reading and writing memoir: A professional development module.* Unpublished manuscript, University of Pittsburgh, Institute for Learning, Learning Research and Development Center.

McConachie, S., Resnick, L., & Hall, M. W. (2003). *The case for disciplinary literacy.* Unpublished manuscript, University of Pittsburgh, Institute for Learning, Learning Research and Development Center.

Mehan, H. (1979). *Learning lessons*. Cambridge, MA: Harvard University Press.

Mihalakis, V., McConachie, S., & Petrosky, A. (2006). *Response to literature: What is identity and how is it developed? A seventh grade unit of study prepared for the Los Angeles Unified School District*. Unpublished manuscript, University of Pittsburgh, Institute for Learning, Learning Research and Development Center.

Mihalakis, V., Seitz, A., McConachie, S., Petrosky, A., Hall, M. W., & Carpenter, B. (2006a). *Research/exposition: Read and write like a reporter: A tenth grade unit of study prepared for the Los Angeles Unified School District*. Unpublished manuscript, University of Pittsburgh: Institute for Learning, Learning Research and Development Center.

Mihalakis, V., Seitz, A., McConachie, S., Petrosky, A., Hall, M. W., & Carpenter, B. (2006b). *Speaking out: Persuasive speaking and writing: A tenth grade unit of study prepared for the Los Angeles Unified School District*. Unpublished manuscript, University of Pittsburgh: Institute for Learning, Learning Research and Development Center.

Moffett, J. (1968). *A student-centered language arts curriculum, grades K–12: A handbook for teachers*. Boston: Houghton Mifflin.

Nystrand, M., & Gamoran, A. (1991). Instructional discourse, student engagement, and literature achievement. *Research in the Teaching of English*, *25*, 261–90.

Nystrand, M., & Gamoran, A. (1992). From discourse communities to interpretive communities. In G. Newell & R. Durst (Eds.), *Exploring texts: The role of discussion and writing in the teaching and learning of literature*. Norwood, MA: Christopher-Gordon.

Nystrand, M., Gamoran, A., Kachur, R., & Prendergast, C. (1997). *Opening dialogue: Understanding the dynamics of language and learning in the English classroom*. New York: Teachers College Press.

Petrosky, A. (2006). Inquiry teaching and learning in an environment shaped by behavioral standards and high stakes testing. In W. Sawyer & B. Doecke (Eds.), *Only connect: English teaching and democracy*. Kent Town, South Australia: Wakefield Press.

Popkewitz, T. (2004). The alchemy of the mathematics curriculum: Inscriptions and the fabrications of the child. *American Educational Research Journal*, *41*(1), 3–34.

Postman, N., & Damon, H. C. (1967). *The languages of discovery*. Orlando, FL: Holt.

Powell, A. G., Farrar, E., & Cohen, D. K. (1985). *The shopping mall high school: Winners and losers in the educational marketplace*. Boston: Houghton Mifflin.

Purves, A. C. (1991). Indeterminate texts, responsive readers, and the idea of difficulty in literature. In A. C. Purves (Ed.), *The idea of difficulty in literature* (pp. 157–70). Albany: State University of New York Press.

Scholes, R. (1998). *The rise and fall of English*. New Haven, CT: Yale University Press.

Simon, H. S. (1973). The structure of ill-structured problems. *Artificial Intelligence*, *4*, 181–202.

Sosniak, L. A., & Perlman, C. L. (1990). Secondary education by the book. *Journal of Curriculum Studies*, *22*(5), 427–442.

Soto, G. (1990). *Baseball in April and other stories*. Orlando, FL: Harcourt.

Wells, G. (1999). Dialogic inquiry in education: Building on the legacy of Vygotsky. In C. Lee & P. Smagorinsky (Eds.), *Vygotskian perspectives on literacy research: Constructing meaning through collaborative inquiry*. Cambridge: Cambridge University Press.

Woodward, A., & Elliott, D. L. (1990). *Textbooks and schooling in the United States*. Chicago: University of Chicago Press.

Chapter Seven

Apodaca, R. E. (2007, December 14). *Austin ISD case study*. Presentation to the Institute for Learning, Learning Research and Development Center, University of Pittsburgh.

Apodaca, R. E. (2008). *The AISD Learning Walk: Increasing learning and building community*. Austin, TX: Austin Independent School District.

Bill, V. L. (2007). *Content-focused coaching practices in mathematics*. Unpublished manuscript, Institute for Learning, Learning Research and Development Center, University of Pittsburgh.

Brandt, B. L., Farmer, J. A., & Buckmaster, A. (1993, Fall). Cognitive apprenticeship approach to helping adults learn. In D. D. Flannery (Ed.), *Applying cognitive learning theory to adult learning* (pp. 69–78). New Directions for Adult and Continuing Education, no. 59. San Francisco: Jossey-Bass.

Bruner, J. (1977). *The process of education: A landmark in educational theory*. Cambridge, MA: Harvard University Press.

Childress, S., Elmore, R., & Grossman, A. (2006). How to manage urban school districts. *Harvard Business Review*, *84*(2), 55–68.

Coburn, C. E. (2003). Rethinking scale: Moving beyond numbers to deep and lasting change. *Educational Researcher*, *32*(6), 3–12.

Coburn, C. E., & Russell, J. L. (2008, September). District policy and teachers' social networks. *Educational Evaluation and Policy Analysis*, *30*(3), 203–235.

Collins, A., Brown, J. S., & Newman, S. E. (1989). Cognitive apprenticeship: Teaching the craft of reading, writing, and mathematics. In L. B. Resnick (ed.), *Knowing, learning, and instruction: Essays in honor of Robert Glaser*. Mahwah, NJ: Erlbaum.

Conley, D. T. (2007, March). *Toward a more comprehensive conception of college readiness*. Eugene, OR: Education Policy Improvement Center. Retrieved March 24, 2009, from http://www.s4s.org/upload/Gates-College%20Readiness.pdf.

Conley, D. T. (2008). *College knowledge: What it really takes for students to succeed and what we can do to get them ready.* Hoboken, NJ: Wiley.

Correnti, R. (2008, March). Professional development as a lever for changing teacher practice [Entire issue]. *University of Pittsburgh Learning Policy Brief*, *1*(2).

David, J. L., & Greene, D. (2007a, October). *Improving English language arts instruction in Los Angeles High Schools: An evaluation of the Institute for Learning-LAUSD ELA pilot program.* Palo Alto, CA: Bay Area Research Group.

David, J. L., & Green, D. (2007b, October). *Improving mathematics instruction in Los Angeles high schools: An evaluation of the PRISMA pilot program.* Palo Alto, CA: Bay Area Research Group.

Elmore, R. (2008). Leadership as the practice of improvement. In B. Pont, D. Nusche, & D. Hopkins (Eds.), *Improving school leadership, Vol. 2: Case studies on system leadership.* Paris: Organization for Economic Co-operation and Development.

Elmore, R. (n.d.). *The (only) three ways to improve performance in schools* [video recording]. Cambridge, MA: Harvard Graduate School of Education. Retrieved March 8, 2009, from http://www.uknow.gse.harvard.edu/leadership/leadership001a.html.

Goldman, P., Johnston, J., Micheaux, D., & the Fellows of the Institute for Learning. (2001). *The Learning Walk routine: A tool for getting smarter about teaching and learning* [video recording]. Available from Institute for Learning, Learning Research and Development Center, University of Pittsburgh.

Hughes, E. K., & Smith, M. S. (2004, April). *Thinking through a lesson: Lesson planning as evidence of and a vehicle for teacher learning.* Poster presented as part of a symposium, Developing a Knowledge Base for Teaching: Learning Content and Pedagogy in a Course on Patterns and Functions, at the annual meeting of the American Educational Research Association, San Diego, CA.

Institute for Learning. (2008). *The Learning Walk suite of tools* [version 2.0]. Pittsburgh, PA: Learning Research and Development Center, University of Pittsburgh.

Kotter, J. P. (1996). *Leading change.* Cambridge, MA: Harvard Business Press.

McLaughlin, M. W., & Talbert, J. E. (2006). *Building school-based teacher learning communities.* New York: Teachers College Press.

Penuel, W. R., Fishman, B. J., Yamaguchi, R., & Gallaher, L. P. (2007, December). What makes professional development effective? Strategies that foster curriculum implementation. *American Educational Research Journal*, *44*(4), 921–958.

Petrosky, A., McConachie, S., & Mihalakis, V. (2007, June). *DL ELA professional development module.* Pittsburgh, PA: University of Pittsburgh,

Resnick, L. B., & Hall, M. W. (1998). Learning organizations for sustainable education reform. *Daedalus, 127*, 89–118.

Resnick, L. B., & Hall, M. W., & The Fellows of the Institute for Learning. (2003). *Principles of learning for effort-based education*. Pittsburgh, PA: Institute for Learning, University of Pittsburgh.

Resnick, L. B., & Spillane, J. (2006, September). *From individual learning to organizational designs for learning*. Leuven, Belgium: University of Leuven.

Smagorinsky, P. (2008). *Teaching English by design: How to carry out instructional units*. Portsmouth, NH: Heinemann.

Smith, M. S. (2001). *Practice-based professional development for teachers of mathematics*. Reston, VA: National Council of Teachers of Mathematics.

Smith, M. S., Bill, V. L., & Hughes, E. K. (2008). Thinking through a lesson: Successfully implementing high level tasks. *Mathematics Teaching in the Middle School, 14*(3), 132–139.

Staub, F. C., & Bickel, D. D. (2003, August). *Developing content-focused coaching in elementary literacy: A case study on designing for scale*. Paper presented at the biannual meeting of the European Association for Research on Learning and Instruction, Padova, Italy.

Staub, F. C., West, L., & Bickel, D. D. (2003). What is content-focused coaching? In L. West & F. C. Staub (Eds.), *Content-focused coaching: Transforming mathematics lessons* (pp. 1–17). Portsmouth, NH, and Pittsburgh, PA: Heinemann and University of Pittsburgh.

Stouch, C. (1993). What instructors need to know about learning how to learn. *Applying Cognitive Learning Theory to Adult Learning, 59*, 59–68.

Talbert, J. E., & David, J. L. (2007, July). *Evaluation of the Disciplinary Literacy-Professional Learning Community (DL-PLC) Initiative in Austin Independent School District: Interim report*. Stanford, CA: Stanford University.

Talbert, J. E., David, J. L., & Lin, W. (2008, August). *Evaluation of the Disciplinary Literacy-Professional Learning Community (DL-PLC) Initiative in Austin Independent School District: Final report*. Stanford, CA: Stanford University, Center for Research on the Context of Teaching.

Wenger, E. (1998a). *Communities of practice: Learning, meaning, and identity*. Cambridge: Cambridge University Press.

Wenger, E. (1998b, June). Communities of practice: Learning as a social system. *Systems Thinker*. Retrieved March 24, 2009, from http://www.co-i-l.com/coil/knowledge-garden/cop/lss.shtml.

Appendix C

Petrosky, A. (2006). Inquiry teaching and learning in an environment shaped by behavioral standards and high stakes testing. In W. Sawyer & B. Doecke (Eds.), *Only connect: English teaching* and *democracy*. Kent Town, South Australia: Wakefield Press.

Smith, M. S., Bill, V., & Hughes, E. K. (2008). Thinking through a lesson: Successfully implementing high-level tasks. *Mathematics Teaching in the Middle School, 14*(3), 132–138.

Stein, M. K., & Smith, M. S. (1998). Mathematical tasks as a framework for reflection: From research to practice. *Mathematics Teaching in the Middle School, 3*(4), 268–275.

Stein, M. K., Smith, M. S., Henningsen, M. A., & Silver, E. A. (2000). *Implementing standards-based mathematics instruction: A casebook for professional development*. New York: Teachers College Press.

INDEX

English, L. D., 80

English language arts (ELA) classroom, 129–161; arc of instruction, 145–146, 220; classroom culture and socialization of intelligence, 156–157, 212; comprehension, 147–148; comprehension and sorting questions, 141; design features, naming, 142–144; difficulty questions, 141; DL design principles, 209–212; DL principles in action, 155–159, 220; ELA study, encouraging, 136–139; equity in reading and literature study, 137; formative and summative assessments, 141; gender readings, reflections on, 154; gender study, 153–154; guiding questions, 141; I-R-E (initiate-respond-evaluate) instruction, 136–137; identifying significance tasks, 141; inquiry, 129–131, 144–154; inquiry case study, 145–155; inquiry learning, 133–136; instruction and assessment, 157–159, 213; instruction/methods of inquiry, incorporating in the classroom, 138–139; interpretation, 148–151; knowledge and thinking, 155, 209; learning as apprenticeship, 155–156, 210; lesson and unit design features, 140–142; lesson/unit design features, 220; literary lens, using, 153–154; nominal theme, 140; overarching questions, 141; pedagogical rituals and routines, 220; principals' support, 159–160, 159–161; project, 139–144; retrospective assignments, 141; rigorous texts, 138, 141; significant moments, 148; step-back tasks, 141; teachers as mentors of apprentices, 156, 211; text selection, criteria of, 220; unit architecture, 142–143, 220; writing tasks, 141; written responses, creating, 151–153

Evidence-based explanations, writing, 221

F

Fair and credible evaluations, as principle of learning, 25

Farmer, J. A., 190

Farrar, E., 138

Fellows of the Institute for Learning, 23, 24, 92, 112, 185, 190

Fillmore, L. W., 16

Fishman, B. J., 189

Fitzsimmons, S., 20

Focused curriculum, 13

Frederiksen, J., 72

G

Gallaher, L. P., 189

Gallimore, R., 27

Gamoran, A., 18, 137

Ge, X., 72

Geisler, C., 20, 66

Gelman, S. A., 18

Gender readings, reflections on, 154

Gender study, 153–154

Gerstle, G., 41

Godley, A. J., 3

Goldenberg, E. P., 65

Goldman, P., 185

Gonzalez, E. J., 7

Goos, M., 17, 65

Graham, S., 2

Greene, D., 4, 189

Grigg, W., 2

Grob, G. N., 36

Groff, C., 2

Grossman, A., 186

Grossman, P., 138

Grossman, P. L., 17

Guided reflection, 27, 191, 194–195

Guiding questions, 141

H

Habits of thinking, 21–23, 30; mathematical, 69; synchronizing within a discipline, 21

Hall, M. W., 11, 23, 24, 71, 89, 92, 138, 139, 167, 190

Handlin, O., 41

Heath, S. B., 17

Henningsen, M. A., 7, 66, 81

Hess, F. M., 8

Hiebert, J., 64

High school biology class: charts, 112, 115, 117, 121; coach discussion cycle, 109; cognitively wrestling to advance understanding, 112–114; DL science classroom, 107–122; knowledge and thinking, building through explanations, 115–123; planning/reflecting on the lesson, 109–110; student draft explanations (table), 116; student final explanations for claim and reasoning (table), 118–120; teaching from the planning, 111–112

Hirschfeld, L. A., 18

Historians: conversations with each other, 36; role of, 35–36; thinking as, 34–39

Historical narratives, 35

207; conceptual framework, 91; conceptual navigation chart and graphic organizer, 221; and connection of science concepts/nature of science to students' lives, 87; deep foundation of usable knowledge, 91; DL design principles, 204–208, 221; DL science and the nature of science, 92–95; and everyday experiences, 90–91; evidence-based explanations, writing, 221; features of classroom inquiry in science, 94–95; features of science, 94; gains in achievement, 88; high school biology class, 107–122; how students learn science, research on, 89–90; instruction and assessment, 208; knowledge and thinking, 204; learning as apprenticeship, 205; learning science as a process of inquiry, 91; lesson protocol, thinking through, 221; metacognition, 91; national standards in science, 94; ongoing informal assessment during instruction, 106; path to DL science, 123–127; physics classroom, snapshot of, 88–89; planning and facilitating high-quality professional development, 221; principles of learning (POLs), 92–94; science inquiry, 93–94; scientific explanations, role of, 106–107; scientific inquiry, 95–96; scientifically literate students, 88; seventh-grade life science classroom, 96–105; student preconceptions about how the world works, 90; teachers as mentors of apprentices, 206; testing of assumptions, 92; vision, developing, 88–89

Science for All Americans (American Association for the Advancement of Science), 93–94

Seitz, A., 139

Self-management of learning, as principle of learning, 26

Setup phase of a lesson, 78

Seventh-grade life science classroom: accountable talk moves, 96–105; collecting/recording data, 103; data analysis (session 3), 103–104; data tables, creating, 101–102; lesson, reflecting on, 104–105; scientific investigation, designing (session 2), 101–103; scientifically oriented question, developing (session 1), 98–101; student learning, reflecting on, 104–105, *See also* Science classroom

Shanahan, C., 2

Shanahan, T., 2

Shane, P., 87

Share-and-discuss phase of a lesson, 78–80

Shepard, L. A., 72

Short, D. J., 20

Silver, E. A., 7, 65

Silver, E. A.., 66

Simon, H. S., 139

Slavin, R. E., 2

Smagorinsky, P., 192

Smith, M. S., 7, 66, 78, 183, 221

Snow, C. E., 2, 16, 20

Social studies classroom: analyzing the architecture of a lesson, 222, *See also* History classroom; defining rigor in, 222; DL design principles, 197–199, 222; planning/facilitating high-quality professional development, 222; unit of instruction, thinking through, 222; unit planning guide, 222

Socializing intelligence, 31; English language arts (ELA) classroom, 156–157, 212; history classroom, 53–54, 199; mathematics classroom, 202; as principle of learning, 25–26, 28; science classroom, 107, 207

Sosniak, L. A., 138

Soto, G., 144

Sourcing heuristic, 35

Spiegel, S. A., xxv–xxvi, 87

Spillane, J., 184

Squires, A., 89

Staub, F. C., 194

Stein, M. K., 7, 66, 79, 221

Stewart, R. A., 2

Stigler, J. W., 64

Stodolsky, S. S., 17

Stouch, C., 193

Strong early reading skills, and later more complex skills, 2

Stylianides, G. J., 65

Sustained implementation, 4–5

Systemic practice of DL, 167–196; cognitive apprenticeship, 189–190; district vision and organization, building, 167–171; DL systemic leadership in action, 171–173; learning as apprenticeship for students, 190–191; observation and feedback routine, 184–188; preparation stage of DL implementation, 178–179; principals' instructional leadership, actions suppor5ting, 181; professional learning, developing, 189–195; school organization, building for DL, 173–178; sustaining DL in schools and classrooms, tools for, 183–184; teacher professional learning communities and observations, scheduling, 181–183; understanding/implementing, 178–184

T

U

V

W

Y

Z